GIVERS AND
LIES

PET CARE GIVERS AND FAMILIES

Getting the Most from Dog Playgroups, Walkers, and Pet Sitters

Robert M. Berkelhammer

ROWMAN & LITTLEFIELD
Lanham • Boulder • New York • London

Published by Rowman & Littlefield
A wholly owned subsidiary of The Rowman & Littlefield Publishing Group, Inc.
4501 Forbes Boulevard, Suite 200, Lanham, Maryland 20706
www.rowman.com

Unit A, Whitacre Mews, 26-34 Stannary Street, London SE11 4AB

British Library Cataloguing in Publication Information Available

Library of Congress Cataloging-in-Publication Data

Berkelhammer, Robert, 1955–
Pet care givers and families : getting the most from dog playgroups, walkers, and pet sitters / Robert Berkelhammer.
pages cm
Includes bibliographical references and index.
ISBN 978-1-4422-4815-1 (cloth : alk. paper) — ISBN 978-1-4422-4816-8 (electronic)
1. Pet industry. 2. Pet owners. I. Title.
SF414.7.B47 2015
636.088'7—dc23
2015011687

♾ ™ The paper used in this publication meets the minimum requirements of American National Standard for Information Sciences Permanence of Paper for Printed Library Materials, ANSI/NISO Z39.48-1992.

Printed in the United States of America

CONTENTS

PREFACE

This book guides pet owners and pet professionals to achieve high levels of caretaking, customer service, and behavior change for pets. The best changes occur within healthy hierarchical systems: the pet family system, the pet care company system, and the system of the dogs and cats themselves socializing with one another in different settings. Domesticated animals are troubled by hierarchy breakdown: war, terrorism, earthquakes, tsunamis, hurricanes, floods, unemployment, underemployment, substance abuse, divorce, illness, and mental illness. Pet companies can help pet families to restore healthier functioning during lifestage transitions.

The son of a veterinarian, I've worked since 2007 as a pet care professional, and I have the distinction of having assisted in over 1,100 sessions to date in one behavior modification playgroup for dogs. I have pet sat in homes, visited cats while owners traveled, walked puppies and dogs while owners worked or parented, and completed bird care visits. I also have years of systems experience as a parent, holistic health counselor and therapist, and the perspective of a trained guidance counselor.

This book clarifies what a successful dog behavior modification playgroup should look like and why. Correctly managed playgroups don't just put the dogs together and let them run around; they need guidance and oversight by well-trained playgroup professionals who set limits, praise, and use redirective discipline. A successful pet care company follows effective respectful protocols, especially when dealing with special-needs populations such as rescue dogs, puppies, sightless dogs, and cats and dogs with injuries or age-related medical conditions.

This book discusses, in depth, the standards for pet sitting, dog walking, and cat and bird visits. Pet owners tend to be hard on themselves, feeling guilt and separation anxiety when they leave their pets. For that reason, this book emphasizes communication among the pet care company owner, the field professional working directly with the pets, and the pet family. The book presents sample questionnaires, notes, and activity logs that the pet sitter can use to keep communication strong.

Transitions, both lifestage and minor, can be particularly difficult, both in how changes in the pet family affect the animals and vice versa. This book provides specific strategies for dealing with puppies, pets with health issues, and pets in the last stage of life, as well as guidelines for when it's appropriate to bring a new pet into the home. There is even a section on one divorced family's successful sharing of a dog between their two homes, with the help of the pet company.

This is not a dry how-to book. Throughout, I bring the scenes of the dog behavior playgroup, pet sitting, cat visits, dog walks, and a bird visit to life, punctuating the narrative with vignettes of some of the astonishing animals I've cared for:

- Mookie, the ambassador, the large, gentle Labrador mix who took it upon himself and with staff intention to socialize a Tibetan Terrier puppy at playgroup.
- Bronzeback, a chocolate Labrador who went blind after many years in playgroup, and how we gently brought her back into the group via a bell system helping her whereabouts.
- Cumin, a Rhodesian ridgeback-Viszla mix brought along by stages into dog walks and playgroup after a loving adopted family rescued her from a misery-filled life.
- Chantelle, the Havanese I walked after learning of the murder of a close pregnant friend.
- Sadie, an elderly Pekingese who passed away in her sleep while I was pet sitting and how I worked with the grieving owners over the phone.

I hope this book will inspire new pet companies to start up internationally and raise or maintain standards of existing pet companies. I would like to see the five areas of pet service outlined in this book included in the curriculum of vocational schools' agricultural track study. Additionally, doggy daycare needs inclusion in vocational school curriculum. Finally, I believe traumatized rescue dogs can be partially healed through attending behavior modification playgroups. The scientific study of this needs clinical research, and I would like to be a part of this.

I believe the hearts, souls, and minds of the animals and their owners are visible on the pages of this book. The animals have told their stories through me.

ACKNOWLEDGMENTS

There are many whom I thank:

My family: my veterinarian father and musician mother, Dr. Albert Morris and Eileen Sperber Berkelhammer, brother Stephen (musician and pet professional), sisters Lisa, an acupuncturist, and Beth Tiana, an editor.

My children! Amanda-Rose, Talea Eliana, and Rafael Josiah. May you let God's love and abundance guide you throughout your life and the lives of your children and your grandchildren!

The mothers of my children: Dr. Laura Shakun and Att. Cara Cheyette.

Linda Horsley, proprietor of Personal Comforts Pet Care, Marblehead, Massachusetts, for her seasoned knowledge of dog behavior modification playgroups, pet sitting, dog walking, dog boarding, cat and bird visits: www.personalcomfortspetcare.com (781) 631-7964.

Personal Comfort Pet Care colleagues and friends Ann Sweeten, Christine Stuart, Ann Marie Segal, Jean Hamburg, Joan Gross, Lauren Kapp, Sally Libby, Dawn Matchette, Fraffe Welch, Dot Stanley, Shelia Fischer, and Barbie Barnum.

Brooks and Ned Williams, proprietors, Creature Comforts Pet Care in Marblehead, Massachusetts, for North Shore excellence in pet care services and 2013 winner of Marblehead Chamber of Commerce business of the year: www.ccpaws.com(781) 990-0081.

Writers, editors, and cinematographers who encouraged me to write: my editor, Janet Ruth Young; Julian Thompson, Phyllis Karas,

Mayra Dole, William Stevenson, "Professor" Jeff Hoffman, Joel Netsky, Eli Gottlieb, John Mann, Richard Stout, Julia Bobkoff, and Beth Berkelhammer.

Two distinguished holistic clinicians helped me to understand a wellness orientation for pathology and health: Dr. Linda Reynolds for pediatric and adult health—www.iwellnesscenter.com, (978) 298-5753 and Dr. Jeff Levy, veterinary homeopath: www.homeovet.net.

Mentors: Adria Fredricks, Cleve Penberthy, Margo Ouimet, The Crosbys, Joel Koby and Beebe School students, Charlene Bobek and Guilmette School students, Prof. Bill Aldridge, Prof. Rob Knapp, Robert Purdy, George Kosmides, Bob Ibsen, Marcus Lemonis of The Profit, Chef Robert of *Restaurant Impossible*, the Kiwanis and Rotary Clubs, and Paolo Soleri and Arcosanti.

Dan Cherry–Homeopathy; Carol Nelson–Iyengar Yoga, Kevin Mastronardi–Bikram Yoga, Kripalu Yoga Center, Acupuncturists John Myerson, Bernie Augot, Peter Valaskagis, Susan Kane; Muscle therapist–Gary Miller and Thomas Jacobson.

Childhood friends Mindy Wolkstein, Maxine Lefkowitz, Lauren Alexander, Patsy Kragan, Barbara Anspach, David Ketchum, Billy Doane, Peter Grubstein, Bob Hetherington, Toby Keats, Charles Collins, and Steve Allsop.

Friends Steve Hustava, Sam and Dorrie Friedman, Joe and Shirley Kessler, Burton and Jean Apple, Joe Soli, Beth Guidry Hoffman, and D. Mello.

Shubie's, Whole Foods, Trader Joe's, and Market Basket for nutritional support.

I recognize the families: Berkelhammer, Sperber, Rosenfeld, Gelfond, Shakun, Cheyette, Redstone, Bliwise, Fisch, Samuel, Sollander, Weisner, Galor, Spies, Spitzer, Lustig, and Zagnet.

In sacred memory of family members who perished in World War II along with the U.S. and allied soldiers who tried to save them.

In sacred memory of Rohn Finard, Joseph Burstein, and Yuliya Galperina.

1

HUMAN–COMPANION ANIMAL DYNAMICS

The Importance of Healthy Hierarchy

THE IMPORTANCE OF HEALTHY HIERARCHY

Hierarchy, or power structure, is the foundation for success in the homes of pet families. Pets should never run the home. The pet family's parents need to be in charge of the home, exerting their power and oversight over pets access to exercise, discipline, affection, socialization, nutrition, basic health care, and other vital needs. The pet's parents make all the difference in the quality of life the pet will have over its lifespan. Many times the hierarchy in a home has broken down slightly or extremely, and pet professionals are needed to help the pet owners organize more success for the pets and family. The family pet hierarchy may be destabilized by crises and lifestage transitions. It can be affected by marriage, childbirth, adoption of children or animals, relocation, natural disasters, illness, substance abuse, divorce, underemployment, or job loss.

Fortunately, pet sitting, dog behavior modification playgroups, dog walks, doggy daycare, and cat and bird visits offer important remedies for many hierarchy problems. Hierarchy issues can also arise between the pet owner and the pet professionals. Whether you are a pet family owner or pet professional, the more cats or dogs you are taking care of, the more important a healthy hierarchy is for the health and happiness between people and pets.

A pet professional entering the home of pet family system encounters established protocols and beliefs that have developed over time. Pet professionals and pet owners can agree, disagree, and theorize about what pets need, in what order, and in what proportions. But when you don't have consistent structured exercise, socialization, discipline, and affection in the pet's home, all types of chaos can manifest themselves. Homes in which animals have consistent exercise, discipline, and affection, and socialization are homes with healthier marriages, more joyful parents, and better-adjusted children. Figure 1.1 shows different ways pet owners can relate to their pets.

In the first and second sections of the figure, either the owner and pet are on the same level or the needs of the pet are more important than the needs of the pet family owners and children. In these households, the owners see themselves and their pets as largely emotional beings for whom feelings are more important than principles about exercise, discipline, affection, and socialization of animals with family members or other animals. Pet owners may believe that affection is the most important of the principles named above. A pet owner may be anxious about their pets feeling unhappy, and that escalates into spoiling dogs with a lack of exercise and discipline. These pet owners have gotten their priorities mixed up and put the carriage in front of the horse. Accordingly, the pets, not the pet owner or owners, are in control in the home.

SIGNS OF HIERARCHY BREAKDOWN

Situations in which pets are in control can range from temporary and slight to mild and severe. Homes where pets have severe control over family life include pets on any surface they choose—chairs, couches, tables, and desks. Dogs may surf the kitchen counters and stove top for food and face no redirective discipline from their owners. Cats may eat from their own plate or bowl directly on top of dining room tables, or from a bowl on the dining room floor instead of a bowl in the kitchen near their water bowl. In the kitchen, cats may be seen resting on a counter next to a cutting board or walking over a cutting board that

1.

OWNER ↔ PET

(equality between owner and pet)

2.

PET

↓

OWNER

(pet dominant)

3.

OWNER

↓

PET

(owner in control)

Figure 1.1. Ways Pet Owners Can Relate to Their Pets

human food is prepared on. A cat may walk on the stove, lick frying pans that have not been cleaned, or drink from a soup pot—clear invitations to spills, bad germs, and burns.

In households shown in the first two scenarios in the figure, pets may be found lying on beds with antisocial effects. In the master bedroom, the privacy a couple needs has been sabotaged by controlling dogs or cats, testing the marriage. Dogs manipulate owners to allow them into the couple's bed. Dogs can force the issue by jumping into the bed and being unwilling to budge. It is difficult to move a medium-sized or large dog off a bed, especially when it plays dead or refuses to move. Dogs may bark viciously at a husband or wife who approaches the spouse in the bed. Dogs removed from the bed may jump right back in or bark and scratch at the bedroom door. Cats can hiss and attack a husband or wife in the master bedroom.

Why do these problems go on as long as they do in marriages and the master bedroom? Often one adult owner in the couple doesn't agree with the lack of pet discipline but feels powerless to change the mind and behavior of the other spouse. One spouse may believe a solution is to have more feelings being expressed back and forth between the dogs and their owners. The other spouse believes that a mutually agreed-upon pet policy is needed in the home. If children side with the more lenient spouse, the other spouse feels more hopeless and helpless.

Out-of-control dogs or cats may eat parts of furniture and window treatments. Urine stains and feces are often visible in some rooms. The family may already have accrued large veterinary bills from pumping out, or even surgery on, the pet's digestive system after the pet has ingested towels, socks, nails, or tacks.

In households depicted in the first two scenarios in the figure, dogs can be hostile to mail deliveries sliding through door slots. Dogs may be aggressive toward visiting family members such as aunts, uncles, and grandparents. Children may fear their own pets, which bark or chase them when they enter the home. Relatives who are frail feel intimidated and may stop visiting entirely.

Further evidence of a weakened hierarchy in a backyard reveals digging, which causes muddy messes, damaged lawns and flower beds, as well as holes that family members may stumble on.

Walking a dog in public can be a harrowing experience when the dog constantly barks, pulls on the leash, and exhibits leash aggression toward cats, dogs, children, and adults. Riding with these dogs in a car can be both earsplitting and distracting as dogs bark and run back and forth in the rear seat or cargo area. Pedestrians, cyclists, and other drivers are distracted by the barking head of a canine jutting out a window.

A bloody dog bite to a person or another animal triggers a whole sequence of problematic reactions and bureaucratic involvement. Puncture wounds in animals and humans need immediate medical care, including antibiotics, sutures, pain medication, and rabies shots. Animal control officers may visit the home.

Animal control officers have the authority to enter private property to investigate situations, whether blood has been shed or not. A dog may be placed under quarantine for a period of time, meaning it cannot be walked off its owner's property until written permission is granted by the animal control officer. Quarantine time periods can vary and be as long as a week or two weeks depending on different factors. Neighborhood tensions escalate as upset neighbors react. Lawyers may enter the fray, bringing greater civility or inciting incivility. Parties may file lawsuits that are based on relevant facts or that are miscellaneous and baseless. The very reason people choose to live in neighborhoods, safety and peace of mind, is altered for a period of time by well-meaning but antisocial dogs.

Adults and children in out-of-control pet families appear helpless in influencing their pets properly. Raised voices, raised hands, avoidance, and denial perpetuate the chaos. At the center of the problem are the owners who are unable to set boundaries or apply proper decisions about socialization, exercise, discipline, and affection. The pet owners' desire for companionship has degenerated into a scenario of unease, anxiety, gluttony, and property destruction.

Neighbors are very aware of the chaos in a home where pet owners are not in charge. Dogs running loose may dig holes under fences and damage flowers on neighboring property that is not fully fenced along its perimeter. Neighbors hear the dog's excessive barking and may feel assaulted by the loud incessant noise as they walk in their neighborhood and pass by the pet owners' home. These neighbors may start walking on the opposite side of the street to avoid the dog. Tensions arise if neighbors call the animal control authorities to complain. The animal control officer can sometimes help families change, but pet owners may become obstinate and unchangeable.

SIGNS OF A SECURE HIERARCHY

Hierarchies are working in the home when the owner is positioned above the pet, as in the third scenario in the figure, not beside or below the pet. The pet owners maintain authority over the pets and the children, and they run the home environment with a loving regard for the overall health of all animals and the people they interact with.

A healthy hierarchy allows relatives, adult friends, and children's friends to relax while visiting. Pets interfering with a visit are placed somewhere else on the property until they calm down. The couple has privacy from both pets and children in the master bedroom because pets and children have consistently been taught to respect privacy. Pets are not overfed, and they act secure because they're receiving the proper proportions of nutrition, exercise, discipline, and affection.

Dogs and other pets are creatures of habit, and when their needs are consistently met, feelings of security reinforce their habitual behaviors. Adults and children use commands like "No," "Down," "Sit," "Stay," "Good, " and "Want a treat?" in a healthy home. By assuming authority over their pets and interacting well with them, children are learning about discipline, boundaries, and setting limits. When children apply authoritative behavior, they learn how to be parents to the pets. The children eventually understand their parents' job of parenting them as they become adults and parents.

A dog barking in the yard is monitored and asked to stop. Children also learn to ask their dog to stop barking. The owner may try hand signals or voice commands to teach the dog to stop barking, or a gentle water spray. If the dog doesn't stop, the owner brings the pet inside. Dog owners living next door to each other may bring their dogs inside immediately when they become overstimulated and bark at each other through the fence between the properties. Dog owners on adjacent properties or near public areas can have some dogs meet each other and develop rapport, which can decrease the excessive barking. (Because I spend a lot of time in parks, I only wish some dog owners who live near parks would realize how antisocial it is for their dogs to be barking for forty-five to seventy-five minutes!)

With stable hierarchy, cats and dogs are not fed from the table at breakfast, lunch, or dinner. They take their meals every day from the same area, which has been designated for them. When owners who preserve limits and discipline talk to pet professionals about the dogs, cats, or birds they keep in their homes, they make statements like, "These are Rover's water and food bowls, and we feed her in this area"; "This is Fee Fee's basket of cat toys. We keep this basket in the living room, and she has a second basket of toys in the basement." This language shows clear strategies for taking care of pets' various daily needs.

In a home with a healthy hierarchy, cats can seek out being touched in certain ways, and their desires will be respected by the pet family, who will inform all visitors how their cat likes and dislikes being touched.

The hierarchy operating in a pet family is the first thing a pet professional identifies and navigates. How do these descriptions reflect the hierarchy in your home?

2

FOUR-LEGGED JOY

All About a Dog Behavior Modification Playgroup

Dog playgroups are not doggy daycare or dog parks, both of which are very valuable resources. Playgroups are shorter in time than daycare and require different skills from the staff. Including round-trip transport, playgroups run anywhere from one to three hours depending on when a dog is picked up on the transport schedule. Doggy daycare can take five to six hours. Some dogs do well with the shorter playgroup; they come home tired but not overexerted or overstimulated, having plenty of energy left for their pet families. Other dogs do very well with doggy daycare's extended day, releasing a lot of energy and relaxing with many dogs. Dog owners today have access to many kinds of committed pet professionals who are offering diverse situations for their dog.

BENEFITS OF A DOG BEHAVIOR MODIFICATION PLAYGROUP

Dog behavior modification playgroups suit the basic needs of most dogs throughout their development stages, from puppyhood to late adulthood. Playgroups provide the physical and psychological benefits of exercise, where a dog finds its unique play style and learns limits through redirective discipline, social skills with other dogs, and pack dog affection. Playgroup socialization and exercise of about one hour, plus transport time of ten to ninety minutes supplements the solitary, boring, and lonely experience many dogs live daily in homes where owners work long hours outside the home, five days a week. Even the stay-at-home mom or dad with young children cannot provide their dog the same benefits as a social network with other dogs.

Behavior modification playgroups provide an excellent environment for rescue dogs to heal some of their intensity and frequency of their trauma from a loving pet family. The following problems may decrease in frequency and intensity for regular and rescue dogs via playgroup:

- Property destruction
- Boredom and understimulation
- Overweight
- Mounting
- Hyperactivity toward dogs in play
- Constipation
- Off-leash aggression
- Lack of confidence
- Leash aggression toward dogs
- Leash aggression toward people
- Excessive shyness
- Depression
- Negative anxiety
- Excessive barking
- Lethargy
- Obsessive playing with people, dogs, and toys

The positive qualities dogs can improve upon are:

- Playfulness: initiating, joining, perpetuating, and enjoying play
- Enthusiasm and measured excitability
- Improved boundary awareness around people and pets
- Increased calm and less barking in cars
- Leaner body areas with positive weight and muscle shifts from increased exercise when being fed properly at home
- Increased peaceful dog presence at home and while visiting family friends and dogs

A behavior modification playgroup helps dogs learn better behavior through modeling what is normal. Normal behavior is reinforced by dogs and staff, allowing dogs to associate socialization with joy and happiness. Redirective discipline by dogs and staff helps dogs improve their behavior. A prospective playgroup dog experiences a protocol of meeting the playgroup director in the director's home with their dog. The dogs mix, and if it is a positive experience, the new dog will be invited to two twenty-minute playgroup sessions. This initial meeting is a safeguard for everyone and for the playgroup director to assess a dog's playgroup readiness.

Dogs with the following issues will not be ready for the initial two twenty-minute playgroup sessions:

- Dogs adopted from shelters that need more family bonding. Dog walks by the pet owner could eventually lead to a dog playgroup as part of this transition.
- Dogs that were bought by the family from a breeder that are in need of more family bonding.
- Dogs with unhealed surgical procedures and not cleared by a veterinarian for playgroup.
- Puppies younger than four months that are not house trained and unable to ride in cars without bathroom accidents.
- Dogs with certain levels and types of aggression that need an animal behaviorist's help before playgroup attendance.
- Dogs who have a healthy dominant guard dog or animal-herding behavior that cannot learn to share space or toys with other dogs safely. (Many of the wonderful livestock-guarding dogs from mountainous countries have a history of being raised from puppy-hood with human beings and are unsocialized around dogs and cats.)
- Dogs without updated rabies, heartworm, or kennel cough treatment.
- Unspayed or unneutered dogs.

Socialization and Exercise in the Playgroup Yard

Basic obedience is reinforced in playgroup and dovetails nicely with playgroup socialization. A basic dog obedience training course is important for most dogs in their early development. A family dog that is learning basic obedience commands is happier, and their pet family functions better. Basic obedience commands like "Sit," "Come," and "Stay" are used. Dogs enjoy basic obedience because it stimulates their brains and they receive pleasure from pet owners' playfulness and joy in giving them commands. Dogs enjoy pleasing their owners, and treat rewards taste great!

Dog playgroups have a main outside area for dogs to run, play, and rest in. The playgroup I work with features two toddler slides, balls for retrieval and play, squeaking toys to bite and carry, areas of large rocks for safe climbing and resting, and plastic wading pools that are empty, filled with water, or filled with sand. Additionally two or three stainless-steel bowls of fresh water are spread around the yard, and dog poop shovels, small and large garbage cans, very strong and protective fencing and gates, and other resources to care for the dogs and stimulate them physically and mentally are available. A basement near the playgroup area contains snow shovels, ice breakers, rakes, a first aid kit, and other stored resources.

Mulch is a very comfortable surface for dogs and allows urine to drain from the top down to deeper areas. Mulch is a toxic-free, playground-rated substance. Mulch covers mud and prevents the dogs' feet and coats from getting dirty. Mulch absorbs shock, softening the impact for dogs that leap, tumble, run, fall, wrestle, retrieve, turn on a dime, stop short, and slide, with their momentum leaving long skid tracks in the mulch, like you see in cartoons. An adjacent indoor cellar for extreme cold weather is available, although dogs do well outside with their winter coats, even to a thirty-degree below wind chill. Playgroup staff keep the door open in very cold or wet weather, providing dogs with the option to play both inside and outside as staff oversee both areas. Valuables and breakable and unsafe possessions are inaccessible by the dogs.

Our playgroup uses a superlative winter coat product called Smartpak with Thinsulate. Smartpak offers a waterproof rain coat and a winter fleece coat. Dogs can wear one or both depending on the weather. The jackets are very easy to fit and remove, very sturdy, and offer protection from cold, rain, and wind when fitted properly. Sturdy Velcro straps easily secure the coats around a dog's chest and torso.

The largest fenced main area of our dog playgroup connects to two smaller entrance areas that can serve a variety of functions. The transition pen closest to the transport parking lot has two gates, serving as the main entrance fenced area for all dogs and staff arriving at drop-off time. Dogs are led on leash from the transport vehicle through the outer gate transition area where the leash is removed. The inner transition gate is then opened, allowing dogs entry into the main fenced area. The transition area is also used for introducing new dogs slowly into the playgroup, for occasional time-outs in redirective discipline, or to allow groups of small dogs time by themselves.

A third fenced area in the far end of the playgroup area allows for more flexibility socializing dogs. The third area allows the most kinetic dogs to run, wrestle, and play if their energy level is much higher than other dogs. Closing the fence for five or ten minutes helps them dissipate their energy without bothering the other dogs. The third area can also support five to eight small dogs that need to be calm and quiet or segregated from larger galloping dogs wrestling and chasing one another. Transitioning new dogs into a playgroup in the transition pen is supported by the third fenced area, holding a few dogs that are acting rambunctiously for five to fifteen minutes until they have calmed down. The staff always avoids allowing overly excited dogs to create distress at the fence of the transition area for a new dog who may initially lack confidence or needs a relaxed, quieter transition. If a particular dog cannot swim in a wading pool for medical reasons, it can be placed in the third area with some friends that also do not have pool access.

The staff also shifts dogs into the third area in order to do landscaping maintenance on the main area like raking leaves and spreading mulch.

Transitioning Newcomers into Playgroup

In the playgroup I assist running, a new dog would be brought from the vehicle last into the transition pen after all the other playgroup dogs that day have been dropped off and attendance has been completed. This sets the newcomer up for success and helps the dog avoid being overwhelmed by strange excited dogs.

New dogs benefit from the director's and assistant manager's careful planning. The director informs the owner who is transporting the new dog or assisting in playgroup beforehand and what transition guidelines, including strategies, may apply for a newcomer and experienced playgroup dogs. I often suggest certain larger overexcited dogs be placed in the third fenced area until the initial excitement calms down between dogs in section two and the newcomer in the transition pen.

At our establishment, the playgroup director or I would sit in a chair in the transition area and bond with the newcomer through quiet eye contact, talk, and petting. We switch off between playgroup leaders to benefit the newcomer bonding with those who run the behavior playgroup inside the fences. The staff person outside the transition fence guides the excited dogs to calm down and play with one another. Full-grown dogs and puppies may lack the confidence when first brought to a playgroup as newcomers. Newcomers' transition area behavior and body language informs playgroup staffers when dogs have lost enough anxiety and developed enough confidence to leave the fenced-off transition pen and enter the larger yard.

A new dog may be too shy without confidence or too out of control to join the main playgroup areas for a few minutes or a number of days. During this transition, the new dog and the pack of dogs look at and smell one another through the transition area bordering the main area. Playgroup dogs model normal behavior for a newcomer immediately. The playgroup directors sets in motion a second stage of transition area socializing by inviting particular dogs into meet the newcomer. Dogs are slowly invited in one or two at a time to embody a mixture of gentle personality and good social skills. Their size is secondary. The newcomer experiences a social excitement and confidence with these new dog connections while transcending unhelpful anxiety. These initial bondings are inspirational as dogs learn to start socializing with other dogs under staff oversight. A newcomer smaller dog may be introduced first to small dogs with a couple of larger dog exceptions. If the newcomer plays well with the first larger dog and vice versa, second and third larger dogs are guided into the small fenced area. Larger dogs transitioning into a playgroup have similar-sized dogs introduced initially before smaller dogs.

Experienced playgroup dogs are also released from the transition area when their numbers are too high for the space, have lost interest in the newcomer, and if a dog is too hyper with the newcomer. A newcomer may have seven or eight dogs bonding with it in the transition area.

Once newcomers start reflecting the body language of consistent confidence as opposed to inconsistent confidence, they are ready for the next stage. The gate separating the transition area from the large fenced area can then be opened.

How long does it take a new dog to transition from the transition pen into the larger area with all the dogs? As long as it takes—whether it's five minutes or fifteen one-hour playgroups over fifteen days. The new dog informs playgroup staff of its readiness to enter the larger group. This can't be forced, and it is an individual process. Body posture showing confidence toward other dogs is a key to readiness for the general playgroup dogs and area. What does consistent confidence look like in a new dog in the transition pen? It is indicated by tail wagging; movement toward other dogs inside and outside the penned area to lick, nuzzle, smell, and play with them; the "play with me" crouch posture facing the fence where veteran dogs are, and dogs reciprocating peacefully. The newcomer reflects consistent confidence by not staying under a chair or overly attached to a staffer in the transition pen. Consistent gazing by newcomers into the larger yard signals the gate can be opened.

The director would then state "I'm opening the gate" to notify all staff members of the change in playgroup status. The gate then remains open, allowing the newcomer to remain or return to the transition area if the dog chooses. Some new dogs may feel more secure knowing this, while other newcomers won't use it but may see it is an option. The newcomer sees other dogs modeling the behavior of choosing to enter, leave, and reenter the small fenced area. This modeled behavior shows that a choice is available to all dogs. As creatures of habit, dogs are secure with routines, and choices are part of their routines. To prevent newcomers from leaving the transition area after being rushed by excited dogs, the staff can place themselves between the newcomer and other dogs.

Repetition of ritual bonding is important for newcomers to feel secure and build their confidence. The director may repeat this short process with a newcomer the next time the newcomer attends playgroup if confidence building seems necessary.

Minimal Minglers: Helping Shy Dogs Socialize

Dogs with a sedentary play style are very active socially. Minimum minglers means they are socializing through sight, smell, sitting close to other dogs, and limited kinetic movement. They are developing confidence and a style of play unique to them and their pace. Eventually, minimum minglers may change their play style radically by running with dogs and wrestling. Minimum minglers may need encouragement to socialize more actively and exercise more expansively in the playgroup yard full of toys, slides, balls, and other stimulating things.

Playgroup staffers approach these dogs, pet them, talk to them, put them on a leash, and walk them around the playgroup area so they receive more exercise, encouraging opportunity for interaction with other dogs. I place dogs on slides and teach them to go up and down. If they are small dogs, the staff may hold them in their arms at times or place them on their laps.

The interspecies bonding between playgroup staff and dogs helps shy dogs become more comfortable mingling with other dogs. A bonding between staff and dogs is part of playgroup socialization. Actively introducing these minimum minglers to wading pools, slides, or ball play may open up an interest these dogs hadn't shown before the staff guided them into the activity. These are just some of the ways a trained playgroup staff helps dogs become more socialized and playful and accelerate their socialization process. But their play style is up to them.

A staff member challenging a dog to try something new may trigger levels of anxiety in the dog's body language. I may walk a dog near a wading pool filled with water and encourage it to jump in, either by guiding it on leash toward the side of the pool or placing it down next to the pool. Some dogs' body language reflects total rejection of the idea of entering the water. Certain dogs actively try to squirm out of the staffer's hands, almost in a panic of high anxiety. If we ignore the dog's total opposition to being led or placed gently into the wading pool, the dog may lose trust in a staff member, running away from the staffer for a period of weeks.

Other dogs show resistance to wading pools but still demonstrate curiosity. They may get tense in the staff member's hands but look at the water with interest and not try to squirm away. Perhaps the dog needs a little time to get used to the present situation, smell the water and the air near the wading pool, or relax in proximity to the excitement of dogs nearby. Dogs that model water wading help build confidence and curiosity.

Dogs that allow staffers at playgroup to guide them into experiencing the water in the wading pools are opened up to an activity unknown to them. A lot of socializing occurs next to and in the wading pools. Many dogs become regular pool minglers. Water is very pleasurable for interested dogs. Dogs, like many humans, enjoy the sensation of cool water in hot, humid weather, and of course, many breeds of dogs have significant histories of working in the water to help humans by hunting, gathering nets, and swimming ashore with messages.

The slide near the pool is another place where much kinetic and general socializing occurs. The slide at my playgroup has two ends, both angled gradually, so dogs can go up and down without building the excessive momentum that could lead to an injury. Small, medium, and large dogs have become regular slide users after a staffer has guided them up or down a few times. Dogs may respond to the staffer's calling their names and encouraging, "Come on down to the wading pools and the slides!" Dogs that become confident on these structures have learned to associate joy and pleasure with the pools and slides.

CASE VIGNETTE: SHANA, THE DOX RETRIEVER

Two dachshunds were regular members of our playgroup. One of the dachshunds, Fredrick, learned to walk and run the whole length of part of the play yard and hop into the pool to retrieve a ball. He loved it— hence the new breed name, Dox Retriever. The other dachshund, Shana, was placed in playgroup by her owner hoping she would learn to socialize more. Her owner told us Shana was shy and a bit grouchy with other dogs when walking in public, unable to relax and barking at other dogs instead of enjoying their company. Shana's owner excitedly told us Shana changed after playgroup socialization. One day a dog in a park was barking loudly and frequently disturbing those present as Fredrick, Shana, and their mom entered the park. Shana would have joined the dog in barking or pulled away to avoid contact before playgroup behavior modification. However, Shana began walking peacefully with her mom and Fredrick toward the other dog and began licking it and making eye contact. The barking dog began to calm down and then stopped barking. Shana's mom was very excited to relay this story of Shana's improved social skills outside the home.

CASE VIGNETTE: MICA'S PLAY STYLE

Mica has an endearing play style. I call Mica the Energizer Bichon! Mica often approaches Goldy, a sedentary Golden retriever, who enjoys resting on a large rock with other dogs. Mica first looked Goldy in the eyes, asking her to play, with no response. Mica then moved to Goldy's flank, giving her a little nip. No response. A second flank nip, no response. Mica then moved to Goldy's shoulder and nipped her. No response. Mica gave another nip to Goldy's shoulder. No response. Mica moved to Goldy's ear and nipped her. No response. A second or third ear nip finally caused Goldy to stand up and play! Mica's play style is remarkable to behold!

LIMIT SETTING AND REDIRECTIVE DISCIPLINE

Playgroup dogs release lots of pent-up energy that they import from their homes and in their bodies. Rescue cats and dogs also carry a lot of pent-up energy from their preadoptive lives. Excess energy occurs in all dogs. Playgroup can help release excess energy through socialization, exercise, and activities. Staff may need to respond to negative behavior using limit setting and redirective discipline, which sets dogs up for successful socialization.

Dogs love socializing with many other dogs in dog playgroups. Stimulating interaction brings out authentic joy, and increased energy levels reflect happiness as they run, wrestle, lick, rub against each other, and communicate in unique ways. Joy and socialization with dogs and cats has a huge kinetic factor, and dog playgroup is a time period of kinetic movement, emotional movement, and socialization maturation for dogs, punctuated by water breaks, bathroom breaks, and rest.

At our behavior modification playgroup, dogs are running back and forth within the fenced confines of the play area, covering scores of yards. Certain dogs may become either too loud in barking or too aggressive with their teeth and body postures. Socialized dogs usually use a normal and playful teeth style that produces no pain, no blood, and no puncture wounds—although in the high energy of playful running and wrestling, mistakes sometimes happen. Socialized dogs also use a biting pressure that creates pain without bloodshed; they may modulate the pressure based on their moods and levels of stimulation. You have probably seen playful biting in puppy play and kitten play; it continues with adult dogs and adult cats and in wild animals throughout the animal kingdom.

Beyond joyful safe oral play, there is biting that looks and sounds too aggressive and can lead to puncture bites and unsafe play. I have learned to intervene immediately to prevent unwanted and antisocial aggression from possibly escalating into bloodshed. By using redirective discipline, I set limits that change behavior and energy in an individual dog as well as in dynamics of the group. Redirective discipline is a basic skill playgroup professionals practice daily, because without the staff setting limits on bad behaviors or praising good behavior, dogs would begin to behave poorly more of the time in a variety of situations inside playgroup, during transport, and at home. Playgroup staff and pet owners don't want dogs that have been well behaved before they came to playgroup to develop bad habits from playgroup and go home acting poorly. Limits and redirective discipline are both staff enforced and dog enforced. An overly aggressive dog snarling or baring its teeth results in staff spraying a little water on that dog's face and saying "No!" The second time the dog bares its teeth, growls, or a makes a snapping sound with its jaw, the staff member probably uses a time-out, isolating the dog in the transition area until it is time for staff to enter that area with one or two dogs to make sure they are getting their energy out in a safe way. Time-outs generally last from one to five minutes, depending on staff discretion and their assessment of a situation, and they make an important corrective impression on most dogs.

Another approach to discipline a biting dog is for a member of the playgroup staff to quickly slide his or her hand over the dog's snout and nose, giving a quick pinch to the nose without pulling and saying "No, No!" Dogs don't like this, so it can help change their behavior. Then we closely observe the dog to see if it calms down. We also use this technique when a dog consistently humps other dogs or barks too frequently. We sometimes also use small plant spray bottles at a dog who is breaking rules and not listening to the staff's directives of "No!" "Stop!" or "Down!" Certain dogs seem to be undeterred by water spray, but many respond by stopping the behavior for a period of time—how long depends on the dog.

Dogs generally don't like to be scolded, no matter how gently you scold them. Many breeds are extremely sensitive to the human voice and how loud it is. I generally find softer voice tones more effective than louder voices. Of course there are some dogs who ignore what the pet professional or pet owner is saying, and that is why other tools like eye contact, a whistle, or nonverbal signals are worth trying. Experienced pet behaviorists are invaluable resources for owners dealing with ingrained, hard-to-change behaviors caused by aggression, anxiety, and fear.

We use redirective discipline to give dogs new options, new activities, and new forms of exercise at playgroup. Dogs learn to associate good behavior with pleasure and fun. Balls, squeaky toys, wading pools, and slides are some of the exercise and activity tools our directors often choose.

Balls and Toys

Balls and toys can increase and redirect energy and fun. Conversely, balls and toys are taken away if overstimulation occurs or if dogs need to play more with one another. Dogs retrieve balls safely at playgroup, but a small percentage of dogs retrieve recklessly, nearly running into or under other dogs, potentially causing damage to leg ligaments. For reckless retrievers, I throw balls in the direction where few dogs are standing to minimize crashes.

Excessive group energy of running dogs or play may become overstimulating for the dogs and can verge on escalating beyond control. This can be decreased by throwing the dogs' balls or toys to distract them from chasing one another or from other unwanted behaviors.

Our playgroup has a metal container of at least twelve balls and other toys for chewing and retrieving. These toys and balls are either quiet or have squeak sounds. Dog balls and dog toys vary as to how easily they can be chewed apart and become dangerous versus being very hard to bite apart. Some metal ball containers are designed with built-in handles that allow staffers to retrieve balls on the ground by holding the container above a ball and pushing down, which forces the rubber ball through the bottom of the ball container. This keeps staffers from having to bend over to pick up those scattered loose balls. This design protects pet professional's hands from excited dogs that are lunging at balls on the ground while the staff member is trying to pick the balls up. Staffers sometimes take the balls away but leave the toys for chewing to decrease excessive group energy.

Retrievers, hunting breeds, and other breeds will often sit or stand near a staff member just waiting for balls to be thrown. Many dogs enjoy chasing balls thrown the length of the playgroup yard. I especially enjoy watching and listening to a dog catch a fastball in its mouth! What a popping sound!

After a period of time, balls often stir up an excessive group dynamic energy. A few ball-obsessed dogs can tire or distract staffers from other concerns at playgroup. Taking away the balls and leaving chewing toys restores calm. The chew toys still allow a lot of pleasure and distraction for dogs that usually need ball play. Dogs become attached to some toys for periods of time and will stand in front of the toy container waiting for a staffer to pick out a specific toy and throw it to them. A dog may become attached to a squeaky green rubber toy for four weeks and then lose all interest in it, becoming transfixed instead by a cherry-red toy of a different shape for the next two weeks of playgroup visits.

Wading Pools and Slides

My company's playgroup has four children's wading pools for dogs in the late springtime, summertime, and early fall. They can even be filled with snow in wintertime or turned upside down during a hail storm, allowing the dogs to watch with great curiosity the little white balls bouncing off the blue pool bottom with a snap-crackle-pop sound! Water is changed daily and the pools are stored indoors overnight.

Most of the Labradors and retrievers in our group lounge in the pools repeatedly between ball play and socializing in other parts of the yard. It is a joy to see dogs wet themselves, lying down on their stomachs or on their sides, and shake their coats in pleasure or rub against a fence or the ground afterward, becoming covered with dirt or mulch! The pools placed near the slides are magnets for socialization, water pleasure, cooling, and exercise.

Toddler slides placed near the pools are another magnet for social-ization and exercise for the dogs. Placing slides near wading pools al-lows dogs to see other dogs modeling the use of both facilities. Some dogs proceed directly from using the slides to visiting the wading pools. A personal joke I make is that on hot days the Labs, Pointers, and retrievers use the wading pools, but the poodles don't because they "don't want to have a bad hair day."

One slide is a three-sectioned design, with two slides connected by a level platform. One slide is about twenty-four inches long and leads up to the platform for sitting or standing. In front of the platform is the entry to the larger slide on the opposite side of the short slide. The larger slide is about seven feet long and descends at a gentle downward angle. Small dogs like Yorkies, Bichons, chihuahuas, and dachshunds are able to jump onto the lower end of the big slide and often climb to the top! The second slide has one slide steeper than the other, with a platform on top with walls full of holes and room for dogs underneath at ground level to hide out.

Dogs have individual styles for using the two slides, and they look excited as they find their slide style. Some dogs walk up the big slide, proceed to the platform, and walk down or jump down the small slide. Other dogs do just the opposite, moving up the short slide, standing on the platform, and then, with or without assistance, place their front legs on the slide, hopping up so their hind legs are also on the slide, and then either sliding down, walking down, or some combination of both. Still other dogs jump over the lower end of the longer slide or enter on the lower end. Special needs dogs are escorted on the slide by staff holding their harness.

"Let's Take a Walk"

"Let's take a walk" is a redirective discipline phrase I use to stop a behavior and encourage something fun and acceptable. "Let's take a walk" increases the energy of sedentary dogs. Experienced staff learn how to instantaneously change group dynamics, group focus, and atten-tion to improve playgroup when necessary. I leash up dogs who are less prone to walk the length of the playgroup area on their own.

CASE VIGNETTE: BRONZEBACK—REINTRODUCING A NEWLY BLINDED DOG TO PLAYGROUP

Bronzeback, a chocolate Labrador, had been in dog playgroup over many years. Like the scales of a small-mouth bass, her hair color shone bronze in the sun. Bronzeback's bond with me was powerful. She became very excited at pickup, her tail thumping powerfully as she jumped up and down on her rear legs.

One weekend, life hit Bronzeback and her family hard when blindness took her sight. Bronzeback was changed forever. What didn't change was her owners' commitment to providing her with a wonderful pet family home full of the love and continuing playgroup. Continuing playgroup would help Bronzeback develop independence while blind, maintaining exercise, socialization with dog friends, and experiencing the joyous excitement she had always showed when I would arrived for her at the house. The reasonable challenge of playgroup with her familiar dog contacts would allay some depression and negative anxiety a blind dog experiences, keep her in physical shape, and bring her social joy.

Playgroup reentry began with me successfully walking Bronzeback at her home four days a week for four weeks. I felt honored to accompany her on her walks, carefully approaching doors and stairs.

The first day in returning to playgroup, I placed her comfortably in the front seat of my car near me and my familiar voice. I brought her early for a walk around the playgroup yard before picking up my other transport dogs. Bronzeback's tail and nose lifted into the air as she smelled the scents left behind by the dogs in the mulch and against the fences. She sniffed the thick mulch around the perimeter. Bronzeback's excitement persisted as she recognized her old place, full of dog smells and happy memories. I offered her some water and let her lead me around the yard as she smelled vigorously. After twenty minutes, we reentered my car and went to pick up the other dogs on my schedule. Bronzeback's excitement level increased gradually as more dogs filled the transport vehicle. Bronzeback's head lifted as she heard their sounds and smelled their smells. Some dogs looked over the gate between their back seat and Bronzeback's front seat, gave her a smell, and tried to nuzzle her as she repeatedly leaned up to meet them with her nose. Dogs are creatures of habit, and Bronzeback was back in a routine she had thrived in for many years, ever since she had started playgroup! I was happy that Bronzeback's owners were not letting her blindness prevent this wondrous playgroup routine from continuing to light up everybody's life with her indomitable spirit.

I arrived at playgroup and unloaded all my dogs with the transport drivers except Bronzeback. Our playgroup director signaled me to bring Bronzeback into the transitional area. She opened the door and Bronzeback clearly remembered her voice, becoming very affectionate and excited. The director and Bronzeback bonded for five minutes, wagging her tail like a fast-moving metronome.

Many excited friends of Bronzeback had gathered, poking their noses through the fence into the transition area to greet their old friend. Mookie, the ambassador dog at the playgroup, had assumed his usual endearing "Play with me" stance toward Bronzeback, who was smelling his nose through the fence, barking and whining enthusiastically, wanting to greet her friends in the larger yard as she had done hundreds of times before her blindness.

I let selected dogs into the transition area to greet Bronzeback. Mookie and Sporter, both large Labradors, were the first of five dogs to greet Bronzeback. Bronzeback and the dogs greeting went smoothly. The next step was the director leading Bronzeback into the larger area on leash. We told Bronzeback's owners we would keep her on leash for safety reasons, including the leashing dragging behind her. Stepping on a leash can prevent a blind dog in a fenced yard from walking into a fence. My boss or I stayed with Bronzeback for most of the session with her and other dogs. As the hour went on, great happiness permeated the session for Bronzeback, the dogs, and staff. Bronzeback's owners were overjoyed at her progress and reintegration into playgroup. They felt some relief about her condition as they saw her joy when I arrived daily for playgroup transport. Bronzeback's disability continued to make her anxious for months after restarting playgroup, but the return to her routine ameliorated some of her anxiety as well as her family's.

A system of bells and directional commands helped Bronzeback at playgroup and walking to and from my transport vehicle. Bells worn by playgroup staff allowed Bronzeback to orient herself geographically near stairs, doorways, and fences at playgroup. The bells helped her feel more independent, relaxed, positively stimulated, and less anxious with her blindness. Directional commands accompanying the bells' sounds included "Right—good Bronzeback," "Left—good Bronzeback," "Move on—good Bronzeback," and "Heel—good Bronzeback." Bronzeback's delight and ease in playgroup was evident, through her willingness to be led on leash, follow bell sounds and commands, and an increase in her walking speed.

Bronzeback achieved another stage of transitional progress after two months of attending playgroup three to four times weekly. She became comfortable wandering around herself off leash, allowing her to learn where fences and gates were through smell, memory, and occasionally bumping into structures. We allowed Bronzeback off leash for five to ten minutes at a time before picking up her leash and walking her. Bronzeback began wrestling again with Clipper, a Golden retriever friend she had relished before her blindness. Clipper is a highly socialized dog who approached Bronzeback with gentle physical contact, leaning into Bronzeback and signaling for her to begin wrestling. This prevented her from having to find Clipper to make contract for wrestling. Other dogs in playgroup didn't follow Clipper's perfect technique.

The next stage for Bronzeback was being off leash during most of the playgroup. Bronzeback's directional memory was sufficiently advanced, rarely walking into walls, gates, or fences. Relaxed body language replaced tension in her body language, evident in her slow sauntering and curious smelling. A person unfamiliar with Bronzeback wouldn't know she was sightless except when she slowly negotiated fence gates, home doors, and stairs. Bronzeback learned to pass through a fence opening the majority of the time; only occasionally did we have to bell prompt to change her direction. Very windy days seemed to upset Bronzeback's directional memories in the playgroup yard, perhaps because familiar smells were altered by the wind.

One of Bronzeback's many wonderful days at playgroup occurred when she engaged in a conversation with another dog for about forty-five seconds. The two alternated dog talk, sitting and standing close face to face. Bronzeback was very animated during this exchange. A month into playgroup, Bronzeback started to greet transport dogs with a lick or bark after placing her front legs over the seat top.

Bronzeback loved the slide at playgroup, starting at the bottom. "Step up," I guided with a firm grip on Bronzeback's harness as she stepped onto the slide. The first half she walked up herself. I placed my hands in two places in front of her chest and above her shoulders for safety reasons at higher steeply angled slide area. She was safe from falling off the slide with my grip in case she had an impulse to jump or slipped.

Bronzeback enjoyed stillness standing on the slide top, lifting her head, listening to sounds, and quivering the sides of her nostrils. I would play a game with her by making loud smelling sounds, which she responded to by raising her nose and smelling. I commanded her from the slide top "Move on, pool," and Bronzeback walked gently forward down the small slide searching for the pool's location. She listened for sounds and smells she associated with the pools: wet dogs, water splashing, balls being thrown in water, dogs retrieving them, a dog shaking its coat, a noisy hose filling the pool up. The smells and sounds that register in a blind dog's nervous system may map out directional knowledge. Dogs that have recently gone blind that are exiting a door and walking stairs with an adult are held by the harness strap covering their backs for maximum body balance and safety to avoid tripping or crashing. Once the blind dog is familiar and demonstrates skill and safe stair walking with adults, the leash can be held firmly instead of the harness. Please don't assume a dog who is recently or experienced sightless will remember the location and spacing of stairs leading to the front or rear doors of the home. Changes in moods and adrenaline levels can cause a fall on stairs—for instance, if a dog is very eager to enter or leave the home. Bronzeback was incredibly excited at playgroup pickup time and returning home, anticipating her family's attention or a bowl of food.

PLAYGROUP DYNAMICS: STAFF AND LEADERS

A romanticized view of dog behavior modification playgroups exists. Working with dogs and their owners is fun, inspiring, and difficult. In playgroup, I have a commitment to dogs' socialization. Playgroup professionals are required to work hard, have patience, and be responsive to the director's and assistant managers' directives and protocols. Enjoying ambiguity and uncertainty helps. Running a dog playgroup is not as difficult as running and teaching a classroom of kindergartners for an hour and fifteen minutes, but challenges occur!

A dog playgroup is successful when it includes multitasking and wisdom while loving the dogs. Multitasking includes transporting dogs and overseeing the always-changing multitude of behaviors in a dog pack in differing weather conditions. Group dynamics in playgroup between many dogs and staff is a daily learning experience. The more you think you know, the less you know!

Playgroup is not an extended social time for playgroup staffers running the group. Social talk between the group director and manager of a nonpet-care nature is limited to discussions to help the dogs receive the oversight needed. Dog transporters are asked to socialize away from the yard after they drop off or pick up their dogs. Staff running the playgroup are challenged daily by multitasking during both the first fifteen and last fifteen minutes of every group. Transporters engaged in nonpet company questions or talk in the transition area distract the playgroup staff and irritate the dogs.

Routines for Starting and Ending Behavior Modification Playgroup

The following is a partial list of what playgroup staff should accomplish in the first fifteen minutes inside the yard:

- Remove leashes from dogs they transported.
- Start overseeing all the dogs' behaviors and energy.
- Remove from storage two poop buckets.
- Watch dogs for pooping and clean it up.
- Remove from storage a metal toy and ball holder.
- Dump out balls and toys.
- Fill two bowls with fresh water from a hose.
- Take attendance.
- Remove from storage four wading pools.
- Fill pools with water in warm weather or leave empty in cool weather.
- Kick balls around for some retrievers while staff are busy.
- Set limits on any dogs that are barking too much, humping, eating mulch or leaves, engaging in unhealthy biting, and so on.
- Continue taking attendance until all dog transporters have dropped their dogs off.
- Close the third fenced section until all dogs arrive for playgroup, so it is easier to contain and clean up poop.

- Fifteen minutes after attendance is completed the third section is opened up, where an additional slide and wading pool are.

Additional staff responsibilities during playgroups include:

- Rake unleveled mulch out of the yard corners formed by running dogs and hard rain.
- Rake leaves and twigs. Leaves make it harder to see poop, and dogs shouldn't be chewing twigs.
- Use ice crackers and snow shovels to clear walking paths, gate paths, and the playgroup yard and applying pet-friendly salt when necessary.
- Placing one to three crates for small, medium, and large dogs in the yard on very rainy, snowy, or cold days. Crates are also used for new small dogs who seek a cave like structure until thirty to sixty days have passed for transitional comfort.
- Fit weather jackets to dogs in weather with thirty-degree wind chills or less except for certain long-haired dogs.
- Short-haired mutts and breeds like Vislas and Rhodesian ridge-backs are susceptible to playful bites, breaking their skin when pack dogs run in playgroup in warm weather. These bites are not meant to draw blood; however, it is harder for socialized dogs to modulate and coordinate their bites when running. Pet owners should provide a T-shirt that is fitted and tied to the dog for skin protection. A jacket is used in cold weather.
- Smartpak with Thinsulate jackets are placed in different sizes across the top of the transitional pen facing the playgroup yard. Transport drivers can easily fit appropriate jackets for their dogs at drop-off time.
- Playgroup staff write the dogs' names inside their jackets worn to playgroup to avoid mix ups.

Playgroup Director and Assistant Manager

Through February 2015, I have been the daily assistant manager for 1,455 playgroups. My boss, who owns the pet care company, is the director of the playgroups. Dog playgroups need a strong hierarchy of leadership to function properly on site. Leadership puts the needs of the pet owner and dogs first and establishes clearly written protocols for staff integration.

You should look for good playgroup leadership when placing your pet in a playgroup, such:

- Loves working with animals, dogs, and pet owners.
- Understands acceptable and unacceptable behaviors by dogs in playgroup and how to redirect dogs with positive regard, positive reinforcement, and skills to decrease antisocial behaviors in playgroup.
- Refers pet owners to skilled animal behaviorists and trainers who help animals heal and change through positive regard and reprogramming versus heavy-handed corrective training. (Heavy-handed is necessary for some dogs, but is beyond the scope of this book.)
- Hires staff members who have cleared a background check and have a history of either raising children, raising or caring for animals, or in some other way proves they would act responsibly with other people's dogs, staff, and pet owners.
- Is insured and bonded, carrying insurance to protect themselves and staff from litigation when unavoidable accidents take place with dogs and other companion animals being cared for by the company.
- Interacts effectively and respectfully with diverse pet owners with many different opinions and styles of ownership, through verbal and written contract agreements.
- Handles conflict well with pet owners, showing unconditional positive regard to create a win-win situation for the pet owner, pet, and pet company staff.
- Guides different staff personalities and styles to work together in meeting the present and ever-changing behaviors of dogs in playgroup. Leadership sets limits on staff members and teaches them how to improve their decision-making skills and strategies in working with animals and one another. The playgroup director gives the staff more responsibilities in the business as competence and merit are demonstrated.
- Is able to say no to clients whose situations pose challenges beyond what the director and the staff can accommodate.

- Provides written protocols regarding all aspects of the playgroup for staff. Written protocols reduce stress for all employees and support the staff's learning pace and style.

Playgroup Staff

A good playgroup can be judged by its staff. Hiring the right staff to fill in for the absence of the director or daily assistant manager is important. Ideal playgroup employees are physically strong and confident about being around running dogs, because muscle-skeletal injuries can occur. Ideal employees are committed to learning to work well under directives and pressure, love dogs, enjoy colleagues, and are committed to excellent customer service for dog owners.

Good employees understand the playgroup director is in command. Autonomy and consensus exist, but the director is by necessity at the hierarchy top, and what he or she says in a playgroup needs to be followed.

The healthy hierarchy avoids problems. For example, an inexperienced or stubborn staffer may not understand the importance of giving a dog a time-out for chronic poor behavior during a playgroup. Instances of excessive growling and jumping forcibly into other dogs' faces with one exposure of snarling teeth earn a time-out. The playgroup director asks a staffer to lead the dog into the transition pen for a time-out. If the staffer, not realizing the need for the dog's time-out, were to voice opposition to the playgroup leader's decision, the leader should ask the staffer to please follow the instructions now and then talk about it later as time allows. Time and quick effectiveness with a dog pack is tantamount to keep the peace and model good behavior and consequences for poor behavior.

A couple asked me, "Can a team such as a husband and wife or two friends direct a playgroup together as co-leaders?" Yes, up to a point. However, in emergency situations, action needs to be immediate and discussed preemptively, with strategies already planned out. You cannot have co-leaders disagreeing on how to break up a dog fight. The larger dog pack becomes overly agitated and a danger to themselves, each other, and staff.

Staffers who are lifelong learners can be more fully present with playgroup dynamics ebbing and flowing. Lifelong learning influences decision making on intervening or not intervening with a dog or dogs. Respecting the authority of the playgroup director or assistant manager by taking directives is vital in playgroup. Staff members who do not take directives well and have authority problems will not be able to function consistently as a team player. Team players, in the true meaning of the phrase, are pet professionals who become better at what they do as a group. Trying to become the best employee possible should always be one's goal.

Visitors to Playgroup

Playgroup visitors are limited to those confirmed by the playgroup director. Otherwise, dogs become very distracted and bark excessively. Dogs become distracted by package deliverers, mail carriers, or repair people visiting a home near a playgroup area. Lawn mowers, leaf blowers, and people near the playgroup perimeters cause distractions, and dogs lose their focus on the playgroup energy and activities.

The playgroup director decides, based on a dog's reactions, whether the owner needs to be totally out of sight while watching the playgroup or perhaps close by but visually shielded by trees. If a new dog even picks up the scent of its owner and overreacts to it by looking for the owner, that dog will be distracted from its normal assimilation to playgroup.

Dog playgroup is not a time for cell phone use unless the playgroup director has to respond to business emergencies. Food cannot be eaten by playgroup employees, otherwise dogs become distracted and compete with one another to steal the food, causing chaos.

A spring water bottle or thermos can be drunk from briefly on hot days but kept out of reach of dogs who may chew and grab plastic bottles or apparel holding a thermos. Gloves placed hanging over the fence top can soon become clamped in a dog's mouth.

Group Energy and Inner Quiet

Talking quietly to dogs in the playgroup promotes interspecies relaxation, kindness, good behavior, and calm. Talking quietly is more conducive to effective discipline and limit-setting. Excess energy and exuberance can be transformed by talking quietly, thus creating a calmer playgroup. Talking too loudly sometimes creates negative tension and teaches the dogs to be loud themselves, and they may respond with excessive barking. Dogs may reject certain commands like "Come," "Sit," "Stay," "Down," and "Off" if stated too loudly. Calm and limited talking allow for the staff's eyes, ears, and attentions to relax amid the almost nonstop group dynamics in playgroup, while scores of interactions take place every few seconds between the dogs. If the staff and visitors are talking excessively, playgroup employees may have to speak more loudly than they should. Talk that is unrelated to what is present at playgroup decreases calm. A quality of inner silence helps playgroup staff be in the moment.

Problems can arise in a very short time, and being calm, quiet, and aware allows for quicker solutions and less escalation. The attention of two calm alert staffers is better than just one. Four eyes instead of two eyes and four ears versus two ears help playgroup function better. Seeing and hearing playgroup socialization lets staffers witness inspiring socialization.

Ending Playgroup

Ending playgroup is a slow transition, which starts twenty minutes before 1:30. The following activities take place during this time:

- Poop buckets are gathered and the plastic bags in the buckets are dumped into a large garbage can, which is secured.
- Garbage bags are taken to curbside on appropriate days.
- New plastic bags are placed in the poop buckets and placed into the overnight facility. Rubber bands can be used to seal the plastic bags around the circumference of the pail or bucket.
- All toys and balls are replaced in their metal carriers, hosed off, drained in the yard, and stored.
- Pools are drained and stored.
- Jackets are stored inside and hung up according to size to dry and air out. Dogs are leashed up and attached to harnesses if they have them. Leashes are placed in separate groups assigned to the appropriate transport drivers, hanging over a fence on the side of the entrance pen.

The playgroup workers leash up the transport drivers' dogs first, before their own transport dogs. I place the loops of attached leashes around the tops of the fence points to secure dogs to that area, encouraging them to rest and calm down during the remaining ten minutes. Certain dogs dislike when playgroup ends, and they begin a hyper play style of running around in circles stirring up other dogs who mostly want to relax. Staff will often let them do this unless the running is unsafe for the dogs and staff and leashes are applied.

THE FOUR DYNAMIC DOG BEHAVIORS

I read a book by a historian William Irwin Thompson titled *The Edge of History*. Thompson believed four patterns in human relationship existed throughout human history. After assisting in over 1,200 playgroups, I have applied my own interpretation of behavior I see in dog playgroups and transport.

1. Leader: Initiate an independent behavior while interacting with other dogs or staff. These actions include eating, drinking, exercising alone or with other dogs, gathering leaves and sticks, and performing bodily functions. For example, a dog approaches a playgroup staffer with a rubber squeaky toy, drops the toy near the staffer, and starts to run, waiting for a throw before the toy is even picked up. The toy is thrown and the dog redirects its running toward the flight and changing the location of the toy. The dog picks up the toy and runs back to the staffer, asking to repeat the throw–retrieval process, and runs again to wait for the throw.

2. Follower: A dog sees another dog engaged in play and starts to run with the dog down the playgroup yard, not to intercept the toy from the leader but to enjoy being part of the action kinetically and socially.

3. Bystander: A dog decides to sit and watch the other dogs retrieve throws from playgroup staffers. This dog's socialization maturity may be undeveloped, and it is watching dogs model behaviors it may develop in the future. The dog may be just relaxing and watching. Other bystanders simply don't have a play style that

would involve retrieving balls or following other dogs that are retrieving them.

4. Opposer or Rebel: A dog runs in front of the staffer who is trying to throw to another dog and steals the toy out of the staffer's hand. The staff throws another toy to the desired dog and the rebel dog runs to intercept the toy from the other dog or runs away with the toy without returning it to the playgroup staffer.

The four behaviors are interchangeable as playgroup dogs make choices and react differently in a pack. A playgroup dog can move from being a leader to a follower to an opposer or a bystander in a short period of time. The dogs' playgroup joy in these roles of socialization is obvious as they run, wrestle, sniff, explore, relax, lick, listen, see, use the bathroom, drink water, play with toys, occasionally bark, make new friends, use wading pools, engage in slide play, greet and play with old friends, and bond with staffers. The old adage "If you don't use it, you lose it" also applies to dogs, who are deeply nourished by structured contact with a dog social system in behavior modification dog groups. Modern domesticated dogs have lost the dog packs they used to run in, but they haven't lost the ability to relearn their innate social skills by attending dog behavior modification playgroups.

I remember one playgroup ending when I had three dogs on a leash and I was about to open the gate door and leave the main yard. Slipper, a large female Newfoundland who had never ridden in my vehicle, pushed toward the gate front, wishing to follow me out. I placed my relaxed hand on her forehead and gently pushed against her advancement. Slipper quickly moved backward and out of the way instead of pushing forward and running around my hand! Socialized dogs in playgroup learn the routines in playgroup protocols. Soon Slipper would be guided out by her transport driver.

CASE VIGNETTE: THREE PLAYGROUP ANGELS: ABE, MARY, AND SHAKESPEARE

I had never pet sat for three dogs at once before. The first time was for three sweet dogs. I think of them as my three angels. Shakespeare is a large Golden retriever with reddish hair. Mary and Abe are Labradoodles of medium size with apricot coats full of curls, who lived with a devoted owner on the Atlantic Ocean.

I will never forget meeting them. "The Doodles' eyes were so unique and beautiful," I said to the owner.

"They have people eyes, the eyes of a human being," the owner mentioned.

"They do look like the eyes of a person!"

I was stunned. I had never observed this in a dog, and I was seeing for the first time something surprisingly lovely, expressive, and poignant.

Pet sitting for the three angels and transporting them to playgroup filled my days with enjoyment and appreciation for their unique magnificence. Shakespeare was a very endearing and popular fellow at playgroup. His large, reddish-bronze body exuded excitement as he rushed to the gate to mesh with his friends, stirring up a bees' nest of anticipation in the playgroup yard. Shakespeare conveyed leadership qualities of physical strength and presence when he stood by himself on top of the rocky area in playgroup. Shakespeare's owner told me about his gentleness with puppies and children, gently licking them like a mother removing birthing mucus. Shakespeare often initiated a mediator role in group dynamics by intentionally moving into a group of dogs on the verge of excessive rough play, calming them down through his internal charisma and physical stature and distracting them by reminding them about relaxed play. Shakespeare sported a happy fatigue after playgroup when he asked me with his eyes to toss his carrot snack close to him while stretched out on the floor, avoiding a retrieval. Shakespeare ground the carrot into orange wood shavings before licking them off the floor.

Shakespeare could play with unknown children for over an hour at a time. One day Shakespeare played football with a child he had just met. The child would throw the football and Shakespeare would run after it and then sit or lie down near the football, waiting for the child to run over and pick up the football, because Shakespeare had realized his mouth couldn't grasp the oblong width. Once the child ran to the football and picked it up and threw it again, Shakespeare ran and sat beside it again. The child's father was amazed at this unknown dog's social grace, gentleness, and focused play.

Shakespeare had a routine he completed with great pride when I unlocked the front door and entered his home for transport to playgroup: he picked up his blanket from the floor and walked around the living room with it in his jaws, his head held high.

Shakespeare's siblings Abe and Mary were also endearing. Have you ever sat on a couch and had two cats come and sit on the couch arms? Abe and Mary do this same thing. They are too big to fit on the couch's arms, but they lie there anyway, with their bodies spreading onto the surrounding areas of the sofa. Abe and Mary would gradually slide off the arms to move toward the couch ends and start licking my hands.

In my car, Mary was always ready to peer over the gate separating the front seat from the dogs' riding compartment in the back. She placed her front paws on the fence divider and her eyes widened as she looked around. She repeated this posture when people were walking down the road in front of her home, peering through the window with her paws on the kitchen sink in front of the window. This pet family owner and her three angels were an inspiration for me! I love their hearts!

PLAYGROUP GUIDANCE: AVOIDING RARE BLOODSHED

One day a rescue dog named Bishop started playgroup. Bishop embodied high-energy testosterone, thus he was seated up front with me, separated from other dogs to minimize tensions leading to possible aggression. Bishop had growled in troubling ways toward staffers in transport and at playgroup. Staffers kept close oversight over him and often would talk with him before he entered an automobile and during the drive. I made eye contact and voice contact with Bishop in a kind and authoritative way before and after I seated him in my vehicle. Staffers helped Bishop learn they were in charge, not him, and he was learning to follow a social playgroup order of rules, behaving peacefully with high vitality, running and enjoying the rewards of social joy.

Another transport day I placed Bishop and another high-energy male dog, Pogo, in the rear seat. Bishop and Pogo behaved well during transport, with affectionate, roughhousing, and playing behaviors. I walked them into the transition pen at playgroup when another dog that was already in the main yard, Margin, began growling and rushing toward the fence aggressively. Bishop and Pogo reacted to Margin's aggressive barking by rushing toward the fenced areas separating the transition pen from the main yard. The playgroup director quickly instructed staffers to leash Margin inside the rear third section until he calmed down. Bishop and Pogo were retained in the smaller transition area with their leashes on, to keep them segregated from the large playgroup area until they calmed down. Margin was able to quiet down. Calm was restored, and playgroup staffers let Pogo and Bishop out of the transition pen into the larger pen, where we closely guided all three dogs, making sure calm was maintained. Staffers were ready with spray bottles and could step on the dog's leashes if necessary to set limits. Possible rare bloodshed was avoided.

Consistent barking is not allowed in our playgroup. Barking dogs receive hand signals, words, petting to calm down, a ball to play with, the statement "Let's take a walk," or a water spray. The small handheld water spray bottles discourage barking and other unwanted behavior. Small barking dogs are picked up and comforted as part of a redirective discipline strategy. Time-outs are also used. Stubborn barkers learn they are not in charge or they refuse to learn to change their barking behavior. Excessively barking may reflect excitement, anxiety, fear, confusion, pain, territorial instincts, self-defense, a desire to play with or protect others, or being overwhelmed. Playgroup attendance decreases barking as dogs play in a group, enjoying protocols that support healthy stimulation.

Harvey, a gray miniature poodle, was the smallest dog in playgroup. During winter dog playgroups, staffers would tuck Harvey inside their jackets, carrying him around like a newborn baby. This was comforting and warming for Harvey. He was transported in a small carrying case that looks like a roadside mailbox. He liked to stand next to his brother, Hurley, a standard poodle who towers over Harvey. When Hurley could not come to playgroup, Harvey was more social with other dogs. Dogs love playgroup and their owners tell us how excited their dogs are when the transport arrives at their homes for pickup. Playgroup attendance and results are a wonderful win-win situation all around!

Very rarely a playgroup dog bites another hard enough to create a puncture wound that produces blood. This can occur with peaceful socialized dogs under proper and vigilant staff oversight. Two dogs with a history of playing together happily may lose control and bloody the other, perhaps an ear wound. How can this be? Dogs were once wild, undomesticated animals. They can turn violent in an instant without any provocation apparent to the humans overseeing them. But dogs have their own reasons for their behaviors. Other puncture wounds occur by accident: for example, a number of dogs seek out the same ball and one unintentionally bites the other's flapping ear. As much as we know about ourselves and animals, new lessons can always being found for people to learn from and adapt to. The key is always to guide dogs through socialization, exercise, discipline, and affection events.

Transporting Dogs for Playgroup

Transporting animals for playgroup involves many responsibilities. Transporters' roles demand strong relationship skills with the pet company owner, the playgroup directors, staffers, pet owners, the dogs themselves, traffic and weather patterns, and personal life challenges. Transporting a new dog to playgroup may be anxiety-producing for the animal. A small percentage of dogs are unsure what to expect and are unwilling to enter a strange automobile without their owners. Dogs can panic as they approach the vehicle or when the door opens. Certain general precautions are necessary.

Every dog should wear a properly fitted harness for the security and safety of both the dog and driver. Collars are not adequate for playgroup attendance. Dogs can slip collars off their heads and run away, get hit by cars, or become lost. The initial interview informs pet family owners about providing a harness. Owners have the ultimate decision about a harness. If the owners persists in sending their dogs out with just a collar, the transport driver should intermittently check the collar for looseness and any ripped material.

The pet owner can bring their dog inside the pet store if possible and ask for customer service to fit the correct harness. Harnesses come in sizes for toy, miniature, small, medium, large, and giant dogs. Many harnesses are difficult and complicated to place and fasten, even before any loosening or tightening is done. The easier the harness is to use, the more likely the dog owner is to use it! Two companies manufacture excellent harnesses that I am familiar with: Softouch Concepts (their models are called SENSE-ible and SENSE-ation) and Easy Walk Harness. Most harnesses have a ring in front of the dog's chest that the transport drivers and owners attach the leash to. A small percentage of harnesses have leash attachments on the dog's back. The dog walker and the dog are safer with leashes attached to the chest ring.

Pet owners may inform the company owner or transporter that their dogs exhibit resistance or other difficulties when entering a strange vehicle with an unknown person or familiar person. High-anxiety dogs may crouch, pull away, or start moving in a tense windshield-wiper movement pattern when it's time to enter the vehicle. Dogs with injuries have special needs that the transporter needs to support. One solution is to attach the leash to the collar after securing it to the front of the harness inside the dog's home. A leash attached to both the harness ring and collar ring is difficult for a dog slip through if panicked. Strategies that help the transport driver feel more at ease during transitions also help the dog feel less ill at ease.

Transport vehicle treats that are readily available (but safely secured from pilfering dogs) are helpful. Treats help new dogs enter the vehicle, even when uncomfortable and unfamiliar with the transport process. I have crouched down next to the open door with treats in my hand for certain dogs, offering them one treat from my hand and holding a second treat up in the dog's field of vision, then placing it on the seat. Transport drivers use voice tone warmth, patience, and kindness when leaving the home with a new dog and repeat the process when the vehicle door is open.

Certain dogs with temporary transport anxiety are enticed into a vehicle that is lower to the ground versus a vehicle with a high-ground clearance, step-up design. High-anxiety dogs may ride in the front passenger seat closer to the transport driver and enjoy bonding. This strategy limits an anxious dog's access to dogs riding in the rear.

The playgroup director sets a transport schedule, deciding which dogs fit into which vehicle. Considerations include dog developmental stages, social skills, size, health, vehicle design, physical condition of the transport driver, and geographic location. Less socialized dogs will sit up front near the driver. Puppies that are crated, or uncrated and younger dogs who could be a behavior problem for socialized adult dogs, less-socialized adult dogs, or puppies need to sit away from one another at times in their development.

I exude a calm authority with the playgroup dogs I transport pick. I am quietly warm and affectionate for most dogs. I look behavior-problem dogs in their eyes and remind them to be good and get along with the dogs in the seating area. I may communicate this before or after the dog is in the seated area. I blow very quietly on my whistle if I sense a possible behavior problem occurring before or after seating. Eye contact with transport dogs is important, as is a reassuring kind word, scratch, or pat. I often play soft classical or country music. Occasionally I use a water spray to redirect growling. Dogs with occasional behavior problems are best unaccompanied by their owner to the transport vehicle to limit territorial issues being triggered. Pet owners who are at home for playgroup pickup should allow the transport driver to walk the dog to the vehicle from outside the home to prevent dogs unfamiliar with the dog from becoming agitated. Rarely is it necessary to pull the transport vehicle over to ask dogs to calm down. Our behavior modification playgroup dogs learn to get along!

Transport drivers communicate with pet family owners for better customer service. They encourage pet owners to write a dog's name on playgroup leashes to avoid a red leash getting mixed up with three other red leashes at playgroup and going home with the wrong dog. Leash identification also expedites the leashing up of dogs at the end of playgroup. Drivers communicate concerns about treats and leashes being accessible upon pick up and drop off and make sure that owners leave checks in a consistent place, with note pads if needed for two-way communication.

At homes with two or more medium to large dogs new to the transport, the driver should walk the dogs one at a time to the vehicle. This creates familiarity of routine and shows the driver how a new dog responds. Two new dogs responding poorly together at pick up creates safety problems for everyone. One dog experiencing some anxiety is easier to handle and keep safe than two or three dogs wanting to run away from the entrance to the vehicle. After the initial routine becomes familiar to a two- or three-dog medium to large dog family and the dogs are comfortable entering the vehicle, all the dogs can be walked out to the vehicle at once. Small dogs are easier to handle. The leash is attached to both the harness and collar rings the first few trips, until the dogs are calm and relaxed.

Sometimes, at pick up, one leash may be missing from a home with two dogs. The solution is take the end loop of the leash that is attached to one dog's collar or harness and thread it through the other dog's collar. This leashes both dogs in a temporary and functional way.

Outfitting the Transport Vehicle

Windows in transport vehicles should be adjusted high enough to prevent a dog from slipping its head into the opening, preventing neck injuries. Adequate vehicle air ventilation year round and well-functioning heating and air conditioning systems are very important. Air conditioning will be essential on hot or humid days, because windows cannot be lowered beyond a safe height. The transport vehicle needs to be in good repair and have a current inspection sticker. The floor should not contain leaks where exhaust fumes can enter the passenger compartment and build up dangerous levels of carbon dioxide.

Drivers should carry two ignition keys on themselves during playgroup transport. Dogs in the front passenger seat could stand on the electric door lock as they look out the window, locking the doors. This could cause the driver to be locked out if he or she had left the key in the ignition. Transport vehicles have a cargo area where dogs enjoy ample room, being denied access to the drivers passenger seat area. Dogs in the front passenger seat need restricted movement toward the driver's side of the vehicle. I always close the front passenger door on folded leashes to restrict dogs from moving toward me while driving. This prevents medium and large dogs next to the front passenger door from licking my cheek while driving. A small percentage of larger passenger vehicles have a bench seat in front. When using this type of vehicle, only small dogs should be seated in the middle of a bench seat so they cannot lick the driver's face.

Never place a leash between the interior window door frame and the window because the window may break if the dog pulls on the leash. Pet family owners use older leashes and older harnesses for playgroup. Wear and tear does occur with dogs chewing on other dogs' harnesses and leashes being closed in door frames for safety.

The transport passenger area should be securely fenced off from dogs in the rear. Playful dogs, small and large, enjoy the exciting challenge of trying to crawl over the gate into the front seats. After all, when these dogs ride with their owners in the front seat, they find things like people food, dog snacks, and a warm family body to snuggle next to.

The gate should feature holes or slats small or narrow enough to prevent dogs' legs from becoming caught. Pet professionals often use child gates that are installed to separate stairway tops or bottoms from inquisitive toddlers, which can be strapped into place in a vehicle with rope. Gates can be metal or very hard plastic. Bungee cords have to be securely attached so they can't accidentally become unfastened and whip into a dog's or person's eyes. (By the way, please don't ever allow young children to play with bungee cords. The elastic properties make them move at a velocity that can injure eyes, throats, and other body parts. Young children may also try to tie each other up with these cords and sometimes innocently place them around necks of children or animals.)

Sedans, pickup trucks, SUVs, station wagons, cargo vans, and minivans are workable transport vehicles. Some pet companies own commercial vehicles for staff use. I have used my own personal transportation, resulting in a great amount of body damage to my vehicle from hitting snow banks, ice banks, and rocks on customers' properties when I had to drive in poor conditions or in the dark.

If a private vehicle is used, the option exists for covering floors and seats with all types of materials to prevent damage from toenails, smells, hair, or—in the rare situation when a dog has an accident—vomit, urine, or feces. There are properly-fitted floor and cargo area mats for most vehicles available for purchase on the Internet.

"Heavy-duty" tarps are sturdier than "all-season" tarps. Small heavy-duty tarps can cover a passenger bucket seat. Newspapers can be used to cover floors or old towels can be covered with newspapers on top of the towels. I replace my tarps every six to twelve months due to toenail rips and dog odors. I remove the tarp about three times a week to air it out overnight after washing it off with soap and water.

Dogs may initially be uncomfortable with certain colorful tarps in a cargo area and may dislike noisy, crinkly-sounding tarp material. I owned a bright blue tarp that influenced three dogs from one home to refuse to enter my vehicle. I knew these dogs spent a lot of time on brown couches in their home, so the second day I placed a dark brown sheet over the tarp to help calm the dogs. After a week of knowing what to expect at playgroup, the three dogs were thrilled about attending and were no longer bothered by the blue tarp. I also placed sheets under the tarp, which decreased the crinkling noise the tarp made when they stepped on it. Heavy-duty tarps soften over time and make less noise under paws.

Dogs often drool on or place their paws on doors, windows, and dashboards. I store window cleaner, paper towels, and disposable wipes in my trunk for cleaning windows, door frames, and seats a couple of days a week.

Seats and cargo areas where dogs enter or leave should be clear of any cargo—no ropes, no backpacks, auto tools, car seats, paper, sandwich bags, aluminum foil, or other items. Dogs are likely to catch a leg or chew on unnecessary cargo.

Dogs rarely become car sick during transport. A playgroup director should inquire about a dog's tendency for carsickness in short or longer trips. The pet care company can accommodate some car-sick dogs by the driver picking up that dog last to minimize transport time. Customer service is all about knowing the pet family and making the adjustments.

Dogs with old injuries to hips, backs, shoulders, and legs may need more assistance exiting vehicles. Pet owners have the responsibility of informing a playgroup director if a dog has a history of surgeries anywhere on its body, including musculoskeletal surgeries that can affect pet visits, pet sitting, and playgroup transport. Ligament surgeries in some dogs may affect their ability to jump safely in and out of vehicles that have higher door levels. Drivers use a technique by which the dog places its front paws in the vehicle and the transport driver lifts the hindquarters inside.

Many dogs are capable of jumping into an owner's vehicle but won't execute the maneuver because of a lack of technique on the part of both the owner and dog. Here is a technique for teaching a dog to jump into a car independently. Hold the leash firmly with the leash hand pulling toward the seat and into the door frame. Don't let the open door hinder your movement. Try pressing the leash arm elbow into your ribs for more strength and protection from strain. Leaning toward the open door, exert more leash pressure. The dog will be expecting help jumping into the car. Don't say anything unless the dog is trained to respond to the words "Up" or "Jump." Try this a couple times. If your pooch won't enter the seated area on its own, try gently pushing with your foot and leg against your dog's hindquarter as you pull the leash toward the seat area. Right-handed adults may need to use their opposite leg to push against the dog's hindquarters. (Pushing isn't kicking, of course.) Coordinating a strong pulling of the leash while leaning toward the seat compartment with a gentle foot push against the hindquarters may change this longtime uncooperative behavior. Treats can also be used to train the dog to enter your car.

Transport Pacing: Start Early and Relax

I start transport early, decreasing worry about arrival time to set up playgroup. Rushing can result in me or dogs tripping on leashes or my hands getting caught in wind-blown storm doors. Traffic congestion and weather conditions like heavy rain, snow, and ice all impact playgroup pick up. Negotiating many different driveways at different dogs' homes, parking your vehicle, and walking to and from the home are challenging in snow and ice. Many sidewalks and driveways will have fresh snow or ice on them, despite having been shoveled once and treated with sand or salt. With snow banks impeding access, driveways may be too narrow for a large passenger vehicle. Respect for the safety of pedestrians is always important when I am visiting over fifty pet family homes weekly, especially when backing out of driveways around neighborhood children. Early school release days can slow the pickup of dogs and regular afternoon school release can affect transport drop off after playgroup ends.

The playgroup I have been daily assistant manager of begins transport at 11 a.m. and drops the final dog off about 2:30 p.m., allowing the dogs to use the bathroom without owner involvement. Certain dogs take a quick pee or poop pee before entering the transport vehicle. Transport time includes many opportunities for structured stimulation: socializing as dogs reconnect with familiar dogs, visiting their dog friend's homes as the vehicle stops to pick up or drop off, and smelling the individual smells from a freshly cut lawn or cedar-mulched flower beds wafting through the transport windows. Below is a typical pickup schedule for a dog playgroup transport driver responsible for three dogs.

At 11:45 a.m., Sophia, a Gordon setter, awakes from a nap as the dog transport driver unlocks the home's front door for pick up. The Gordon becomes excited as she sees the pet professional she has come to know through 112 previous playgroup transports over the past ten months.

(Average attendance at dog playgroup is three times per week.) Familiar positive bonding passes between the driver and Sophia, intensified by eye contact and Sophia's olfactory prowess. The dog becomes more excited as the driver says familiar words. "Sophia, want to go to playgroup? Want to see your dog friends Tess and Domino?"

The transport driver goes into the kitchen, washes and fills Sophia's water bowl with water, removing a treat from a box and leaving it on the counter for after playgroup. "Sit, Sophia." Sophia sits for the transport driver, who finds a light switch and turns on a dim light, struggling to find a harness and leash in the semidark, windowless hall. Multiple leashes and a couple of harnesses hang from the wall, as if in a horse's tack room. The driver connects the harness to the leash, attaches it to Sophia's body, and walks toward the front door, stopping at a table to picking up a check for the week's three playgroups plus one Saturday evening dog walk. (Sophia's owner telecommutes two days a week; Sophia goes to playgroup the three days that her owner works outside the home.)

Sophia sees the transport vehicle, lets out a gleeful bark, and makes a quick dive for a tennis ball on the porch. "Drop it, leave it Sophia. You and the dogs will just fight over it. Leave it home," the driver says. Sophia drops the ball and gives the driver a sad look. "Good drop it. Good leave it, Sophie," she affirms.

The driver opens the car door and Sophia smells familiar dog scents in the empty vehicle. Sophia settles into the rear area of the SUV, smelling a window streaked with saliva from previous playgroup dogs and licking it. Tess is the second pick up on the route. A Hollywood movie is being filmed in town, and cars are being rerouted by seven smiling policemen spaced out over 1,000 feet. Traffic slows to five miles per hour. Large movie set lights line the street, and fans huddle in cordoned-off areas along the fronts of commercial businesses, holding autograph pens and paper. The movie stars are conferring closely together as young people stick their heads out of car windows, yelling the celebrities' names.

The Hollywood movie reroutes the transport driver a quarter mile into heavy traffic, adding an extra eight minutes to the trip. A gray Cape Cod home appears and the driver parks. The key inserted in the door is very hard to turn, as the wood on the old door has swelled in the summer heat. The driver has brought this to the attention of the pet family owners, but oiling the lock isn't working well. Tess is in the dining room under the table, chewing a marrow bone. The marrow bone has been licked and sucked clean of any fat and meat and looks so polished it could be threaded on thick string with other bones for a necklace. A black chow, Tess runs to the driver, licks her hand with her black tongue, gently bites her sleeve, and leads her into the kitchen toward a counter where her treats are kept.

"You are really something, Miss Tess," the driver chides. "Just what your owners *don't* want, with your expanding waistline. Treats after playgroup exercise—not before." The driver checks Tess's water bowl, adds fresh water, leaves a treat on the counter for after playgroup, and fastens Tess's harness and leash that were hanging on shoulder-height hooks at the front door. Tess leads the driver gently down the stairs and wags her tail after seeing Sophia in the vehicle. The tailgate is lowered on the SUV and Tess jumps up without need for a hindquarter lift by the driver. Tess and Sophia smell and lick each other as the vehicle approaches Domino's home. Tess and Sophia love running together at playgroup. Domino is a mixed breed, black-and-white Griffon and Glen of Imaal terrier. He is playing on the front lawn with his owner, and Sophia and Tess press their noses to the window, looking out at Domino and his owner.

Two socialized bondings are occurring at Domino's house. Domino, Sophia, and Tess attend playgroup together three days a week on the same days. (Domino attends five days a week and Tess four.) Domino has attended four hundred playgroups over twenty-four months. Continuity of attendance has deepened the social system experience for these three dogs. That is one form of bonding. The second is a five-way bonding, with Domino and his owner, the transport driver, and Sophia and Tess meeting one another's gaze. The five-way bonding occurs frequently in the warm weather and has become a recurring ritual when the three dogs meet at Domino's home. The transport driver is also friends with Domino's family, forming another bond of positive regard for the dogs to experience. Playgroup fosters multiple bondings for dogs, deepening socialized stimulation.

Transport itself is a joyful socialization process of teaching and learning. Dogs learn better vehicle manners when they associate pleasurable experiences with having their harnesses fitted, walking to the vehicle, jumping into the vehicle, greeting and being greeted by other dogs, and being treated responsibly by a transport driver who sets limits while affirming good behavior.

Domino's mom gives the leash to the driver, respecting a protocol by which owners cannot bring their dog to the transport vehicle. The owners are strangers, and dogs who are already inside may react in a territorial way toward a stranger. During the transport process, I also ask strangers not to stick their hands into the windows to pet the dogs.

Built low to the ground, Domino needs a total lift getting her twenty-five pounds into the rear tailgate of the SUV. Some other dogs entering a rear door entrance of an SUV need less driver support. Tess has moved away from the front of the entrance, making room for Domino, but Sophia has not.

"Move over Sophia. Let Domino in," the driver states. Sophia listens to the command and moves back, and Domino jumps in from the transport driver's arms. Transport drivers teach dogs the command "Move over" so new dogs can enter the transport seating areas. After a few months of playgroup, transport dogs often move over without being asked, as they happily learn success in the socialization routine.

The three dogs greet one another with licks and smells, and Domino growls briefly when he has had enough, which ends Sophia's and Tess's advances. A peaceful growl teaches the dogs limit setting. "Okay now, settle down," the transport driver says. After hearing the growl, the driver sends a message the dogs are okay. The dogs vary their postures in the cargo area between sitting up and lying down with their heads up. Occasionally, one dog rests its head on another dog's back.

The transport vehicle arrives at playgroup driveway as the three dogs see and smell other dogs unloading. The dogs become excited and start whimpering and barking, crowding together in the vehicle without giving one another the space they allowed during transport time when they rearranged themselves in a comfortable, orderly way. The dogs look earnestly at the driver as she exits through the driver's door.

The three dogs formerly rushed to exit the transport vehicle, but they have learned to wait and follow commands from the driver. The driver opens the rear hatch door of the SUV and says, "Sophia, wait. Tess, wait. Domino, come." Domino moves forward to waiting arms of the driver, placing him on the ground with leash in hand. "Sophia, come," and Sophia jumps out of the vehicle herself. The leashes for Sophia and Domino are in the driver's left hand. Tess's leash is squeezed in her right hand. "Tess come, darling." Tess jumps out and all three dogs are walked to the playgroup gate in the transition pen. The driver slips a security rope off the gate top, opens the gate, and walks the dogs into the transition pen area, closing the gate firmly.

Dogs are starting to approach the inside gate where the dogs will pass through when it is opened to the larger yard. Inferno, a large gray collie, and Albie, a German shorthaired pointer, are sticking their noses through the fence, trying to touch Sophia, Tess, and Domino, squealing quietly and wagging their tails with all their might. The driver removes the leashes of two of the dogs, leaving their harnesses on. Domino's harness always comes off per the request of the owner, because Domino is recovering from medically diagnosed skin problems and the harness rubs against his skin excessively when he runs. The driver places the three leashes in one separate group over the fence alongside the larger playgroup yard, allowing playgroup staff to recognize each driver's leashes for efficient leashing up when playgroup ends.

Co-managing the playgroup, I place my body between the dogs inside the yard and the gate, allowing Tess, Domino, and Sophia easier entrance into the yard without being overwhelmed. The three dogs scoot merrily into the larger main area, greeting other dogs who have initiated greeting them! The driver demonstrates a pet professional establishing a healthy hierarchy during transport, supported by the staff in the playgroup yard.

Transitions at Playgroup: Unloading and Loading

Dogs are very excited during unloading at playgroup and more relaxed in loading after the group. Pet professionals protect their bodies from being tripped by leashes or dog bodies when excited dogs pull excessively on the way to the fenced playgroup's exit gates. Dangers increase exponentially for the driver when snow or ice affects traction under foot and under paws. Drivers also have to avoid being in too close contact of dogs that are walked to or from the playgroup yard to nullify out-of-control jumping and play. Transport staffers communicate near the outside gate of the transition pen visually or verbally to make sure dogs off leash cannot sneak out the gate.

A driver who is unleashing dogs in the transition pen cannot have another driver with dogs on leash opening up the outer gate until all the off-leashed pets pass through the inner gate opening to the larger yard and the gate closed. Snow and ice in the transport parking area present additional challenges. Transport vehicles engineered with all-wheel or four-wheel drive to negotiate snow and ice are safer in the wintertime. Pet professionals driving front-wheel or rear-wheel vehicles are wise using four snow tires versus two snow tires or all-season radial tires.

Transport vehicles must enter and exit the parking area carefully to avoid injuring the staff and dogs walking near vehicles. I suggest emergency lights be used when backing out of pet owners' and playgroup driveways. Using the flashing emergency lights offers visual warning for distracted or impaired drivers.

CASE VIGNETTE: A RACE FOR THE SQUIRREL AND THE HARNESS

I use yoga posture mechanics to protect myself and the animals. Two large Labrador retrievers named Favre and Sweetness were in the rear seat of my car ready to exit from playgroup transport. As I opened the rear door to reach for Favre's leash, Sweetness began barking violently at something. His body was turned around as he looked outside the window from the far end of the rear seat. I heard a shaking sound in the tree above the narrow street and saw a squirrel climbing it rapidly. Suddenly, Sweetness ran across the five feet of the rear seat past Favre through the open door partly blocked by my body. Sweetness knocked me partly off balance only to be stopped by my left hand slapping down on his back and grasping enough harness strap to stop him. I remember quickly rotating my shoulders back in a panicked instant when grabbing for his harness, which helped me avoid injury to my shoulder, arm, wrist, and hand, all of which strained against his ninety-pound mass and velocity! This was the first time a dog bolted from my car, and at high speed! I was able to avoid injuring my muscles, tendons, and ligaments by quickly integrating a variation of the mountain pose I learned from yoga science.

My hand was very sore and chafed, and I put Calendula lotion on it for four days. I vividly remember seeing a large Old English sheepdog hit by a car when I was young, and I was thrilled I was able to keep Sweetness from running free in the street. I also realize that not all people transporting dogs have the luck and yoga science body posture knowledge I have. To minimize my time away from the dogs in my transport vehicle, I usually write the playgroup notes in the car before I take a dog into the residence, as opposed to writing the notes in the dog owner's home where our company leaves a notepad for that purpose.

CASE VIGNETTE: BOGART'S AND BACALL'S INITIAL PLAYGROUP

One day an owner and his two Havanese arrived for their initial visit to playgroup. Littermates and two years old, their black-and-white coats were exquisitely colorful and soft to the touch, and their coal-black eyes and charcoal muzzles contrasted sharply with their panting pink tongues. Bogart's and Bacall's mom and dad were distressed and disappointed by the dogs' antisocial behavior walking on leash in their neighborhood and while visiting friends with dogs. Bogart's tendency was to bark loudly, growl, and lunge at times at another dog, while Bacall remained aloof and not open to canine affection or mingling.

No one cares more for their pets than the pet owner, with their immense commitments in time, energy, and financial resources. Many pet owners guard their dogs while walking to prevent them from charging other dogs or to curb their barking. A lack of social success is a source of disappointment for dog owners. They have seen their dog behave so well and affectionately with their immediate pet family members and the human guests visiting the home. Dog owners confronted with social immaturity in their dog's behavior often limit social interactions with their dog-owning friends. Dog owners would enjoy visiting their dog owner friends, but they hesitate when dogs cannot play together well.

Dogs may have evolved from wolves, which are pack animals, and wild dogs themselves were pack animals. This genetic and social history may be what dog playgroup rekindles in dogs in a structured setting. Bogart and Bacall had no socialization history with other dogs. Bogart and Bacall's dad watched from a porch above the playgroup yard during the initial playgroup visit. Bogart and Bacall began interacting with the playgroup director alone in the transition pen. Dogs pressed their noses against the fence eagerly as the dogs surveyed the new world of excitement. After a few minutes of bonding with the dogs, the playgroup director asked that Jemima, a wired-haired terrier mutt, be let into the area with Bogart and Bacall. Jemima sniffed Bacall, who was peaceful in response, gazing back at Jemima, who then approached Bogart. Bogart backed up as Jemima approached slowly, and the director's words "Okay, Bogart" and "Gentle, Jemima" added calm to the transition. Bogart turned away from Jemima, who reapproached Bacall, smelling her tail area. Bacall responding by turning toward Jemima and gazing.

Jemima's social style was to initiate but to maintain distance, perhaps sensing these two new dogs were in transition socially. Jemima returned to the fence and sniffed while a second dog, Barley, a Yorkshire terrier, scampered into the pen with my assistance. Barley approached Bacall, gazed at her face, and then approached Bogart. Bogart was calm while Barley smelled his rear end, and then lunged at Barley with a small bark when Barley approached Bogart's face. "Gentle now, Bogart," I said. Jemima came over to greet Barley, and they licked each other's faces as Bogart and Bacall looked on. Jemima approached Bogart, who let her stand close to him without lunging or growling. Jemima was let out of the pen and a small dog named Surething, a black female poodle, entered with her gorgeous prancing walk and her head held high, looking like she was bred for dog shows. Surething approached Barley, and then Barley stood still, watching Bogart and Bacall as Surething initiated with Bacall. Bacall moved closer to Surething, and they sniffed each other's faces. Bogart looked toward the two dogs and moved a little closer as Surething placed her nose near Bogart. Bogart was peaceful and seemed to enjoy the interaction with this strange, very feminine new dog.

Playgroup moved into the final fifteen-minute transition stage of cleanup and ending. The playgroup director motioned for the owner to come down from the porch. Bogart and Bacall's owner was a little teary eyed. "I've never seen them interact with dogs so well," he said. This was a very sweet, tender, and educational moment for the pet owner. His hope for Bogart and Bacall to become socialized with dogs was renewed.

Bogart and Bacall continued in playgroup, becoming happier and more relaxed around dogs, allowing interaction and initiating interaction themselves. Bogart continued, for months at times, to overreact to dogs approaching his face for social interaction, but the frequency and intensity of his overreactions decreased as he relaxed. Bogart and Bacall learned to enjoy walking throughout the dog playgroup yard, following dogs, and being part of excited social times near the slides, the wading pools, and the big rock in the yard. Bogart began chasing dogs who were retrieving balls. This new behavior of Bogart's was a delight for him and for staffers.

INCORPORATING PUPPIES AND YOUNG DOGS

Parents of young children often feel on certain days that their home is out of control, with the kids acting like an unruly kindergarten class, including loud voices or screaming, dangerous pushing, shoving, hitting, no one listening to anyone, including the parent. Puppies and unsocialized young dogs act the same way when they get out of control in a playgroup. Puppies and young dogs out of control can ruin a peaceful dog playgroup session and model poor behavior for many dogs. Socialized dogs can have their behavior corrected quickly by redirective discipline, but puppies acting poorly need more staff oversight. Additionally, well-behaved dogs can become very overstimulated and upset with puppies acting poorly, especially on days when high energy levels already exist, for instance, in Monday playgroups or in cold and windy conditions.

Unsocialized puppies and young dogs make excessive noise by barking, growling, and engaging in reckless kinetic play. They leap carelessly, without control, into other dogs' bodies instead of performing the controlled leaps common in socialized dogs. Aggressive leaping in other dogs' faces, with overzealous face pawing that includes the use of nails, really upsets socialized dogs. They run at top speed, upsetting dogs of all sizes by decreasing the calm dynamics. A reckless impulsivity is seen when they quickly confront dog after dog to play but are not given the time to play. (Some dog owners may not even recognize these impulsive behaviors as play, because they are only one-sided and usually forced.) The unsocialized dog in playgroup overuses its teeth in a hurting way that doesn't draw blood. I've recognized this in some breeds that traditionally were used as ratters or that herded cattle by biting the backs of the cattle's hooves.

Skilled dog behavior modification playgroup professionals change these unruly situations with younger dogs quickly, by bringing in a third staffer if necessary, and by using smaller fenced areas (the transition pen and section three) adjacent to the larger areas to funnel puppies in and out with selected dogs. Whistles are very helpful for quickly distracting most, although not all, dogs from undesirable behavior within a range of ten feet. A gentle spray from a water bottle is something dogs generally do not like. The following vignette about Frieda outlines the tools that are used in redirective discipline, changing poor behavior into better behavior.

CASE VIGNETTE: FRIEDA IS SOCIALIZED BY MOOKIE, THE AMBASSADOR DOG

Frieda was a mixed-breed dog of about twenty pounds, with an all-white head, a longhaired white-and-black body, and two black socks and two white socks. Frieda was four months old and new to playgroup. Initially, Frieda played too aggressively with larger dogs she met at parks with her parents. (She also had a history of biting one owner's toes, something that could be very painful with the needle-type teeth puppies have.)

Frieda would run up to large dogs, jump into their faces, and paw them near and on their eyes during her first four weeks in playgroup. Mature dogs don't tolerate this, finding the biting and pawing very intrusive, uncomfortable, and not playful.

Socially mature dogs have some controlled and effective ways of teaching lessons to unruly puppies and young dogs like Frieda. Mature dogs often run carefully into a puppy or younger dog that needs to learn how to play better. The socialized dog uses its head or shoulder to push the younger dog onto its side or back, then carefully stands over the dog as it wonders about this strange response to its unruly behavior. I have seen adult dogs push over an unruly dog onto its back and bite its belly painfully to teach a lesson. This lesson is enough for many unruly dogs to curb their impulses for a time and to learn to play more peacefully.

Frieda received plenty of lessons from mature dogs, usually larger dogs like Golden retrievers, a Newfoundland, and a Rhodesian ridgeback. After Frieda was pushed onto her side or back, the socialized dog would sometimes hold her down on the ground with its head for a short time. Frieda looked very surprised about this. This response may be anxiety producing and scary for an unsocialized dog like Frieda. She was being taught lessons by individual members in the dog playgroup assuming leadership roles.

Mature, well-socialized dogs gently wrestle, bite (without drawing blood most of the time), walk, and run gently with puppies, teaching them how to play. While running dogs intermittently do run into each other as they move in the same direction, generally a mature dog models a style of running that doesn't cut off the direction of the younger dog. This allows for longer runs together. It is wonderfully endearing to see dogs in playgroup run twenty to thirty yards down the play area, circle around the slides, and come back another twenty to thirty yards to where they started, then repeat this process.

Frieda was lucky with some socialized dogs who tried to teach her. She wasn't so lucky when she aggressively pursued Tuna, a fantastic loving dog with lots of affection for his sister Kuna and people. Tuna was toy fixated and had some general resource-guarding issues. Resource guarding means that a dog has problems sharing its toys and may also mistake a child's toy as its own, attack a child playing with a toddler's toy, or bite a child who comes too close to the dog's toy or food bowl.

Frieda threw herself into the face of Tuna, encroaching on Tuna's ball space, and received a small bleeding bite on the nose. Frieda was in pain and lost confidence for a couple days, refusing to reenter the large fenced at playgroup drop. Frieda's body language reflected fear and anxiety, so she stayed in the transition pen area with carefully chosen confidence builder dogs until her confidence returned.

Frieda's body language after a couple days reflected increased interest in what was occurring in the main playgroup areas, telling us she was ready to return. Frieda continued to be too aggressive with smaller dogs, and the staff separated her over and over again to try and teach her a lesson as well as to prevent her from being bitten painfully again. Frieda never bothered Tuna again. At least that lesson was learned!

Dog playgroup professionals trained in redirective discipline help dogs develop a wide range of social skills in the dog group context. Keeping a leash on certain dogs makes it easier to redirect their play to other dogs in the yard. Staffers can step on the leash and change their impulsiveness or bring them into a smaller fenced area for a timeout or to be with other selected dogs.

Playgroup staff decided to isolate Mookie, a very large gentle dog, which the playgroup dubbed the ambassador to the playgroup, with Frieda in the transition area to help Frieda learn to play. Mookie was a larger dark Labrador mixed breed with green eyes. Mookie had calmed down considerably after a couple months in dog playgroup, attending four to five times a week. Mookie rarely jumped on staffers anymore, and he walked calmly on leash to and from transport vehicles during pick up and drop off at his house and the playgroup location. He had previously pulled excessively on his leash, with his large frame and approximately ninety-five pounds of body weight, making walking difficult and at times unsafe, especially on snow and ice, or when walking with three other dogs on leash from the transport vehicle to the playgroup area.

Dogs socialized over time with other dogs usually increase normal behaviors and decrease unwanted behaviors. Mookie had ceased excessive barking at playgroup as he had learned to play with other dogs of all sizes and dispositions. His anxiety and excitement-influenced barking decreased through playgroup attendance. If Mookie had any problem behaviors left, it was that he occasionally jumped up onto female staff. Perhaps he was doing this with the females at home too.

I have come to adore many dogs, cats, and birds in all the professional pet roles I perform: playgroup, pet sitting, dog walks, cat visits, and bird visits. Mookie is one of them. Mookie is a very special dog with consistently strong social skills, and his charisma and excitement around the introduction of new dogs into playgroup are endearing for me to witness and guide.

Playgroup dogs become very excited toward new dogs in the transition pen. Their ears and noses go up and their eyes widen, as if a birthday cake had been brought into a school classroom! The dogs press their noses against the fence from their location in the main larger playgroup area. Mookie is usually the leader of the excitement as he runs to the fence, sticks his rear in the air and his nose as close to the fence as possible, whimpering excitably and twitching his tail. Mookie cannot wait to get into the transition pen and greet the new dog!

Mookie and Frieda were segregated together in the transition pen for five to ten minutes during playgroups when Frieda was overstimulated. Mookie towered over Frieda! Mookie's and Frieda's play styles varied, both combinations of standing up and lying down. Frieda engaged in oral play of excessive to gentle biting, accompanied by guttural sounds. Mookie was very patient with Frieda's excessive exuberance, perhaps giving her a chance to dissipate some of her extra energy. Frieda's exuberance was like an emergency alarm starting at a low sound and increasing to a crescendo as she became more physical.

Mookie had two approaches with Frieda's overexuberance. Mookie would let Frieda be wild and dissipate excess energy until he couldn't tolerate it anymore. Mookie also may have sensed Frieda was becoming tired. For five minutes she would attack Mookie with her paws and body and he would gently receive her, wrestling and rolling with her on the ground. Mookie would then become more dominant by overpowering her with his strength.

One day Mookie's lesson plan took a unique strategy. Frieda had been her usual wild self in the transition pen until Mookie gently bit into Frieda's winter coat. After biting into her coat, Mookie began pulling on Frieda's coat. Mookie's pulling put Frieda off balance with her legs, stopping Frieda's rambunctiousness. Frieda looked startled and powerless, unable to move. Immediately Mookie started his next lesson. Mookie slowly dragged Frieda along the ground. Her struggle to free herself was fruitless. Mookie stopped the dragging after about eighteen inches. Frieda appeared startled again and went limp, her head following between her paws. She looked bewildered. Frieda behaved differently after Mookie let go of her coat and body, appearing calmed down kinetically.

I was stunned to witness Mookie's lesson plan for Frieda. Mookie had a wise man's look in his eyes during the gentle biting and dragging. Frieda made gradual improvements in playgroup.

Dogs like Mookie need time to relax after being engaged with an overexuberant dog. I approached Mookie after his lesson plans with Frieda and gave him some scratching, pats on the head, and said "Good Mookie, good Mookie." Mookie enjoyed relaxing on the pine needles after leaving Frieda.

CASE VIGNETTE: NELLIE THE NEWCOMER

The day arrived for Nellie to enter dog playgroup. I felt like a proud uncle taking his young niece to school for the first time. I had joyfully helped provide puppy care for Nellie since she was small enough to fit in the crook of my left arm. I had stroked her head while walking down the front stairs to the backyard before she was ready for stairs. Nellie had a fear of the brick stairs leading to the driveway, and her first descent was with anxious glee, wagging her tail quickly. I remembered Nellie sitting on my lap, licking my hand, and trying to bite me with her puppy needle teeth. I recalled Nellie's head resting on my foot while she slept on the floor.

I recalled the huge scar from her intestinal surgery slowly changing color and disappearing as her body hair grew back over the incision, and how the neighborhood kids reacted to seeing her scar. "Wow, is she sick? What happened?" they would ask. I assured them Nellie was recovering well due to the quick action of her owner, our pet care company, and the veterinarian. Nellie was now almost six months old and growing quickly! What a Golden retriever miracle!

Her owner left a note on Nellie's first day of dog playgroup. The note said: "Nellie may need help getting into your car." She was very reticent looking, awkward, unsure, possibly even unwilling to try a new, unknown adventure. She finally put her front legs up onto the seat and I lifted her hindquarters. My boss suggested I minimize Nellie's time in the car. I decided to pick her up as near to the end of the pickup route as possible and dropping her off first afterward. This could reduce anxiety-induced nausea or pee accidents.

Nellie sat in the back seat by herself on the drive to playgroup until I picked up a lovely older yellow Labrador named Butterscotch. Butterscotch often sat behind a glass storm door and began barking as I shut off the car engine. I helped Butterscotch enter the rear seating area with Nellie. Nellie was quite excited initially to be driving with a second dog in the car; then she became more relaxed. Her head turned more often in the direction of her car mate instead of out the windows. Butterscotch, appropriately named, is a sweet and gentle dog, and both dogs licked each other.

I brought Butterscotch out of the car toward the dog playgroup's fenced areas, leaving Nellie in my car as my boss had directed me.

Many dogs rushed to greet Butterscotch as we entered the large fenced area. Butterscotch licked dogs as they licked her. I returned to my car and opened the car door for Nellie. Nellie was wagging her tail as I brought her toward the smaller transitional fenced-off area.

"Nellie is here. How do you want this to proceed?" I asked the director.

"Bring her into the small pen first and I'll take over with Nellie," she said.

I intermittently watched Nellie in the small pen as I worked with the dogs in the large penned area. On her very first day in the transition pen, Nellie initially seemed anxious and excited with some mild discomfort, lifting her head up and down as she adjusted to meeting her new friends. Nellie smelled dog after dog as they greeted her with strong curiosity and excitement. They smelled her mouth, nose, and private parts. The daily stimulation innate in dog playgroup, including social discovery and play, wind, dog odors, dog sounds, and the staff's talking, were being incorporated into Nellie's capable physiology and psychology. Dogs introduced into the smaller pen by staff were met with kind peaceful interest by Nellie. There were no mutual conflicts or red flags in Nellie's behavior or the dogs behaviors toward her. Nellie's body language became consistently confident after about forty minutes. Nellie turned away from the dog greeters the staffers introduced her to and started to look out repeatedly into the larger yard, where the next whole new world of dog socialization awaited her. The playgroup director opened the gate and Nellie quickly exited into the large fenced area, being greeted by other dogs and responding with her own growing interest and confidence.

A great female bear of a Newfoundland named Slipper was in the group. Slipper is a most imposing sight, lumbering along like a black bear. Slipper approached Nellie and sniffed her as Nellie rolled onto the ground immediately into a submissive posture. With Nellie on the ground, Slipper sniffed her belly, as Tuna and Kuna, the Golden retrievers, quickly gathered around, with Frumpers the Corgi and Sally the Field Spaniel. Nellie stayed on the ground, dwarfed by these full-grown, socially mature dogs sniffing her gently. Nellie didn't seem overwhelmed or too anxious, so staffers didn't disperse the crowd around Nellie. Nellie soon stood up, and she was quite confident for most of the twenty minutes remaining in playgroup as she initiated contact and let other dogs make contact in relaxed, mingling styles. Nellie ran around with wild abandon and joy and thoroughly enjoyed herself, racing in circles and fairly straight lines. Finally, with all her worming protocols completed, she was relishing the beginning of a more structured social life, seeing the other dogs three to five times a week.

Nellie's Big Second Day at Dog Playgroup

Nellie's second day at playgroup was unforgettable for me. Nellie entered the large yard as dogs smelled and looked at her and she returned the favor. Suddenly something occurred with beauty and powerful energy! Nellie ran stride for stride back and forth with the second-largest dog present, a Rhodesian ridgeback named Della. Della and Nellie ran together around the small toddler slide, past the rock ledge near the house foundation, all the way down the yard to the door into the smaller third fenced area, and back again the length of the yard. I watched in awe and excitement as Nellie opened up to her emerging play style in only her second playgroup day. Della towered over Nellie. Della is one of our most athletic of dogs, with a muscular body traditionally used in Africa as a scent dog to track lions. Della exhibits a powerful, graceful ability to hurdle over dogs with her thick muscled hips, and her dark intelligent eyes sparkle in her face. With such aptitudes, it's not surprising that property owners sometimes post signs stating "Warning! Patrolled by Rhodesian Ridgebacks." Della is a leader and teaches other dogs to find their play style by leading gallops down the yard. No one can catch Della unless she allows them. Dogs find their velocity and acrobatic abilities through Della's lead. Adelle, an Airedale, has pursued Della by leaping over the backs of other dogs! Della is in control in playgroup dynamics yet shows wonderful vulnerabilities. A super handsome grayish-white mixed-breed male dog named Flipper challenged Della in running from his first playgroup day. Della's style of play with Flipper changed by including her rolling on her back, something I have never seen her do with any other dog. I felt an almost maternal teaching presence from Della to Flipper, who was absolutely delighted with Della rolling on her back while making intense eye contact with him.

Nellie was becoming confident and opening up to her abilities very quickly on that second day. Nellie's confidence speaks very well of her breed, her breeder, her very devoted owner, and the playgroup's socialization power. Nellie was growing up quickly, finding herself in the velocity of her strides around the fenced perimeters of playgroup, passing many dogs that moved about at their own chosen paces. Fences are wonderful structures; they allow contained freedom.

The playgroup staff marveled at Nellie's second-day exploits. Nellie became one of our most consistent running dogs, along with the Rhodesian ridgeback Della, the Airedale terrier Adelle, Sporter a black Labrador, and Slipper the Newfoundland. These five would speed down the length of the playgroup area in packs of two, three, or four, turning around between the toddler slide and wading pools, and speed back. The power, speed, grace, and dog horsepower in their striding were impressive!

There is no predictable right amount of time, based on any theory, for a dog to make a transition in playgroup contexts. Dogs need to be watched and guided, and their confidence is sure to externalize itself when the time comes. The kind of running Nellie did with Della might occur for another dog after twenty days in playgroup, or not at all. Dogs each have their own styles of play.

Nellie was always thrilled to be exiting the transport vehicle in the parking lot near the playgroup. Dogs see other dogs exiting vehicles or hear and smell fellow hounds. Many dogs, like Nellie, dig in their paws and try to lunge toward the gated dog group areas, causing playgroup transport workers to have to change posture to protect themselves from soft tissue and skeletal injury.

Nellie continued to change and relax around transport vehicle transitions. Playgroup dogs learn calmness and cooperation as car occupants through the playgroup transport pickup and drop-off processes. Nellie began to willingly jump into my vehicle when I would pick her up at her home, and at the end of playgroup, she no longer depended on my lifting her hindquarters. After some anxiety the first eight times exiting my car at her home drop off, Nellie began jumping out of my car with ease.

Nellie exhibited nurturing behavior toward other dogs at playgroup. I saw in transport mutual licking between Nellie and her dog friends in the back and front seats. One of the most tender moments I've seen in transport was her fond gazing at and licking of a dachshund family seated below her on the front floor of my vehicle, Shana and Fredrick.

Certain dogs, like the Newfoundland Slipper, enjoy making squeaky toys squeak until the staff asks them to stop the noise. Many dogs enjoy retrieving toys and engage in small amounts of chewing, whereas other dogs engage in lots of chewing and retrieving. Nellie developed a strong interest in a particular green squeaky toy and enjoyed retrieving it after long throws down the yard. Nellie would choose one of two retrieval patterns. She would either go off by herself onto a large rock to chew on the toy passionately or immediately retrieve the toy standing near a staffer, turn her head away from us, and refuse to drop it for another throw. Nellie enjoyed playing tuggy and allowed other dogs to grab part of the squeaky in their own mouths to start the game. Dogs pull in different directions in the tuggy game, often standing side by side without moving before digging in their legs and using more force.

The toddler play slide became a favorite of Nellie's. She enjoyed following me down the dog playgroup yard as I said "Slide, slide!" Once we were within ten or fifteen feet of the slide, Nellie would run to the top of the slide, furiously wagging her tail at the top. She would exit the slide through the lower hole opening in the wall, opposite the inclined slide ramp, making her one of the few large dogs in playgroup I've seen exit the hole.

I think Nellie is very intelligent in her ability to learn new things. I could see her learning every station on an obstacle course and enjoying it with utter glee! Nellie exhibited how a dog accelerates its social maturation process by attending dog behavior modification playgroup.

FOUR SHORT PLAYGROUP POINTS

Point 1: Protecting the Staff from Accidental Dog Bites

Playgroup staffers can protect themselves from accidental dog bites. Dogs love the stimulation of running after and retrieving toys. Accidental dog bites occur when a staff member has a ball or a toy in his or her hand and has not thrown it yet. Dogs will pursue the toy, and if the hand is held low before or during the throwing of the toy, overexcited dogs may accidentally bite the hand or the hand may brush against teeth when moving. Accidental bites are avoided by holding the toy chest-high with the elbow bent against the body. Height and a partly obstructed view from certain dogs visual angle will decrease problems. Certain dogs will jump up high toward a toy held against the chest.

Point 2: Hyperactivity on Mondays and Windy Days

After assisting in running many playgroups, I have seen behavior patterns repeat themselves on Mondays and windy days. Dogs may lack enough exercise over the weekend, returning to playgroup on Mondays hyperactive and pent up, very eager to bond with dog friends. I see major increases in high-speed galloping, acrobatic running followed by turning on a dime, moody growling, irritability, some bullying, and excessive barking on windy days and Mondays. Windy days may jettison a concentration of smells into a dogs olfactory physiology. A dog's smelling physiology is much larger than that of humans. Comparatively, one postage stamp on a regular-sized piece of paper signifies human's olfactory physiology. The entire rest of the piece of paper signifies a dog's smelling physiology. The intense socialization energy of playgroup inundated with blowing winds is overstimulating. (Kind of like a kindergarten class drinking espresso, and each child with their own puppy.)

Point 3: Puppy Food Preventing Energy Depletion at Playgroup

Younger dogs eat three meals daily for their physiological development, and attending a dog playgroup at midday before they eat a regular lunch may require some portion of a meal before playgroup. The developing dog finishes breakfast in the early morning between 6:30 and 8:30 a.m. and cannot wait safely until after dog playgroup 2:00 p.m. for lunch. The developing dog must have some lunch before playgroup commences to avoid dangerous low blood sugar or some other negative physiological stress from lack of food. Our playgroup is scheduled midday between 12:15 and 1:30 p.m. A solution is for the transport professional to pick up the younger dogs at their home before other dogs if possible and feed the dogs one-half or all of their portion of food, allowing at least forty to sixty minutes to pass before exercise begins. The puppy or young dog is afforded digestion time to pass, while other dogs are picked up at their homes. Owners of younger dogs who eat their food very quickly before or after playgroup can purchase a special feeder bowl to slow eating a meal.

Point 4: Monday's Poop Loop Patrols: Highest Poop Output

I notice more poop cleaned up at playgroup on Mondays than most other days. A psychoanalyst would have a field day (no pun intended) explaining this. Do the dogs save it up over the weekend? What is the relation between socialization and decreased constipation? Socialization in the dog playgroup does, in fact, excite and stimulate the dog's physiology at a different rate than what they may experience resting or walking with their owners.

PARTICIPATION LEVEL: HOW MANY TIMES PER WEEK?

Dog behavior modification playgroups can be a significant part of a dog's life. I believe a happy socialized dog is a tired dog. Socialization and exercise are important for a dog's health both physically and mentally. As we've seen, many pleasurable interactions in playgroup teach dogs to associate happiness and joy with social interaction as dogs are properly guided by playgroup staff.

Many dogs attend dog playgroups three to five times a week. Certain pet owners believe this frequency is best for their dogs' happiness. Other dogs attend less frequently, such as once or twice weekly.

I have observed that dogs that attend one to five times weekly show great delight and excitement in expressing their particular play style, including tail wagging, playful wrestling, licking, and sniffing. Pet owners tell me they see better behavior at home and in public places after attending playgroup. I have seen the same dogs benefit more from attending three to five times a week. Dogs attending frequently encounter more dogs in play and are challenged to develop social skills that would otherwise be unused or underused. The physical stamina that develops in consistent playgroups is an important benefit.

Dogs benefit from consistent modeling of good behavior at playgroup. Behavior change may require the repetition of hundreds of interactions in the context of group dynamics among dogs and staff in behavior modification. This is very different from sitting at home alone Monday through Friday for four to eight hours without people and without a social life with other dogs.

3

A SOUND PET SITTING ENVIRONMENT

In my work, pet visits are a series of twenty-five- to thirty-minute stays in a home, usually once or twice a day or as scheduled according to the pet owners' wishes. The pet visit begins when I close my car door outside the residence and ends when I leave.

Pet sitting is a service in which I live in an owner's home for a minimum of twenty-four hours to twenty-one days while the owners are away for business, travel, vacation, medical treatments, or important family lifestage transitions such as a wedding, graduation, birth, or funeral, among others.

This chapter will lay out most of the requirements and responsibilities that a pet owner or pet professional must consider to make a visit and pet sitting successful. Along the way I'll also introduce the many wonderful cats, dogs, and birds I've had the pleasure of sitting for and visiting.

SADIE, AN AGING DOG, PASSES AWAY DURING PET SITTING

Sadie was an orange Pekingese I pet sat for numerous times. During my last contract with Sadie, she passed away overnight. Her loving parents had spoken to me about her aging issues, and her frailty was mutually understood.

One moonlit night, I walked Sadie, gave her a treat and her favorite play sock, and then I went to bed. The next morning, I went downstairs and Sadie didn't respond to my calls for breakfast. The warming smells of her owners' homemade rice, chicken, and vegetables filled the kitchen. I approached Sadie on her dog bed in the den and realized she was not breathing! Stunned and saddened, I wrapped her up gently in her favorite blanket and called her owners at 7 a.m. after taking several deep breaths to compose myself.

I called the owners and explained the situation. They were distressed, of course, but because we had a good relationship based on respect and mutual understanding, they asked if I could take their beloved dog's body to the vet for handling. They would arrange the meeting themselves and have the vet all set up for when I arrived. When we spoke later, they thanked me and mentioned that they were happy I had found her and not them, which would have been too difficult for them.

This scenario reflects mutual respect between pet family owners and an independent pet professional. Because of my own training, understanding, and regard of both Sadie and her family, I was able to handle a difficult situation with the understanding of distraught owners. The pet family experience was very spiritual for me, and I was glad to remove some burden from a loving grieving pet family.

AUTONOMY IN THE PET FAMILY HOME

The pet owners need to understand that the pet sitter must be the only person in the home while the family is away. This means no family relatives coming over to visit the pets, cooking a meal, taking baths or showers, or having parties. No cousins or aunts or uncles or others dropping by to check the house or see the pets. No college children coming home from college with their friends or crashing at the house during the pet sitting contract. Exceptions have to be made well in advance, written out, and mutually agreed to by the independent pet professional, pet company owner and staff doing the field work, and pet family owner.

There are obvious reasons for this, including legal considerations, the pet's safety, the security of the pet owner's home, and the comfort and functioning of the pet sitter. The pet owners have contracted for pet sitting, and the pet sitter is the one onsite person endowed with onsite responsibility for care of the pets and supervision of the home. Having met the pet's owners, the sitter must use his or her own judgment during pet sitting, without having to consider multiple influences and points of view coming from anyone except the pet owners or the head of the pet sitting service who has spoken directly to the pet owners.

For example, a college student who enters the home while her parents are away might inadvertently leave doors open or unlocked, play loud music, consciously or unintentionally try to take over the pet sitter's responsibilities, have friends over who drink or do drugs, or challenge what a pet sitter is doing. This can become a real disaster quickly, undermining the pet sitter's authority, autonomy, and standards. This type of scenario needs to be avoided at all costs.

I have pet sat in houses where friends of the pet owner showed up and let themselves in without my knowing they had a key. Friends of the pet owners can accidentally let out an indoor cat or a dog that must be leashed before leaving the home. Visitors may feed the pets inappropriate human food that is unhealthy, bringing on an allergic reaction, digestive upsets, or respiratory distress.

A small percentage of pet owners don't understand these concerns and protocols and may try to oppose this policy before the pet sitter begins contracted service. Pet owners should not be surprised if a pet professional will not contract caring for their pets under these conditions. Most pet owners know how to put the health and safety of their pets first. If a disagreement exists about this between both pet owning spouses, one spouse may try to find a pet company that will agree to less-stringent terms while the other takes a wait-and-see position.

Pet owners have some exceptions: painters who are finishing exterior painting and need to come inside to open doors and paint exterior door frames. In a case like this, it's up to the pet owner to make arrangements ahead of time. Pet sitters should not be expected to wait hours for painting to be started or finished. Cats and dogs should not be able to wander loose while the work is being done. They need to be secured ahead of time. The pet owner should explain to the paint company that access to the interior would be limited while the owner is away, and that a sitter will be overseeing the home. That limited amount of time should be decided by all parties: the pet owner, the painter, the pet sitter, and the pet company owner. Ideally, the pet owner should only allow work to be done outside the home during a pet sitters contract. Emergency situations can arise that the pet owner will need to act on during the pet sitting time, such as failures in the heating, electrical, sump pump, roofing, or alarm systems.

In rare cases, a pet owner may wish to hire a pet sitter while work is being done inside the home: interior painting, wallpapering, floor finishing, drapery work, or kitchen remodeling. This work, of course, is time consuming and not a one- or two-hour job. In situations like this, animals need to be crated for their own safety so the work can be done without interruption. These can be very noisy, smelly, and uncomfortable pet sitting jobs. Additionally, pet owners and pet professionals may have allergies to dust and wet paint. Pet owners may need to consider rehousing animals temporarily during major interior work.

Pet owners may not realize that their animals need the work on the home to adjust to their needs also. Dogs and cats have experienced real discomfort living in a home where a room is being rebuilt with the table saws and other loud mechanical equipment. Pet owners might consider having responsible relatives board their cats and dogs during some of the noisier rebuilding stages. Pet owners might also consult a pet professional who boards dogs in a homey situation with couches, no cages, and plenty of freedom to move during the day inside and outside. Remodeling is also an excellent opportunity for pet owners to have dogs attend playgroups for exercise, attention, and discipline outside the home. Playgroups free the dogs from the noise, dust, dirt, and smells of home rebuilding and allow them a higher quality of experience.

Indoor cats have a very negative experience when their owners are away and remodeling is being done on the home. Table saws, hammers, and loud noises from moving furniture all upset cats a great deal. The cats may become withdrawn, scared, aggressive, and unhappy. I have seen calm, sweet cats turn into hissing cats when loud home remodeling goes on for hours day after day. Cat owners need to find better alternatives for their cats in these situations, if possible.

Housecleaners are another group of people who legitimately need access to the home. Pet owners should inform a pet sitter if anyone is scheduled to be in the house for cleaning or other upkeep. The pet owner should let the pet sitter know whether housekeepers have keys to the home, a garage code, or if they would rely on you for entry by leaving a door unlocked. Pet owners should not ask pet sitters to leave doors unlocked while house sitting due to home security.

At one of my pet visit jobs, housekeepers entered the home while I was there and were still working when I left after a daily cat visit. Unfortunately, the housekeepers inadvertently locked a cat in a room in the house. The cat was trapped for about twenty-four hours, until I arrived the next day. The cat didn't show up for breakfast when I called for her. I found her in the closed-off room, which must have reached about ninety-six degrees. There was cat poop on the floor and of course no water bowl. This was a strong healthy cat, so no lasting damage occurred to her. If the cat had been older, with kidney trouble or some other serious malady, the outcome could have been much worse, even death. The cat owner told me it was a language issue with the two housekeepers; they didn't understand her English or mine. Pet owners need to plan well in advance how workers who speak other languages get the correct instructions to ensure pet safety.

SECURITY MEASURES FOR PET OWNERS AND PET PROFESSIONALS

Pet owners may be living in areas where people with criminal intent are scoping out a car, an apartment, a condominium, a home, a dog, a cat, or even a bird. Pet owners and pet professionals they hire don't want to end up in the wrong place at the wrong time. Criminals steal family pets and private property. Many pet owners underuse their security systems. Pet owners and pet professionals have choices to minimize danger for themselves and their pets.

Pet owners can clearly write out their alarm directions and share it with the pet professional. Pet owners can ask the pet professional to keep the information in a locked place. For security reasons, the pet owner's last name and address can be eliminated from the document copy carried by the pet professional.

The pet owner can ask the pet professional to carry identification on him- or herself and in the vehicle used during the pet contract. The pet professional can place a pad of business stationery on their vehicle dashboard in the left corner that names the pet care company they represent with address and contact numbers. The pad alerts pet owners, neighbors, police, and grounds managers who you are. This is helpful when parking at pet owners' homes in apartment and condominium complexes where grounds management allots specific parking spaces for visitors. Pet owners should explain to pet professionals their preferred parking options.

Pet professionals can keep a clipboard with their name, the names of the animals, and the day of the current week on the dashboard. A clipboard sends pet owners, neighbors, and police a clear message that commercial business is being conducted.

Pet owners and pet professionals can be vigilant about having fully charged cell phones inside and outside of pet homes. In an emergency, dialing 911 on a charged, turned-on cell phone takes very little time. Pet owners should show pet professionals where landlines are in their home.

Pet sitters and pet owners should never feel compelled to open a door for a stranger. You can go to a window on the second floor if possible and listen to the reason for their visit. Ask for a business card to be left in the door or on the doormat. Pet sitters can call the pet owner for clarification. If you have a sense the stranger is a cause for concern, calling 911 is a good option. Police are more than willing to send a squad car by for possible assistance and assessment. Police are trained to help you identify situations in which there is a clear and present danger versus situations where danger may not be an issue. Police are skilled public servants, and you shouldn't be hesitant to ask for help. It is better to be safe than sorry when your safety and the security of the home and companion animals are in question.

Tell the police officers who answer the phone that you have a concern as a homeowner or professional pet caretaker visiting an owner's home and you are not sure what to do. Tell them what concerns you and what you are feeling about the circumstances around you. Answer their questions clearly and politely.

If a person with criminal intent really is scoping out a home, pet owners, pet sitters, and pet walkers are vulnerable. When the pet family is out of town and a pet sitter is living in a home, a criminal might notice a change in the family's usual patterns and be more likely to act. To avoid attracting this kind of notice, pet owners can instruct pet professionals to pick up newspapers lying around outside the home if delivery has not been stopped and empty the mailbox if mail hasn't been stopped. Newspapers piling up outside may indicate to criminals that the home could be empty. Returning trash and recycling bins from the curb to their usual places is important. Pet owners can invest in timers for lights or instruct the pet professional to turn on different lights when you leave the residence if there is no automatic lighting system. Pet owners can invest in automatic lighting for outside light fixtures near all doors and gates.

Apartment-dwelling pet owners can inform pet professionals of any people living in an apartment building who should be avoided due to behavior problems. The pet owner can state "There is nothing to worry about, but I would avoid contact with the person who lives down the hall. I'll show you their apartment door." Pet owners can also inform pet professionals of loose dogs in the neighborhood who should be leashed.

CAR SECURITY

Pet owners encourage pet professionals to use their driveways and garages when possible. Vehicles need to be locked when walking dogs or visiting inside the pet owner's residence. Valuables can be stored in trunks to make it harder for criminals to steal a GPS, laptop, DVDs, photo equipment, or other valuables. Pet owner checks can be placed in an opaque envelope. Excess pet family keys can be left in a locked glove compartment during the day and removed overnight.

Pet professionals should not leave their vehicle idling when entering a home to pick up or return a dog from playgroup. Pet professionals should take their vehicle keys with them so that if a dog locks the electronic locks on a door by standing on the mechanism, they can regain entry into the vehicle.

PET FAMILY DRIVEWAY VEHICLES AND BOATS

Any pet family's vehicles and boats are discussed on my initiative before pet sitting. Pet owners should inform pet professionals which cars and boats, if any, will be left on the property during their travels. Cars have disappeared from driveways while I've pet sat without an owner telling me that a relative or mechanic was going to pick them up for use or mechanical servicing.

I once contracted to visit four cats for over two weeks in one home. A few days into the visits, torrential rains occurred. I noticed the next day that one automobile had a window totally open. I went into the car and found the rear right floor area filled with water. The right front floor area also was wet. After removing four floor mats in the front and rear of the car on both sides, I used a large towel to soak up as much water as possible. Then I began airing the car out during sunny weather to help the interior dry. I may have saved the owners a load of money from water damage. I called the pet owners, who of course were grateful I had noticed the open window. For my conscientiousness, I received a generous gratuity from the pet owners after they arrived home. Pet owners appreciate thorough customer service!

Pet owners rightfully expect pet professionals to treat their homes as if they were their own and maintain a high standard of respect and awareness. Great customer service makes the pet professional proud of their efforts that meet, or exceed, the needs of the customer.

BREAKABLE ITEMS IN THE PET FAMILY HOME

Pet owners often contract pet care companies in emergency situations. In emergencies, the pet family may have to leave their homes quickly, not having time to clean up after themselves. I have entered homes where owners had left in an emergency, encountering dirty glasses, opened wine bottles, sharp knives, and plates on side tables next to a couch or love seat, where cats could jump up to reach them and knock them onto the floor. Bottles and glasses have also been left on kitchen counters, easily within a cat's jumping ability. Glass shattering on the floor can precipitate a dangerous situation, causing dogs and cats to cut their paws or worse. Pet owners inform pet professionals about these circumstances and may pay an additional fee for ten to twenty minutes of housework.

Pet owners can also have needs for housekeeping in their homes in nonemergency situations. The occasional extreme puppy or cat mess has taken fifteen to twenty minutes to clean up, and owners always get a call on their cell phone when I encounter this type of extended housekeeping chore to know I have gone the extra mile and to consider calling their veterinarian to make sure the pet is not seriously ill. Pet owners are expected to pay a little more for a visit in extended housekeeping situations.

FLOOR COVERINGS IN THE PET FAMILY HOME

Correct floor coverings in the pet family home are an important asset for pets and pet owners. Additionally, pet sitters, dog walkers, and cat visitors also benefit. Floor coverings help to maintain independence for an aging or physically challenged dog or cat. Installing carpets, carpet runners, or rugs can be a wise strategic decision on behalf of these pets.

The back, hips, legs, and paws of cats and dogs must coordinate with a floor surface in the transitions from standing to lying down or sitting into a standing position. Animals are extremely conscious of their footing on surfaces, and their confidence is bolstered from feeling solid footing and the predictable performance of their body on a surface. Pet homes with hardwood floors and little carpet, wooden stairs without carpet runners, and slippery vinyl kitchen floors offer little support for a weakened pet. A dog or cat may not be able to stand up consistently and confidently on these surfaces or stay upright once standing.

It is heartbreaking to see dogs and cats struggle to do daily things they did for many years with ease. Further muscle-skeletal damage can occur when a dog collapses, quickly losing their balance. Uncarpeted stairs may keep a cat or dog from being able to traverse up or down a stairway safely, preventing them from trying due to a lack of confidence. Carpet and rugs may not be as attractive as polished floors to some pet owners, but they provide more independence for the health-compromised pet.

Carpet runners are very easy to add to those rooms that have only wooden floors, wooden stairs, and vinyl flooring. They will allow a dog to stand upright as well as lie down with more control. They are also a real help in maintaining dogs' ability to move, especially going outside to walk and do their business. A carpet runner three feet wide across a kitchen floor to a back door exit helps a weakened dog immeasurably, including those with overweight or aging issues. It may be necessary for the pet owner to place a leash on the dog so it learns to follow the carpet runners when leaving the home for walks or yard activities. The leash helps the dog become familiar with a safer exit and entry from the home and trains it to use the carpet runner, first with assistance and then by themselves. If the dog is vision impaired, a leash is even more practical and necessary.

Cats with age or injury problems will also benefit from using stairs with carpet runners, so they can continue to have access to more than one floor of the house. Indoor cats benefit from having multiple floors to live on. Multiple floors provide exercise, climbing, visual and sensory stimulation, access to bedrooms, social interaction, and the ability to look out an upper-floor window at birds or squirrels in a tree, while the cat's tail twitches in hunter-gatherer excitement! Cat owners relish seeing their cats enjoying their surroundings!

Basements are a favorite place for some cats who enjoy the cool, damp, dark places near foundations of stone and concrete as well as ceiling and wall crawl spaces. Installing carpet runners on the basement stairs provides more autonomy, exercise, and freedom of movement for the cat. Outdoor carpet can be installed on stairs leading to a yard off a deck, porches, patios, and other surfaces.

PROBLEM EXITS AND ENTRANCES IN PET OWNER HOMES

A pet family residence may have very narrow areas for entering and exiting at the front door. I have found this in multifloor rental apartments and small older colonial homes. Pet owners and pet professionals must avoid stepping on a dog's paws when exiting, tripping over your own feet or the dog's, getting the leash caught on door knobs and on your legs as well as the dog's, having storm doors blow shut forcefully on your body or the dog's, and shutting doors on your fingers.

Often the pet family has adapted to the situation, but it remains a challenge that can be cumbersome and unsafe for the pet professional. Pet owners should encourage the pet professional to do what is convenient for them. The dog's leash may be hung close to the front door, but I prefer to put on the leash and harness at the top of the stairs or away from the front door for less congestion. A dog that pulls excitably in these cramped exit areas is more prone to causing safety problems. Pet owners and pet professionals can try voice commands to see if a dog can wait and be calm as you open the door. The pet owner can inform the pet professional of voice and hand signal commands the dog is familiar with.

Pet owner homes are affected by high winds blowing loose storm doors. Windblown storm doors are a safety problem for a person's body and a dog's legs, paws, neck, and head. Pet owners should adjust or repair storm doors for the good of all involved. A broken storm door doesn't shut properly. The door may cause a lot of noise in the wind, and owners should be concerned about the noise bothering their neighbors. The pet owner may ask the pet professional to lock the storm door with a key. Generally, storm door hardware on older models is inferior to today's hardware and prone to freezing in the wintertime, making use of the key difficult. I have used oil applied through a straw into the lock mechanism to improve performance. Pet owners should prevent pet professionals from struggling with broken storm doors in wintry conditions by repairing or replacing them. Pet owners can provide keys to different first-floor doors if one key doesn't work for a front, rear, or side door lock.

DOGGY DOORS IN THE PET FAMILY HOME FOR EXERCISE AND FRESH AIR

I have never respected the overdomestication of animals, especially dogs. Seeing pet owners at my father's animal hospital impose poor diets and lack of exercise on their pets made a lasting impression on me. Many pet owners may be lounging around their homes watching too much television as their dogs and cats hover about, needing exercise and play. Seeing small, medium-sized, or large breeds known to need one or two miles of walking a day living in small homes without receiving enough exercise concerns me. Some dog owners have so little energy left from work and parenting that a soft couch is more appealing than a mile walk with their dog. This sets the innocent pet up for health problems from becoming overweight and other diagnosis too early in life.

I remember vigorous, exercise-oriented pet owners waiting for their appointments in my father's veterinary office with a Weimaraner or svelte pug on a leash. These were owners who exercised with their animals daily. I also remember pet owners in the waiting room whose dogs had sagging bellies and overburdened leg joints trying to carry the weight, and my father's statements about limiting food, not giving a pet ice cream or meat scraps from the dinner table, and taking walks on a daily basis.

I was introduced to Randy and Dune, two large, gorgeous dogs, by their pet owner. Dune was an Akita and Randy an Alaskan Malamute. I have never seen such hair formation and layering as in the middle and upper hips and shoulders of an Akita. Akitas come from very cold climates in Japan, and Dune was right at home in New England winters with wind chills some days of twenty degrees below zero and average winter temperatures ten to fifteen degrees below freezing for weeks on end. Cold-weather dogs like Akitas have evolved to grow very large amounts of hair with both density and length. When you smooth it out and look at it, this hair resembles duck down from a parka rated for below-zero temperatures. Dune's hip and shoulder hairs were very soft, fine, thick hairs, shorter in length than those on Dune's back. Dune's face looks as if he were part bear and part wolf, with his wide skull and deep-set eyes. It is a face of ancient history, suggesting animals of different species and types, fiercely loyal and protective of their dog families when traveling in packs and loyal to pet owners when domesticated—and a terror toward those harboring ill will to the pet owner's home.

Randy and Dune's owners installed a doggy door that suits the width and height of their two dogs, whose combined weight is easily over 260 pounds. The doggy door is located off a four-season porch that leads directly to the backyard. The doggy door allows Randy and Dune access to the backyard at all times when their owners are home or away. The owners have installed a high, well-built, very secure fence in the backyard, with equally secure hardware locking the two fence doors. These two dogs do not bark much in the yard, something very important for this arrangement in a suburban area where homes are easily within earshot of barking dogs. Their owners have friendly communication with neighbors and have been told Randy and Dune bark infrequently.

The pet owners are so comfortable with their doggy-door arrangement that I visit Randy and Dune daily when their owners were out of town, but I have never been contracted for pet sitting there. I arrive twice a day to feed them, socialize with them, and clean up the yard. It is a glorious site to watch this magnificent Akita and Alaskan Malamute sunning themselves in the backyard, stretching their legs and lifting their noses into a head wind. The sun lights up their coats into hues of chestnut and burnt reddish brown, reminiscent of autumn leaves, as if they are standing next to a bonfire.

Doggy doors afford pet owners a hands-off option for when they are home or away from home. They are something an owner should consider if the dogs are not chronic barkers and the yard is professionally secured with a strong, high fence and gates. Fresh air is very relaxing for dogs and is also cleaner than a lot of the air inside homes, where carpets give off mold, mildew, and unhealthy air pollutants. A doggy door doesn't automatically ensure that the dog is exercising as much as its breed may need, but a dog gets more exercise when a doggy door is available to allow it to go outside than waiting for the owner to come home and walk it. Doggy doors also allow immediate outside access when the dogs hear a stimulating sound or sight, be it a car driving up or a person making noise on the street. When visiting Randy and Dune, I often found one of them sleeping outside on the porch or patio, receiving lots of fresh air and sunshine.

Doggy-door models are being updated and introduced frequently, so there are a variety of models to choose from with differing features. All doggy doors should have strong hardware attachments, be fitted to a door that is in good condition without any rot or cracks, and be flush with the door frame. Unless a pet owner is a skilled carpenter, it is best for an experienced carpenter to install the door. The carpenter can assess whether hardware different from what is sold with the door is best for a pet owners home. Most doggy doors come with a removable door that you pull out or install in a matter of seconds, depending on your needs. If you want your dog or cat to stay inside, you slide in the solid door covering the doggy door. You reverse the process for outside access. Some doggy doors are held on by hardware attached to magnetized borders that fit flush against the metal frame, making the door stay shut during wind gusts and when your pets are not using it.

Cats will, of course, use the doggy door, even if they have a cat door installed where they live. If an owner is without a cat door and has installed a doggy door, the owner should train the cat to come into the house when called. One way to do this is to tap a spoon against a bowl and call the cat, then reward it when it returns home. Entice the cat into the house with a treat if it won't enter on its own. Repeating this method increases the likelihood that your cat returns to the safety of your home whenever you wish, especially for overnight hours when you close and lock the cat door, keeping all your animals safely inside.

COLLARS, HARNESSES, AND LEASHES IN THE PET FAMILY HOME

Inspecting animals' collars, harnesses, and leashes is an important part of beginning the pet sitting job. It can take place at the initial meeting with the pet owners or before pet sitting, pet visits, or dog playgroup activities begin. The condition of this equipment is crucial not only for the pet who wears the leash but also for other pets in the home or outside in the neighborhood. Pet owners will be aware of some existing problems in hardware and may ask for guidance about purchasing new products for their cats or dogs.

Pet owners are aware that dog collars, leashes, and harnesses wear out over time. A broken harnesses or leash creates big problems. For example, very friendly dogs that have the best social skills with children and dogs can break loose from a broken collar or frayed leash, develop a pack reaction toward a dog on a leash, and attack it viciously.

Not only should the equipment be in good repair, it must also be the right size. It is quite common for a puppy to grow so quickly that its harness needs to be loosened so it can breathe normally and walk unimpeded by the straps on its chest and under its legs. Pet owners are often so busy that pet professionals may find themselves in dog playgroup writing a note that will be left for the owners about a harness or collar being too small or on the verge of needing to be replaced.

Conversely, harnesses can be overly loose, increasing a dog's likelihood of tripping and falling while on stairs or while running, resulting in painful injuries and very expensive surgery. The pet owners can learn to check the harness in place to make sure it is not too loose or tight.

Outdoor and indoor cats need to have collars that are not fraying or ripped. Their tags should be attached without any visible weakness in the hardware between the tag and the collar. Indoor cats need collars loose enough to be comfortable but snug enough so that they avoid getting their necks snagged on protruding objects like knobs, nails, or bolts, as well as being swung around by the collar by the house dog.

Pet owners know to always remove harnesses after a walk to prevent dogs from catching their jaws on the harness, causing breathing problems. Additionally, the harness can shift position off leash, greatly increasing the risk of a walking injury to the leg and hip joints and the ligaments connecting bone to bone. Dogs may also chew a harness that is left on, leading to weakness and breakage. A harness that breaks when you are guiding a dog away from cars or other dogs wanting to play is the last thing a dog owner or pet professional wants to occur. It is also expensive to keep replacing harnesses that a dog has chewed to the point of structural failure. Plastic hardware on collars can also get chewed up when dogs play with one another as well as when the owner leaves a collar within a dog's reach. Metal hardware is preferable.

Leash materials include leather, rope, cloth, flexible plastics, and metal. The pet owner will have increased durability with their dog and cat collars, leashes, and harnesses if they are stored in rooms that are heated rather than on unheated porches, because gradual weather damage can cause the metal to rust and the other materials to weaken.

For safety's sake, pet owners should store leashes, collars, and harnesses out of reach of dogs and young children. Leashes in the hands of young children may accidentally end up around the necks or limbs of children or dogs. Hang leashes on adult-high hooks by their handles. Or you can hang the circular opening device that attaches to the collar on the hook so it cannot be pulled off or reached by young children.

DOORS AND WINDOW SECURITY IN THE PET OWNERS HOME

Pet owners are under transitional stress when preparing to travel. They may leave their home in a rush due to being overwhelmed by responsibilities. Pet owners appreciate the pet sitter securing their home on arrival. The first thing I do after arriving at their home, after feeding, watering, and walking the pets, is to make sure the home is secure. I often find first-floor or basement-level windows, doors, and sliding doors unlocked. Deck doors are notoriously prone to broken locks, and they are frequently left unlocked by busy parents and other relatives or people who tend to children. It is also common for people other than homeowners (relatives, children, and housekeepers) to use the sliding doors in a home and forget to secure them. Improperly closed doors and windows can also interfere with the activation of an alarm system.

Pet owners appreciate that I make notes about an unlocked door or window and inform the pet owners when they return home. I check the owners' home to see if it looks like there had been a robbery. I walk through the home to see whether drawers are open and things are abnormally messy, which may signify theft. Of course, the rooms of some teenagers often look like a robbery could have taken place, with clothes and video equipment all over the floor as a matter of everyday lifestyle! Pet family owners may leave their houses unlocked on purpose, but owners should inform pet professionals of this in advance.

PET FAMILY GATES AND FENCES

Pet owners have a wide range of concerns regarding fencing and gating their yards. The pet owner should clarify this in the first interview with the pet sitter. I inform the pet owner that I check all yard gates each day when pet sitting. If I am visiting, I check the yard gates if I bring an animal into the yard. If I am playing with and exercising a dog off leash in the backyard during a twenty-five-minute pet visit, I check the gates. If I am visiting to walk a dog around the neighborhood and return it into the house, I do not check the gates.

The pet owners' yard may have two or three gates, leading to the back, front, and side yards. Some owners heavily secure their yard gates with locks or wire when they leave town. I like extra security on yard gates when I am solely responsible for dogs during pet sitting contracts. Pet owners may show you an open padlock they place in a gate mechanism, which keeps the latch from lifting unless the padlock is removed. People unrelated to the owners' family may enter the yard and leave the gates open by mistake. This can occur during deliveries of heating oil, dry cleaning, meter checks, gutter work, or snow removal. Gates may be left open by housekeepers, painters, roofers, or general contractors. Pet family homes along heavily walked school routes experience occasional balls that were accidentally thrown into the yard by children. Secured gates should remain closed, despite an innocent intruder's attempt to retrieve a ball.

Time, weather, extremes of water, snow, ice, wind, and mud slides weaken gate hardware. Pet owners are often aware of this and make the necessary improvements on gates. Wooden fences also may become loose and break, creating dangerous protruding surfaces for animals who habitually jump up and down against the fence because something nearby is exciting them, such as a neighboring dog or a cat, chipmunk, squirrel, or raccoon. Pet owners appreciate being informed of areas where nails or screws have come loose, wooden boards have shifted position or could shift, or where a dog's paw, leg, or collar could become punctured, scratched, or caught, causing playful jumping leading to strangulation, torn flesh, or broken bones. Document these problems with a note to the owner.

In some cases, dog owners don't have their yards fully fenced. From a safety point of view, it is better for both dogs and outdoor cats when owners fence the entire backyard to attempt to keep out skunks, raccoons, dogs, coyotes, fisher cats, and foxes. Fences also send a message to human trespassers that a gate has to be opened and closed for them to enter private property.

Foxes, coyotes, and small black bears are now found in some suburban areas in the United States. Although fencing a yard is not a guarantee that unwanted critters will be kept out, fences deter and at least slow down many animals. It is also safer for dogs tethered on the property to be protected by a full fence in case an aggressive animal or a wild animal such as a rabid raccoon attempts to enter the yard.

Certain pet owners use interior child-safety gates to keep pets out of certain areas of the home. Safety gates that rely on pressure, rather than hardware attachments to keep them strong and immoveable, never belong at the top of stairs. They should be fitted only inside doorways, with rooms on the same floor on each side of the gate. An animal or toddler at the top of the stairs with a pressure gate can push the gate forward with their paw or leg trapped in it and roll down the stairs and become injured.

CHOCOLATE TOXICITY AND HUMAN FOOD ACCESS IN THE PET FAMILY HOME

Chocolate in certain quantities is toxic for some pets, especially dogs. During pet sitting, I sometimes find chocolate candy on cocktail tables and on top of other furniture where dogs could reach it. Chocolate is also sometimes scattered about in children's rooms, including under beds, which may not be closed off during pet sitting or pet visits. When I see this, I confiscate the chocolate and put it out of the animals' reach, in a high drawer or on a high shelf. Old bags of Halloween candy are placed outside of dogs' and cats' access behind a closed cabinet or closet.

The same caution should apply to lawn products containing cocoa in mulch. Dogs can become sick after ingesting cocoa mulch. Check the label first before purchase. Pet owners often have food stored on counters in plastic or paper bags. Small dogs can jump up on counters or larger dogs can surf counters and access bread, cookies, pastry, chips, and lunch bags. Pet owners should store food out of the reach of their pets. Pet owners can discourage cats on top of stoves and counters with a spray from a house plant water bottle.

PET OWNERS LIMITING WILDLIFE

Property owners can do several things to decrease the likelihood of wild animals being on the property. Animals are attracted to the food smells and tastes in trash. Keep trash in containers that cannot be forced open. Put trash out the morning of the day of pick up instead of the night before. Do not feed wildlife such as geese and ducks. Feeding wildlife teaches creatures to change their normal behavior of finding their own food through foraging, hunting, digging, swimming, and whatever evolutionary techniques their species uses.

Homes, decks, and outbuildings are often built with open crawl spaces under foundations and porches. Pet owners can close these areas off with strong nonflammable fencing material to keep wildlife as well as dogs and cats from entering the spaces, nesting, and raising babies. Fencing off these areas makes the property safer for children and keeps flammable dry leaves from being blown in during the fall months.

Compost vapors may be a constant attraction for some wildlife, although scientists may disagree on which ones and to what extent. Compost needs to be covered and be inaccessible to wildlife. Bird feeders sometimes spill seeds on the ground, attracting smaller wild animals that are preyed on by foxes, coyotes, and bears. Foxes and coyotes may pursue and kill domesticated outdoor cats. Pet owners with indoor-outdoor cats may wish to use bird feeders that spill very little seed. Black bears are also commonly seen around bird feeders. During fruit harvest times in the fall, clearing fallen fruit from the ground is a way to attract less wildlife to your property. In areas where there are hawks and eagles, small dogs can fall prey to these birds if left alone off leash outside without pet owner oversight.

PET FAMILY SUMP PUMPS AND WATER TURNOFF

Pet owners should inform pet professionals about sump pump locations inside the home during the initial interview. Sump pumps decrease water flooding into cellars. The pet owner should walk the pet sitter through the basement to indicate where the sump pump is, and show the outside pipe or pipes that water flows from while the pump is working. The pet owner should write down the necessary contact information for the sump pump professional who can repair the pump if there is a flood emergency. It is helpful for the pet owner to explain the regular working noises of the sump system and show where expelled water exits on a property during normal sump operation. The pet owner should also point out where the main water valve shut off is in the basement.

WHEN TO IGNORE PET OWNERS' INSTRUCTIONS

Occasionally, a pet professional may need to ignore pet owners' instructions. Letting dogs off leash is an example. A pet owner told me during the initial meeting, "It's okay to take Milo into the front yard before bedtime without leashing him. Milo uses the bathroom in the front yard and comes back in the front door if you stand here on the porch."

Pet owners know their animals better than anyone, and pet professionals follow owners' guidelines. However, one night Milo got spooked and ran off. Dogs had begun barking down the street before I took Milo outside. I turned my back for thirty seconds to retrieve his leash inside the doorway and Milo disappeared. I searched the home's foundation, shrubbery, and a neighbors' yard. I felt like an utter fool as my worry escalated. Milo's neighborhood was full of raccoons, skunks, coyotes, foxes, and moving cars. What if something happened to Milo? I was scared and anxious. I called the police and gave them Milo's contact and general description.

An hour later, which seemed like three in cold, rainy weather, a car pulled up and a person carried a wet, shaking Milo to my waiting arms. Milo's address had been on his collar. Milo jumped high off the ground and licked my face as I greeted him. I wrapped Milo in a towel, on my lap, and held him there until he dried off and relaxed, which took about two innings of watching a slow baseball game. That was the last time I let a dog off leash in an unfenced area.

Dog owners don't know how their dog may behave or react with a stranger. Dogs in unfenced yards, tethered to a rope, or out loose can be in danger. Thunder, motorcycles, speeding cars, snow sliding off the roof onto a patio where a dog is resting, an adult slipping on the ice nearby, a person yelling or young people cheering, a garbage can being slid out of a garage to the street corner, emergency sirens, car alarms, or even a whistling teapot can startle some dogs. Smaller dogs can easily be spooked by wild animals.

When I meet the pet family during my initial interview, the pet owners show me the entire yard as well as the integrity of the fence hardware. Over the phone dog owners have told me the yard is totally fenced, only to find this is untrue on my inspection. The unfenced area might be a ledge five feet above a driveway, but it is not fenced. Five feet is an easy jump for a medium or large dog, especially in pursuit of a squirrel, chipmunk, cat, another dog, or a next-door barbecue grill full of juicy steaks sizzling away. In New England, dogs enjoy stealing hotdogs off barbecue grills! Certain yards for small dogs have fences a grasshopper could jump over. Twelve- to eighteen-inch-high fences may be suitable to border flower beds but cannot contain an adrenaline-charged small dog pursuing a squirrel.

CLEANING UP AFTER A DOG ON PET FAMILY PROPERTY

Most pet owners are responsible about cleaning up after their dogs. However, a small but significant percentage of dog owners don't pick up their dogs' poop from public or private property. This antisocial behavior builds up dog waste exponentially, is unhygienic, and unsightly. I occasionally clean up poop dog owners have neglected. When I clean up poop in front of a business sidewalk, I go inside the business and tell them I cleaned it up. They are always appreciative! I do this because I care about the neighborhoods I work in. I also make sure people I meet on my neighborhood walks know I have cleaned up some stray poop on residential sidewalks or streets. This accomplishes a number of things.

First, it eliminates germs and waste easily tracked about by unsuspecting dogs, cats, adults, and kids on their shoes, bicycle tires, and athletic balls. Second, if we keep discussing this health problem with our neighbors, it may encourage others to become more responsible. Talking among neighbors is the best way to become aware of which dogs and owners leave messes behind. Sometimes this oversight isn't just blatant thoughtlessness. It may be that a pet family is in distress due to circumstances out of their control, and they need some help from neighbors or family members until things return to some semblance of normality.

Neighborhood dog owners can start by writing down the description of loose dogs, taking pictures of them and the owners who don't clean up after their dogs, and then submitting those photographs to animal control officers with the name of the street where the poop was left. Let the police or animal control officer in your town know license plates of the cars dogs return to after pooping on a beach, in a forest, or at a playground.

A small percentage of pet owners' children are walking the family dog without carrying a poop bag. Pet owners should remind their kids to carry poop bags. I have often given these teenagers a poop bag to use when I see them walking away from the poop pile their well-trained, obedient dog has left. Dog parents need to train their children. It may be necessary for adult dog owners to attach a poop bag dispenser to the leashes used by the family members.

Condominium and Apartment Communities Poop Science

I walk dogs in different condominium communities. Pet owners have informed me about groundskeepers and I have introduced myself to them. I enjoy showing the groundskeepers the unused poop bags in my pockets to empathize with them about the fact they frequently pick up poop. Pet owners in condominium communities often show me where the poop bag dispensers are located in plain view for dog walkers to use. Some dog walkers don't comply and ignore bagging a dog's poop. If you live in a gated community such as a condominium complex, you might report repeat offenders, both the dogs and their owners, to the groundskeeper. Responsible pet owners might leave some clean poop bags in a neighbor's storm door in hopes that they may get the message!

Let's look at the statistics. In a condominium community, approximately half the units are home to one or more dogs. One hundred units with fifty dogs may house two dog owners who consistently neglect poop patrol. If the three dogs owned by these two tenants are pooping two times daily and just one poop is not cleaned up on an average day, this accumulates to seven poops littered on the grounds every week, or thirty poops a month. When snow melts and spring occurs, a lot of old poops can be seen when snow disappears.

I really dislike seeing people walk their dogs in public spaces like parks, especially baseball fields and football fields. Children end up walking and sometimes rolling in urine-covered areas. It is impossible to clean up all of a poop that is moist or wet, and park visitors frequently step in feces that were only partially picked up. I wish dog owners would train their dogs to do poops on their own property, not other people's private property or public lands. However, some dog owners do not allow their dogs to poop on their property.

I am conflicted that some dog owners encourage me to take their dogs to parks, ocean beaches, and other public places. This presents a quandary for me because often some dogs are reluctant to relieve themselves along the way before arriving at the park.

Are Dog Parks a Solution for Pet Families Owning Dogs?

Dog parks are wonderful resources and may present a partial solution to the dog waste issue. At dog parks, like-minded people who love and respect dogs and their owners can gather, their dogs can play with one another, and poop is picked up by owners. The dog waste is concentrated at the park if people drive to the park as opposed to walking their dog there. Dog parks strengthen the community of dog and pet owners where they live. This is good for all involved. Like-minded people teach and learn from one another and improve the quality of living for pet families.

One problem with dog parks is location. Neighbors may object to dog noise and traffic congestion caused by the presence of a dog park. I can understand both points of view on dog parks, especially when people who oppose having one near them feel controlled and without any power to stop the park from being built. Responsible dog owners can make a real difference in the acceptance of dog parks by keeping their dogs from running loose and crossing over into private property if fences are not present.

Animal control officers have many responsibilities and serve an important public service. They often have to drive to beaches and public forests right after sunrise to ticket dog owners who bring their dogs to these areas illegally. Let's decrease the time pressure on animal control officers by cleaning up after our own pets and speaking up to others who don't.

ICE BLOCKS AND ICICLES

Pet owners should inform pet professionals of any ice conditions on their property and in the neighborhood. I always look for icicles when approaching or leaving exits in the wintertime. Icicles are generally visible to the naked eye. Pet owners and pet professionals can slowly leave a doorway and scan upward looking for icicles that could fall. Gutter ice blocks formed in gutters are rarely visible. Gutter ice blocks look like the snowline or ice-line resting in gutters! They are undetectable, except when melting occurs and a small amount of snow or ice may hang over a gutter line. This overhang will not have icicle points.

On one week-long pet sitting job, I didn't see the large ice blocks along the gutter line. There were no snow guards (small vertical metal structures) to prevent the ice from sliding off the roof. I was returning to Surething's condo apartment after her walk. Surething is a gorgeous black small poodle with a gait made for Westminster dog shows. I stopped to talk with a neighbor three doors down from Surething's unit. I heard a large crash about sixty seconds into our discussion. We turned our heads and looked down toward Surething's unit. I wondered if my car had been hit by ice. Only forty-five seconds passed until I approached the three-foot-wide by seven-foot-long path leading to the front door, formed by the parking space gap between my bumper and shrubs.

Three large blocks of ice rested on the path exactly where Surething and I walk in and out of the residence six times a day. One block weighed over thirty-five pounds, the other two weighed over twenty pounds each. Cracked pieces of ice also lay on the pathway and on the hood and bumper of my car. Surething and I avoided serious injury by a matter of a minute or two. Surething could have had her back broken.

Pet families and pet professionals need to look for any slightly overhanging snow that may actually have turned to ice on the roof. These blocks of ice on roofs are often invisible, until they start moving, which makes noise. You must look up for them when exiting a residence, and if you can't see them, you should listen for them and move quickly. Most residential exits lead away from the rooflines, whereas a higher proportion of apartment and condo buildings may have pathways along the perimeter below gutter lines.

COPING WITH SUMMER HEAT

Like our bodies, cats' and dogs' bodies are largely water, full of healthy substances that have a vital physiological role in keeping the blood, organs, and systems working well during spring, summer, fall, and winter. Summertime poses specific needs for pets as well as people. Dehydration in animals is very dangerous. It decreases the body's ability to normally cool itself, causing higher body temperatures that can be fatal for dogs and cats.

During the summertime, I am surprised how many pet families homes don't have a second water bowl in case the first bowl of water is overturned or drained by cats or dogs. Pet owners can purchase bowls that are heavy, thick, and flat on the bottom as opposed to bowls that are rounded and light that can be easily spilled upon animal contact.

Bowls in sturdy metal racks are also quite stable, and many medium-sized dogs have two water stand bowls. Cats do not generally have water stands. They require floor-situated water bowls. Pet owners know certain rescue cats prefer a water bowl on a bookshelf or to paw running water out of a sink under your watchful eye.

Some pet owners have delegated their children the responsibility for providing water to family cats and dogs. At times the water bowl may be in a child's room. Children forget things easily, so pet owners should supply other water bowls in addition to the one in the child's room both in the summertime and year round. If children are in charge of the family bird, parents should oversee the maintenance of water and food levels in cages by visually checking those levels while walking past the cage twice daily.

If you have a puppy or a mature dog crated in your child's room, verify that water is in the crate when no one is home. You can leave a list of the child's responsibilities on a wall near a commonly used entrance or near the breakfast table. Write pet chores on the chart and have children check them off when they're completed, but make sure you *see* a filled water bowl in the crate in a child's room. "Trust but verify" is a good standard for teaching children how to be responsible for their pet chores.

I have been an unhappy witness to pets crated without water in children's rooms. I rectify the situation immediately by placing water in the crate and letting the pet out to another water bowl in the home. Then I leave a note for the pet owners about the waterless crate situation.

Most pet owners whose dogs cannot tolerate summer sun and heat know this and tell pet sitters and pet visitors without being asked in the initial interview with the pet owners. Some dogs that are intolerant of heat have medical conditions that produce excessive panting and physical weakness in summer. (Cushing's disease is one such ailment.) Older dogs or dogs with medical conditions need to be kept cool in shaded areas outside and to be in rooms with air conditioners or fans during the hotter times of day. Heat-challenged house cats may be shut out of certain very hot rooms in the home by the owner. The pet owner may ask the pet professional to keep curtains or blinds closed between 11 a.m. and 5 p.m. during pet sitting while the sun is hottest.

I was one informed by a pet owner: "Please don't walk Lassie in the sunshine or the shade this week while you are here. She can sit out front in the yard for short periods of time, where she uses the shady bushes and trees. We'll show you how to work the air conditioner to help her keep cool." Heed this type of guidance from the owner and respect the owner's wisdom about the dogs' and cats' special needs. Applying the pet owner's strategies is part of excellent communication and customer service.

Pet owners can help a dog walker plan ahead for dogs with summer heat problems, especially in urban yards lacking shade trees or building shade. Pet owners can pack a dog thermos or a dog-friendly drinking apparatus. Keeping dogs on leash prevents hot, thirsty, and curious dogs from drinking foul water they find in road gutters, mud puddles, buckets, fresh water ponds, industrial runoff, and paint cans.

Pet owners may know if their dog likes to be sprayed with a gentle hose flow in their yard. A dog walker must have control of any hose spray apparatus to prevent powerful water pressure hitting the dog's eyes or interior ears. The pet owner can inform the pet professional about hose play and cooling water in hot humid weather. Dog lovers know it is a wonderful sight to see a dog of any size shake its wet coat. Dogs or puppies need vigilant oversight and should be prevented from chewing a water hose or drinking water from the hose. Drinking water from the hose is a bad habit for dogs. Dogs drinking from a hose can get upset stomachs and become obsessed with drinking. This interferes with normal hose play and the owner's or caregiver's normal use of the hose. Instead, keep a bowl outside filled with water.

Some dogs enjoy ice cubes to chew on in wintertime and summertime. I see this in dog playgroup in the wintertime when we leave clean water overnight in water bowls and then break up the frozen ice in playgroup the next day. In hot weather outside, pet owners can supply their dog with ice cubes and watch their response.

Water bowls in warm rooms are subject to some evaporation and quicker contamination and unfriendly germ buildup. During summer pet sitting, the pet owner can expect a pet professional to change the water bowls twice a day, unless multiple dogs and cats share common water bowls and need more frequent changing. The bowls can be cleaned intermittently with hot water and soap. In winter, spring, and fall, I change water once a day during a cat or dog visit, totally emptying the water bowl, rinsing it out, and filling it. I know many pet owners are not cleaning out water dishes thoroughly, because I see discolored water mineral stains forming over time on the inside of the water bowl.

Pet owners might use filtered water for their cats and dogs. Pet owners should point out the filtered water apparatus in the kitchen for the pet professional's use. Municipal water supplies are not qualitatively what they should be, and filtered water is easier on organs like the kidneys and liver, and ultimately on an animal's blood chemistry and immune system. Cleaner water helps an animal's detoxification system function normally for longer periods of time as the pet ages. Higher quality filtration systems generally contain fewer impurities and put less stress on an animal's physiology of digestion, allowing the animal's body to build up a better quality of fluids to nourish its blood chemistry as the blood circulates throughout the body. Too many additives, unhealthy toxins, and other impurities that may withstand boiling temperatures may be in our tap water, entering the systems of cats and dogs.

Water filters come in all price ranges. Pet family owners should consider this important investment for spouses, children, and pets. Better filters cost upward of a couple hundred dollars and can be professionally installed below your kitchen sink in the cabinet or above the sink alongside the faucet.

Pet owners might get their dogs a summer haircut for better hygiene and to keep them cooler. Haircuts are recommended at different intervals for different breeds. The less some breeds are properly groomed, the dirtier they become and the more unhealthy bacteria, leaves, sticks, and dirt can permeate their coat. This contributes to overheating in the summertime, as well as to rashes, excessive odors, and more household mess. Pet owners may find it easier to keep up with proper nail cutting and ear cleaning when they follow an overall schedule for dog care including baths and grooming. Many cats enjoy being combed by their pet family, including children, deepening the interspecies bonding.

Pet owners should ensure that if they use a dog playgroup, the transport vehicles are kept as cool as possible. The pet professional should keep the passenger windows partly open when leaving animals in the vehicle in order to pick up or drop off a dog. (Transport vehicle windows need to be left high enough to prevent any dog from jumping out or getting its head caught in the window.) I use the air conditioner if needed for dog playgroup transport. For certain dogs that labor in heat,

I pour a small amount of water on their heads in transport to cool them, along with using the air conditioner.

4

CARING FOR THE PET

PET OWNER OPTIONS: PET CARE COMPANY OR INDIVIDUAL PET PROFESSIONAL?

Pet owners have an increasing number of individuals and pet care companies at their disposal to access for help with pet sitting and pet visits. (Pet visits for companion animals can include dog walks and caring for cats, horses, ponies, sheep, goats, cattle, rodents, birds, reptiles, or fish.) In general, pet care companies offer pet families more services than individual pet care professionals do. This chapter explains partially what both have to offer. (If you visit or own and care for farm animals, feel free to e-mail me any experiences, strategies, and stories you have about your work. Obviously the scope of this book contains little on farm animals and I would benefit greatly from your expertise. I would like to know the written quality-control procedures farm animal owners expect of people who tend to their animals.)

Pet families can choose many reputable individuals who have their own pet care business and are not part of a pet care company. People who work independently are often highly committed to animal welfare and care and act skillfully with other people's pets and companion animals. Conversely, many independent pet care professionals work part time for both themselves and part time for a pet care company. Independent professionals who provide dog walks, cat visits, and pet sitting should have references from people other than their families and friends to document their maturity skills. Pet owners can ascertain whether independent professionals are bonded and insured. Demonstrated skills develop over time. A lower cost should not be the main reason a pet owner chooses one individual over another individual or a pet care company. Anyone can charge less, but experience makes the difference.

How can a pet owner decide whom to hire? The owner of a pet care company has a body of work and a reputation in the geographic areas their business serves and should be able to assign a pet professional they believe is the right fit for a job. Veterinarians and animal shelters often have knowledge of independent individuals and pet care companies in their geographic area.

One advantage of a company's service for the pet family is the larger number of staffers. Backup staff members are an important option a pet care company can provide that may be difficult for an individual to provide. Every pet professional has limitations regarding time availability. For pet care professionals, as for other people, snow emergencies, automobile breakdowns, vacations, family matters, and other situations can come into play in their lives. Two or three additional pet company staff can be assigned to dogs and cats for backup to adjust seamlessly to these situations. The backup staff members of a pet care company will meet a pet family and receive keys, verbal instruction, and paperwork instructions. This backup protocol supports the pet family and readies the staff to step in smoothly if the regularly scheduled pet visitor or pet sitter has an emergency and cannot arrive to walk or pet sit. It has not been uncommon for me to visit a new pet family as a backup staff, and never or rarely be involved in pet care for the family. Pet families appreciate staff teamwork in a well-run pet company.

Pet owners can experience last-minute schedule changes while on vacations or business trips. Pet owners may need extended time to be away, and additional staffers at a pet care company have more options to be able to fulfill the pet owners' last-minute needs. Pet families flying home during the winter time from the western United States to the eastern United States are often flight delayed. The pet owners may call the pet company to ask for an additional walk, a meal, or one or two more nights of pet sitting. The independent professional may not have the flexibility that a pet company can offer in these circumstances. Independent pet professionals may have one backup person for emergencies, whereas a pet company may have three backup staff members for emergencies.

Full-service pet care companies offer pet visits for dogs, cats, and rodents as well as pet sitting, dog playgroups, doggy daycare, pet boarding, and other services. Companies serving rural areas may offer some degree of farm animal service.

MAKING FRIENDS WITH A PET: HEIGHT AND MIMICRY

I learned about mimicry while studying didactic marriage and family systems as applied to individuals and their families, and I apply this skill when working with animals and their owners. Different animals need varying time periods to become comfortable with a stranger. Strategically, it is a good idea to sit on the floor with some cats and dogs the first time you meet them. I always do this with my independent clients and for the pet care company I work for. I first get a sense of approaching owners' cats or dogs during the initial telephone conversation. I might ask, "What is the best way to greet your cat (or dog)? Could you leave a treat the pet likes in the mailbox for when I arrive? That way I can bring it into the home for the pet as soon as I see it." I then apply mimicry throughout pet sitting jobs, especially with shy or aggressive cats and dogs.

Pet owners appreciate this respect for their experience and their animal's individuality. Without having met the owners or their pet, you are recognizing them as the authority on their companion animal and presenting yourself as a lifelong learner and a seasoned professional.

I enter the door of the pet owner's home and greet the pet owner verbally or with a handshake and then sit down on the floor or kneel in the hallway, saying hello to the cat or dog. I encourage the pet owners to speak in a calm, soothing voice. If there are two pet owners and only one greets me at the door, I may sit down immediately if the cat or dog is visible. This depends on what I have been informed over the phone about the pet's levels of nervousness, anxiety, and shyness. I am much less intimidating sitting on the floor for a shy and nervous pet, especially with a trusted pet owner or two nearby. If the cat or dog stays in the room and doesn't run into another room, the pet owners and I patiently let things play out, allowing the socialization to begin between the animal and me. A dog or cat that runs into another room during my initial visit will be given time to come back before a pet owner brings it back. I may suggest to go with the pet owner to find the pet, and I will then sit down in that room on the floor. This respects the animal's spontaneity and unburdens the pet owner from feeling he or she has to host me in the living room.

I don't sit on the floor the entire meeting, but certainly part of it. My height doesn't tower over the pets as much. In the floor position, I am not too much higher than many dogs' eyes and much closer to small and medium-sized dogs than if I were standing. Many dogs approach me at some point in the initial meeting with their owners and lick my hands and try to lick my face.

Cats are also less intimidated by me when I sit on the floor. I become a much less threatening presence with shy cats and a more inviting lap for confident animals. It is a very good experience for all when a cat walks up to me, takes a peek, and walks over rubbing against my legs or near my legs upon exiting the room. Having the pet owners see me sitting on the floor shows them I really want to learn how to be with and work with them and their pets, not just impose myself on their pet family without interest in their inner lives, personalities, and behavior patterns. The pet owner notices gladly that you are not presenting yourself as an expert with an arrogant, know-it-all attitude, but rather as a lifelong learner.

Pet sitting and pet visiting transcends showing up at a pet's home and going through the motions of caring for animals without really caring for them. Most pet professionals I know make clear verbal and nonverbal contact in a caring way with the animals they work with. Pet sitters and pet visitors try to replicate as much as they can of the pets' experience with their families. In the human mental health field of family systems therapy, "joining the system" is a behavior approach a family therapist uses to mimic, in a respectful way, the person the therapist is working with. For example, child therapy may be located in a room with age-appropriate toys like dolls, trains, and building blocks. The family therapist may slump their posture when an adult patient slumps in his or her chair or the couch. If a patient yawns or stretches, the therapist may also yawn and stretch. These behaviors create respect and trust so that a working relationship can develop and therapeutic changes can occur.

Similarly, pet professionals can sometimes respectfully imitate and mimic the people and animals they work with. When I ask the owners about how to approach their pet, I am joining with the parenting system in a pet family. When I sit on the floor and become more even with the animals' eyes, I am joining with the animals by mimicking them. I am looking at them and they are looking at me. I may be looking more softly at them instead of staring similar to the way the cat or dog is looking at me, away, and then again looking at me. Animals often don't like extended stares and prefer more soft gazing. I often fake a yawn when a cat or dog yawns and make eye contact with the animal after the yawn, congratulating them for yawning with a pleasant scratch or pat. I might shake my head after a dog shakes its head. A dog or cat may be wet with water or its ears are bothering it. They may scratch their ear or shake their heads. I would also imitate this by shaking my head or scratching my ear, saying something empathic and kind toward the dog or cat. I may whimper or bark when a dog whimpers or bark. When a dog makes various guttural sounds when it is playing, I may do the same. I feel more connected with the animal and the context I am in, be it pet sitting, dog walks, dog playgroups, or cat or bird visits. I believe this imitating gains the animals' trust, allowing me to be more effective with them in many different situations and to learn how to play with them. This is how I let companion animals train me to enjoy myself with them. They show me to a certain extent how to remain a lifelong learner and not to overly rely on my previously learned knowledge.

CAT VISIT: FELINE IMPRESSIONISTIC PAINTING

I began visiting three cats one summer. The pet owners had provided themselves and their three cats with a beautiful new home eight months earlier. I decided to sit on the floor in a sitting room off the kitchen as soon as I arrived. The owner told me Filo was like a dog and would greet me at the door and follow me around. This was true. Filo, a gray Persian cat with green eyes, appeared quickly with her turquoise bell tinkering on her collar. She stretched out her body from head to toe as I scratched her. Her thick fur felt like combed dense cotton balls with healthy oils mixed in. I sat on the floor playing with Filo for a couple minutes until a second beautiful cat appeared, a long-haired tabby named Pucker, with dark rings and streaks of color in his torso and tail. Pucker initially approached me slowly and carefully before he rubbed against me or let me scratch him. I didn't raise my arms to reach out to him until he was very close to me because I learned that he could be scared away with arms raised. Pucker's owners told me to keep my hands low and close to the floor, with my palms face up where he could see them, putting him at ease.

I threw some toys near Pucker and Filo before I looked for their housemate, Wheely. Many cat owners have ample toys for their darlings, and they can tell you if a certain toy appeals to one cat more than others. Cat toys include balls, mice, squeaky toys, imitation peacock feathers, and others. There were two toy baskets in this home, one on the first floor and a toy box on a finished third floor. Filo liked to be held in my arms, and I did this while looking for the third cat. Wheely is an exceedingly beautiful short-haired black cat with jade green eyes and four white sock leg markings. Wheely carried himself in a slow curious way, his head lifted up, his eyes scanning the horizon, noticing lava-red silk drapes moving slightly in the wind in a dining room window or cocking his ear when the heating system vibrates a brass grate in the master bedroom.

Wheely's favorite seat was a dark felt green sofa in the living room. His physical and internal beauty framed by the living room's furnishings reminded me of Impressionist paintings by Mary Cassatt, the great American painter. I felt a strong sense of family when I visited these three remarkable cats in their parents' home. The cats were very secure in their parents' love. The strong bond between them and their parents, and their physical beauty as cats resting and playing in a beautiful home, was very inspirational to me. Wheely's favorite toys were a string attached to a plastic stick and a short tunnel about two feet long, big enough for him to walk through it. I teased him with the string, flicking it in and out of the tunnel until he lunged into the tunnel and started grabbing and biting the string. I repeated the flipping of the string in and out of the tunnel for a few minutes for his playtime. This safe aggressive play helps cats adjust better when their owners travel.

When pet visiting these cats, I usually took five minutes to sit downstairs and play with the cats again after my chores of the cat visit are over. Repeating healthy rituals is important in successful pet care.

I visited the three cats six times over a period of six days during one contract. On the seventh day, I entered the home and within thirty seconds all three cats met me in the rear hallway near the door. What a great surprise—something they most likely do with their owners. I felt honored that perhaps they were becoming more comfortable with me. Or maybe they were just curious who entered their home, perhaps hoping it was Mom or Dad? After entering the house and being greeted by the three cats, I walked to the living room. They joined me and we sat for five minutes where their owners often sit with them before I started the chores of feeding them and cleaning their litter.

RESCUE CAT VISIT

The bodies of animals and people have an intelligence, presence, and energy that reflect learned behaviors and a source much greater than ourselves. Within these learned behaviors are capabilities for greater actions of coordinated skill. Several examples of this come to mind: Bill Russell, blocking a shot and simultaneously directing it to a moving teammate "in the paint," triggering a fast break of a defensive board turnover; the first time a nursing mother dog lies down and provides milk to eight puppies; a harpsichordist playing hundreds of notes a minute of Scarlatti's keyboard music; a Maine bald eagle lifting out of its dive from perch-scarred waters, holding its food in talons as it readies to land in a treetop before ripping off the perch skin and eating pulsing flesh; a sightless person, aided by a cane, using her abilities to walk a new street full of side-street curbs, commercial shops, and noises signaling the bustle of daytime or nighttime; Randy Moss on a deep pass from Tom Brady, elevating higher airborne than the three defenders surrounding him, his hands feel the spiral texture of over inflated pigskin, and his fingers close like a velvet vise on laced leather, protectively tucking the ball into his ribs—touchdown! Every day in our world, people and animals ascend to higher states of adaption, action, and accomplishment. We are remarkable. Americans in particular have led the way in rising to new levels of skill.

I have never seen a domesticated cat move like Comet. Comet has a lightning-quick presence. What was special was his energy and how he moved. It was unmistakable—Comet the cat moved like a squirrel. I noticed this immediately when I saw him the first time. I went to meet his mom and three great cats, Mr. Lattimor, Bif, and Comet. Their mom was a strong proponent of proper shelter adoption and prepped me well about Comet's eccentricities. All three cats were from a shelter adoption. I didn't see Comet for the next fifteen house visits after seeing him with his mother!

"You may never see Comet when you visit here. It's okay. That's how he is," his owner assured me. "You might try running the water in the kitchen sink. Comet hears it when I am here and may come out to jump up on the sink and paw some water to drink. He lived long enough on the streets that he must have drunk water from puddles with his paw." "Which paw does Comet use?" I asked. "The right paw," she informed me.

Comet is quick and light on his feet. He scampers the way a squirrel scampers, moving from closet door to kitchen food bowls, retreating more like flowing water than an animal with weighted bones, skin, and organs. I see that Comet's tail functions in a hypercoordinated way to help him balance his speed. Comet has to be in charge of a situation and will only let you see him in his mom's apartment if he wants you to. Comet is a split-second mover. Once I saw Comet in the hallway along the kitchen; I blinked and he was gone. He was not in the kitchen where I looked quickly but probably down the hall, or was he in the living room in the closet? I couldn't find him.

Comet's legs seem like they are lifting up almost as soon as he places a foot down. It's similar to the Feldenkrais method of movement, which teaches runners to focus on lifting one leg even as the other foot touches the ground. The lifting focus makes movement easier on the body's joints and can support more efficient movement. Comet's body doesn't collapse in gravity like many cats' bodies do. When Comet's foot touches the ground, it actually extends from the hip, muscularly lifting the legs quickly after touching down. Comet could scurry across water if he could avoid sinking. Comet's speed of lifting his legs is quicker than other cats' walking. It's as if he learned to walk on tacks, fire, or eggshells before he was adopted. It is as if Comet rarely had time to slow down and relax or be safe. Comet lived on the streets in an asphalt jungle. Comet's nervous system was wired by the syncopated rhythm of cars, buses, trucks, and other environmental influences. Comet is like an ancient jungle cat living in a modern apartment.

I unintentionally mentioned walking on eggshells. Comet did live on the streets for a while. Animals living on the streets are on guard much of the time. There can be scarcity of food and water as well as competition for food from both other stray animals and the adults who try to keep cats and dogs from prying open garbage cans. Animals can attack one another for the spoils of hunter gathering. Lack of a home with affection and physical comforts can make for a very fear-based animal.

"Hello, Comet. This is Bob talking to you. Which closet are you in today? The bedroom closet? The living room closet? The office closet? The hall closet? Shall I run some water in the sink for you and you can jump up on the sink and use your paw as a drinking tool?" This is the routine I follow whenever I visit Mr. Lattimor, Bif, and Comet.

The fourth time I was contracted to visit Comet, Mr. Lattimor, and Bif, Comet started letting me see him. This was approximately the seventeenth day I had entered the home, after a year of intermittent visits without ever seeing Comet on my own.

I had trouble seeing Comet's colors clearly. He had short gray hair with a white-diamond-haired chest and three white socks on three legs. Hyperalert, Comet watched every move I made as I slunk down to the floor and watched him watching me. I stayed down to try and prolong this unexpected Comet sighting. His eyes were of a wild animal, beautiful with a steely gaze used for hunting and gathering, not a soft gaze. (Did his gaze soften when his mother petted him? Yes, I imagine so. A softened gaze for only his beloved mother.) Comet didn't move for over sixty seconds. He gave me a smirk and disappeared down the hall into a large walk-in closet. Finally, I could see where he disappeared to.

Returning the next day for my daily visit, I changed my voice, sounding higher pitched like Comet's female owner. Surprisingly, Comet appeared quickly to look out the sliding doors with a view of the ocean and islands. I was thrilled he was out, and I left his mom a note telling her this. I felt like I had accomplished something.

I stopped in my tracks about twenty feet from Comet and he refused to approach any closer, trying to hide behind kitchen areas. The salty moist smell of Marblehead waters entered his nostrils as he acknowledged a bird outside the sliding doors by bobbing his head up and down slightly watching its flight. I sensed he had eyes in the back of his head as he quickly turned his gaze toward my direction, where I had slunk to the floor into a crouch. Perhaps Comet's sense of smell or his hearing had lassoed my presence in his brain. I should have stayed hidden, for he was off in a blink under furniture, through the hallway door near the kitchen entrance. I retraced the areas where he had been. Comet had moved so quickly, and there was no sign of him, which is normal for this cat squirrel. Zero for me, the failed trapper being unable to read footprints in carpet fibers.

Comet is still very wild. He has the perfect adopted mother, who has provided many large closets for Comet to live in. The closets are all a minimum of two doors, which he slides opens at his will and disappears into, jumping up on storage boxes and shelves. This is a perfect exercise wonderland for a squirrel cat still on the prowl, multiple levels like a tree, darkness in a closeted forest with cracks of light. The cat squirrel lives! There are closets in the master bedroom, second bedroom, living room, and hallway. I often ended my visits by stating aloud, "Comet, I'll be visiting tomorrow, and if I don't see you I'll talk to the closets!"

CASE VIGNETTE: READING COOKBOOK RECIPES TO MINI THE CAT

Cat visits take a different turn when a cat is upset with its owners' travel and shows that upset to the cat visitor. Hissing, trying to scratch when approached, the formidable moan of hostility, and pee or poop accidents may all be signs of unhappiness with parents leaving cats behind. Besides the cat being unhappy, the cat visitor can take on some unpleasant tension from the situation. Pet professionals want to succeed all the time, and sometimes we base that on unattainable standards. The pet owners' knowledge about their pets' behavior provides me with a more realistic understanding of what to expect in my professional pet care.

"Mini may or may not show herself to you when you visit," her mom informed me. This was the case with Mini, a very beautiful mixed-breed cat. Mini was pitch black, with three full white socks and a half of a sock on the remaining foot. Mini had beautiful green eyes, and she twitched her tail like a conductor's baton when I approached her, before running under the multicolored master bed in her owner's apartment, hissing loudly. This occurred day after day, except for the first day, when she was willing to be scratched briefly before rubbing her whiskers and chin against the brush her owner had instructed me to leave on the kitchen floor for Mini's pleasure.

I decided to finish the chores on the remaining six visits and then read a newspaper or book to Mini for about ten minutes. Some days I read Mini the town newspaper. Other days I would read from a cookbook about preparing fish or chicken. Mini would come out from under the bed during a number of these reading sessions and walk slowly to a dresser and crawl under it, sometimes peering out at me as I sat with the reading material in a chair. I considered this a success and something positive for Mini! Mini received some human contact in a strong, reassuring, vocal way. Did the broiled codfish recipe interest her? I'll break bread and eat cod any day with Mini!

Reading to Mini also relaxed me and helped me feel somewhat successful in bonding with her. Mini certainly experienced me as relaxed, which was good for her well-being. Cat owners should feel assured the cat visitor will attempt to bond with their feline.

CAST VIGNETTE: DAKOTA'S CHANGES IN BEHAVIOR WHEN HER OWNERS TRAVELED

I refer to pet owners as parents in the pet care company I work for as well as in my independent business. The term *parents* helps us understand the place pet owners hold in the hierarchy of their pet family system. The parents have responsibility for pets throughout their lifestages. The stages proceed from choosing a particular pet to how a pet is raised and supported in its last stages of life. This is the family system the pet sitter, pet visitor, dog playgroup transport driver, and playgroup staff enters into instantaneously during their initial and ongoing contact with pet owners.

Dakota is a gorgeous ebony-colored standard poodle with grace and power on and off leash that embodies ease and coordination. Dakota, like all standard poodles, is highly intelligent and very alert to her surroundings. Dakota has a strong athletic body and bright intelligent dark eyes that shine. Dakota is tall at the shoulder and her movements lend the impression she could swim long distances, climb steep rocky trails, and be a supremely effective watchdog for her family.

I met Dakota and her owners on the front porch where Dakota initially seemed guarded and protective of her parents, who informed me that this reaction was normal for Dakota. Dakota's owners showed me around the house.

"Here's our kitchen. This is where Dakota's and the cats' water bowls, food bowls, and food are kept. Also, here's the refrigerator and stove for your use," Dakota's mom explained. "I place these bread boards over the stove burners and knobs so the cat can't accidentally turn on the stove. She likes to walk across the stove searching for good-ies."

"I understand cats can get into all types of things. I always unplug toaster ovens when they're near paper towel rolls when I pet sit. I have some morbid fear the cat may step on the toaster oven control and the paper towels hanging down from the wall holder might catch fire," I said laughing.

I have a communication style with some pet owners that is quite open and forthcoming. I say much less when pet owners seem rushed by their schedules and say very little to me, although I do repeat back to them some of the things they said to let them know I respect what they are saying and to give them an opportunity for clarification. People's homes are among their most personal and prized possessions, and a pet sitter needs to treat a tour of the home with great care and respect.

As we walked around, I noticed that Dakota stood very close to her mother, who had told me Dakota was a one-person dog, that person being her mom. The door to the backyard was right off the kitchen. We went outside and Dakota's father showed me the front gate. "It's impor-tant this gate be latched and closed to keep Dakota safe," he instructed me. "If you could water these backyard shrubs and the flowers off the front porch once a day we would really appreciate it," he said.

"I sure will," I said, making a note on my ever-present clipboard. I carry the clipboard, pad, and pen when I meet owners and their pets to record everything I need to know while I am in their home. Doing so shows the owners you are serious, focused, and organized. On some days when I am tired from writing, parenting, and working, the clip-board gives me extra support for my memory. Dakota's mom took us back into the house.

I suggested to Dakota's owners that I see if Dakota would follow me through the kitchen and into the backyard, without her parents, to play ball and give her a chance to warm up to me and prepare for pet sitting in a couple weeks. "That is a good idea," they concurred.

"Come, Dakota. Follow me, sweetheart," I said as I proceeded outside. Dakota followed me into the backyard and played ball, wagging her tail, playing fetch, and then following me inside afterward to see her parents. She appeared quite comfortable around me. I was excited and looked forward to pet sitting Dakota.

Surprise! Pet sitting for Dakota was like two people living in the same house without talking to each other and not getting along very well. I walked in the front door that Friday afternoon ready to pet sit through Sunday. Dakota ran from the dining room, past me, and up the stairs to the second floor before I could say anything!

"Hi Dakota, sweetheart. How are you?" I called out. No response, no movement as Dakota stood statue still on the second-floor landing. I followed Dakota upstairs to the second floor and she sprinted past me out of a bedroom and ran downstairs to the first floor.

"Dakota, is everything all right?" I asked aloud standing on the second-floor landing. I often talk with the pets I sit for and visit. It may put the pet more at ease, as it does me. My talking is a form of healthy stimulation for pets. It also resembles the stimulation pets receive each day from their family members. With their pet owners gone, they have lost the daily exposure of their family speaking to one another and to them. Pets must adapt to this loss, and I hoped my talking aloud would ease the transition for both of us.

Needless to report to you pet owners, the whole weekend went like this, from Friday afternoon to Sunday afternoon. I was never able to pet Dakota, scratch her, or play ball with her. The only touch she received was brushing my legs as she ran past me on the stairs, and when I reached out to touch her a couple times she growled, which totally surprised me. This was a new experience. Dakota became Dakota-San, my new teacher about adaptability and respecting dogs for who they are, not who we would like them to be.

The only way I was able to let Dakota into the backyard for bathroom and exercise was to prop open the back door and rear storm door and go up to the second floor (which would inevitably bring her downstairs) and then walk toward Dakota as she cowered in the dining room or living room. Dakota would zoom quickly into the kitchen like she was on a race track and run outside to do her business. Wow, this was a total learning experience for me! I felt powerless, uneducated, and surprised.

I would watch this graceful, powerful dog do her business and smell the flowers once she was outside. As you know, dogs love smelling. Despite her unease with me, Dakota ate and did her bathroom routines normally. The weekend presented something contrary to the initial meeting with her and her parents. Dakota also lives with a beautiful cat, who, the mother told me, might act very aloof. To the contrary, after I gave the cat a long scratch of her neck and back areas the day I arrived, she followed me around part of the weekend wanting more scratching, which I gladly gave her.

Not Personalizing Rejection

Dakota is a fantastic family dog that has loyalties to those she knows and loves. It is unreasonable to expect dogs like her to feel or act differently toward strangers. People own dogs for many reasons, particularly for companionship and to guard the home. I was a stranger in Dakota's home. Her owners told me that she is a one-person dog and closer to her mother than father. Thus the owners gave me a heads-up with some valuable information.

I rarely personalize a pet's reaction to me. I rarely let myself feel like I was not needed, not wanted, or not doing the right thing. I never let myself get upset. I learned to enjoy the lessons I was receiving about this family and this remarkable standard poodle. I was afforded a unique opportunity to cultivate detachment and accept lower expectations because things were different from what I had hoped and envisioned them to be. I was there to take care of the dog of a client who contracted with a pet care company I worked for. The dog was not there to take care of me or my needs—something that pet care owners and professionals need to understand.

Animals, like people, are their own beings and have their own ways of reacting to people and nature. Pet professionals who act emotionally needy toward animals can be unhealthy for all involved.

Pet owners can rest assured that a very high percentage of the time dogs will be quite comfortable with a pet sitter who is kind, gentle, direct, and playful and who offers food, water, and a happy presence.

DIFFICULT BEHAVIORS WITH OWNERS AWAY

Pets may act differently with a pet visitor or sitter than they will with their families, as the marvelous Dakota did. Pets familiar with the sitter through previous pet sitting, cat visits, dog walks, or dog playgroup transport may behave differently than they will with their beloved owners.

I met a wonderful older dog named Mr. Dog, whom I was to walk four times over two weekend days. Mr. Dog's owner instructed me "Just ask Mr. Dog to go outside with you and he'll get up and go. Or you can offer him a cookie treat and walk toward the door with it and he'll follow you outside." So how do you think things worked when I started my first visit?

I arrived at the home and tried both tactics that had been successful for Mr. Dog's owner. Mr. Dog just sat on the floor, looking at the treat but not budging. I walked up to him, rubbed the treat on his nostrils, and stepped away. No movement from Mr. Dog, not even a blinking eyelid. What do I do now, I wondered?

Mr. Dog didn't have a collar on, nor was I shown the collar or the leash by his owner, because Mr. Dog supposedly obeyed his owner's spoken commands. I should have known better and asked the owner to show me where the leash was. I looked around the house and found a collar and leash, which I fitted to Mr. Dog. I gently pulled on the leash and Mr. Dog didn't budge. "Up Mr. Dog, up," I said. I sat down and scratched my head. Often if something that is supposed to work with an animal doesn't work, I will repeat it before trying to come up with something different. I stood up again and exerted some tension on the leash. "Up Mr. Dog, up," I said. Mr. Dog stood up and followed me outside, did his business in the backyard, and followed me inside. I repeated the leash approach three more times that weekend with ease.

Traveling pet owners have told me their animals may punish them upon their return. Cats may miss the litter pan and soil the floor near the pan. Cats may isolate themselves from their owners, avoiding normal physical contact except to eat and drink water. Separation anxiety may influence these behaviors.

Most dogs and cats respond well to pet professionals. Pet professionals who try to harness, leash, or medicate a pet that is experiencing anxiety may find quick movements toward the animal counterproductive until they become familiar with them. Swift movements may quickly use up any capital of trust the pet professional might have with this pet that would help them come to you or allow you to approach them that day or in the future. Certain anxious animals do well with slow confident movements accompanied by a soothing voice and nonstaring look, including leashing and harnessing, when less time and ambiguity is involved. The pet visitor determines what works for each animal on any given day in the early stages of building trust with a dog.

Confidence building between a pet professional around dog and cats who are agitated and fearful takes time. I work with many rescue cats and dogs and always approach them slowly and with kindness. If you have the option of a fenced yard versus walking a dog, choose the fenced yard until the dog becomes more comfortable with you. Try making friends in the yard through play, toys, and gentle voice.

Certain owners will mention to the pet professional about unusual behaviors from previous times they have left town. A cat owner informed me of how her cats react when she is away. "Genghis and Ariel tend to hibernate, eat less, and drink less. I think they miss their mama—me," she said. Another cat owner told me, "Henry tends to go off by himself for days at a time in the house. He likes to get up into ceiling crawl spaces or sleep on the windowsills in the basement. You may not see him during your week of visits, but you'll know he's okay by his water being drunk, his food being eaten, and his litter being used."

Cats may isolate themselves and not show up for days at a time after their owners leave on a trip. Pet sitters should look carefully at the levels in cats' food and water bowls and litter trays to make sure cats are active, normal, and busy with food, hydration, and elimination. If you don't see the cats and you see signs of very little water, food, and litter pan usage, the cat may be suffering from major medical problems. The pet professional must then look for the cat and make sure it is not sick. For this reason, I ask cat owners who are traveling to close off some rooms to minimize the number of places where cats can hide. Cats that have access to a first floor only versus the first and second floors will make things much easier for the cat visitor.

Pet professionals should be calm, gentle, direct, and solution focused with other people's animals, the way the pet owner would be with their pets when not traveling. Generally speaking, loud voices and verbal anxiety can scare dogs and cats.

Redirective discipline can be necessary for the good of all involved, so situations don't escalate to the point where people and animals are hurt by out-of-control pets. One dog in the home triggering the other dog into excessive aggressiveness means peace needs to be restored by the pet professional. Two dogs fighting must be pulled away from each other without the pet professional being hurt, and then an assessment must be made as to what trigger or triggers fueled the conflict. Puppies and young dogs may have to have their noses gently pinched to deter them from unacceptable behavior like biting other dogs.

Dog owners may unconsciously shift excess responsibility for guarding the home onto dogs when the human family is outside the home. Dogs have a deeply ingrained territorial guarding nature and they want to protect the home and their human family.

I have had the experience of walking around a neighborhood and hearing excessive barking by dogs whose owners are not home. The noise of excessive barking is a real disturbance of neighbors' peace of mind. Neighbors should be able to enjoy their time at home, but overly stressed dogs with free rein of their home often come to the windows and bark at pedestrians passing by. I can hear and feel the energy of unmet needs that dogs that bark excessively carry inside themselves. Neighbors may feel conflicted about this antisocial behavior committed by barking dogs whose owners don't know any better. Neighbors often don't want to make the effort to talk to the dog owners, nor do they call the animal control officer in the vicinity. One solution is to leave an anonymous note politely informing the dog owners of the excessive barking that occurs when they are not home and how the noise disturbs the quiet routines of others' homes.

Dogs and cats have tremendous smelling capacities. A strategy for decreasing separation anxiety for cats and dogs during pet owner travel is to leave behind unwashed clothes the pet owners have worn. Cat and dog owners can spread some clothes they have worn onto a bed in a master bedroom, children's beds, and cat or dog beds. The smell of the owners or children is one part of the pet's environment that makes it feel loved and secure. I also encourage pet owners to call home and I will let the animals hear their owners' voices by using cell phone speaker technology. Dogs often want to lick the phone when they hear their owners' voices over the speakerphone.

SOLUTIONS FOR PROBLEM BEHAVIOR

Adult dogs that have been house trained often benefit from being crated a certain number of hours a day, perhaps two to four hours maximum. (Pet owners can confer with their veterinarian, dog trainer, or breeder about under- or over-crating.) Crating allows dogs to take time off from feeling that they have to be watchdogs and protect the home. A crated dog has a place that is solely its own where it can rest, sleep, drink, and eat, unburdened psychologically when its owners are out. Dogs are very loyal and such good protectors, but owners should not ask too much of their dog friends. Dogs enjoy closed-in places like crates, dog houses, and rugs on floors near furniture like beds, tables, and chairs. Dog owners can use a crate consistently but with limitations if they are consistently away from their home over two to four hours. A responsible family friend or pet professional is an important option to remove the dog from the crate, walk the dog, and offer some human socialization and geographic connection outside the home in the neighborhood. Pet owners should consider a place in a room of their home to convert for their dog, including an open crate the dog can use at its discretion. Child safety gates can be used to place a border across the doorway of an area set aside for the dog. This could be a laundry room properly cordoned off to keep the dog and the home safe.

Pet owners can utilize limited daily crating to house train puppies. Dogs prefer a certain level of cleanliness and don't like sitting in urine or feces. Thus, dogs learn to wait until they are taken outside. But be ready for puppy action! Don't hesitate between removing your puppy from the crate and getting outside. Some pets, be they puppies or elderly dogs, will soil the floor if they have to wait even thirty seconds. Pick the puppy up from the cage to delay the peeing until outside. Have your shoes and jacket already on and the leash already attached to the harness as you approach the crate. Open the crate, secure the harness, and walk directly to the door and exit. If the yard is fenced, let the dog outside right away to pee, then secure the harness and begin your neighborhood walk.

Certain uncrated dogs engage in property destruction when bored or suffer other negative stressors. Conversely, dog owners crate some dogs too many hours, weakening their muscle tone and cardiovascular health and hurting their moods. Excessive crating may indicate a number of problems in the pet family home, including the owner's misunderstanding of their pet's needs in terms of exercise, socialization, and affection. The owners' life circumstances may be challenged by job loss, illness, divorce, or relocation.

Pet families can utilize pet care companies for help by arranging well-timed visits for dogs and cats. A cat or dog visit can be arranged as seldom as once a week or as frequently as twice a day seven days a week.

ThunderShirts are fitted to dogs to decrease anxiety and foster calm in a variety of contexts, including thunder and lightning storms and daily living transitions. ThunderShirts were originally invented for children with behavior concerns. Pet owners can place the ThunderShirt on their dogs for the dogs' peace of mind.

Dog behavior modification playgroup is another solution A pet service offering dog playgroups can pick up your dog at your house and transport it to the group, where for approximately one hour, depending on the particular playgroup, dogs can learn to socialize and play with one another. The time in playgroup transport benefits your pet, allowing your dog different stimulations with people and dogs as well as fresh air. This is an excellent way for dogs to learn to relax, become less shy, become less aggressive toward other dogs and people, and to mature into better household behaviors. Rescue dogs with trauma behaviors can thrive in these contexts. Additionally, a doggy daycare center will afford the dog owner a flexible schedule for important dog socialization.

Although separation anxiety is common in pets, some pets suffer less from separation anxiety than from boredom. Boredom in dogs can result in property destruction that causes owners much aggravation and money. Pet sitters, dog walkers, and cat visitors need to report any damage they see to owners. Owners should move objects that tempt their dogs, such as pillows, newspapers, shoes, blankets, electrical cords, and magazines, out of the animals' reach.

If I am pet sitting and see property destruction, I remove access to certain objects. Many dogs simply need more healthy stimulation through exercise and dog socialization contact. Obedience training or a small obstacle course in the backyard can be helpful. Dogs enjoy going through tunnels, running up and down special seesaws, hurdling over raised bars, and performing other physical challenges. Dogs have brains, and they need challenges that are designed for them to succeed. A tired dog is a happier dog.

CATS AND THEIR HIDING PLACES

Pet owners can rest assured that pet visitors and pet sitters generally complete a head count of cats each day when visiting the home. Completing a head count is a little like a schoolteacher taking attendance in homeroom soon after the students arrive at school. By taking attendance, the schoolteacher knows which children are present and which are absent or late. A daily head count not only tells pet visitors that the cat is present, but it also lets us know that a cat is healthy or appears abnormal.

The exception is when cat owners have stated that they don't expect this because of their cats' shyness and lack of interest in human contact. "Don't worry about Napoleon, you may not see him for a couple days at a time," owners have told me before leaving town, but this runs counter to my viewpoint as a pet visitor and pet sitter. I will look for a cat or cats in the home and write in my daily log for the pet owner whether or not the cats were in hiding.

Cat owners know where most of their cat's hiding places are. The hiding places are as varied as a house is different from room to room. Pet professionals must write down when meeting the cat owners where cats hide in the home. Owners can also write a list of or take photographs of the places where their cats hide in the home for their own future reference. The pet owners should also be sure to leave a strong working flashlight for cat visitors. The flashlight will light up a cat's eyes when the animal is hiding under a couch or bed, in a closet, or basement ceiling crawl spaces, outside in the yard at night, under a porch, up a tree, under a car, or wherever the hiding place may be. The pet visitor may not see the feline without the beacon lighting up a cat's eyes and body. This is very important if the cat is injured or unconscious and may need immediate help.

Some of cats' favorite hiding places are:

Basements: Unfinished crawl spaces, insulation crawl spaces in both attics and basements, cool or damp foundation areas, inside boxes, next to heating systems.

Closets: Top shelves, middle shelves, closet floors behind hanging clothes or closet boxes.

Laundry area: Behind or beside washers and dryers when not operating, inside a dryer with an open front door.

Bedrooms: Under mattresses, inside the fabric area covering underside of mattress (accessed by climbing through rips in the fabric and resting on the wooden frame), floors under beds, under linens and bedspreads.

Bathrooms: Inside dry bath tubs.

Living room: In plastic crates, behind sofas, and underneath sofas and love seats, on top of television and radio electronic equipment that warms up.

If I don't see one of the cats while I'm sitting for two or more cats in the home, with the owners permission, I close the cats into one room or set of rooms with a window, food, litter box, and toys. I then put out fresh food and fresh litter in a litter box in the other part of the home the unseen cat has access to. When I detect that the unseen cat is using the litter box and eating food, I know there is nothing to worry about.

Cats that are outdoor cats come and go as they please, except when their cat door is locked. Pet companies and independent pet professionals handle outdoor cats in their own way. Some pet professionals don't want the possible problems that arise if an outdoor cat becomes sick and cannot return home to let the sitter know it is injured. These sitters or cat visitors may ask the pet owner if the cat can be kept in the home during visits. The pet owners decide what they want, and it is up to the pet professional to decide how flexible he or she can be. Other pet professionals may go along with the owner's wish that outdoor cats be allowed outside as long as the owner understands it is his or her choice and that the pet professional may not see the cats on some days and cannot be held responsible if the cats encounter problems outside the home. A waiver absolving the pet professional of responsibility for outdoor cats is a good idea.

The decision that the cat can be outside while the owners are traveling should be written into the contract to attempt to eliminate liability for the pet company. With my own independent clients, I bring this up over the phone before meeting the family. I follow up on this during the initial visit. I prefer cat owners to limit their cats to two floors with some rooms shut off on the second floor. Basements and attics should be denied access for cats. I need quick access to cats when I visit to bond with them through food and water changes, connection through toys, my voice, and scratching if particular cats are amenable. Medication dispensing is also simplified when cats are denied access to the whole house.

CASE VIGNETTE: THE FLIGHT OF RICKENBACKER

Cat owners should inform pet professionals if their cat is an escape artist. Cats can sprint out or into doors opened for a couple seconds when pet families and pet professionals enter or leave their home. Cats not wearing a bell may not even be heard or seen while escaping the home. This is a big safety concern for indoor cats as well as indoor-outdoor cats the pet owner may want confined to the home on any given day. Pet owners and pet professionals can beat these escape artist cats at their own game by following certain strategies.

My favorite, most brazen cat escape artist was Rickenbacker, a male calico long-haired beauty who cuts a gorgeously handsome feline presence wherever he appears in his home. His owners told me how Rickenbacker waits patiently for them to open a sliding door to the deck leading to the backyard for the family dog Smooch, a Bluetick Coonhound, to exit. Rickenbacker readies himself to sprint from his launching pad atop the dining room table to the door as they open and shut the sliding door.

If the cats were in charge of the home, a voice sound would loudly state over an amplified speaker system: "Cat control tower to Rickenbacker. You are cleared for dining room table runway take off. Pet sitter on horizon. Approach closing sliding door with cat-warp speed to exit house with Smooch!"

Before I started to place Rickenbacker in a room by himself when taking Smooch outside (when I could find Rickenbacker), I would say "Here Smooch, come Smooch. Let's go outside."

Smooch would give his customary deep baritone howl, loud enough to help tree a fleeing raccoon. Smooch would run over to the sliding door where I stood with my hand on the handle as I peered looking into the dining room and hallways for a Rickenbacker sighting. No Rickenbacker. Smooch usually stopped his barking and I unlocked the door.

The door begins sliding three inches open. No Rickenbacker. The door slides then inches open. No Rickenbacker. Smooch pushes past my leg and I begin to exit the door backward, peering into the dining room, when suddenly I see a blur of calico hair running on the dining room table in front of the sliding door.

When did Rickenbacker jump up on the table? I extract one leg out the door as my heart begins to race. I tighten my hand on the cold steel handle. Rickenbacker achieves quite a bit of speed across the dining room table and takes off flying through the air without resistance, his underbelly hanging between limbs stretched out in opposite directions. I extract my other leg outside the door onto the deck and begin sliding the door as quickly as possible. I see Rickenbacker's four hairy landing gears engaged as his legs pounce off the carpet after landing and he leaps toward the now closed glass sliding door, his face looking shocked and surprised as the wall of glass forces him to apply his brakes on all wheels. "Beat you at your own game, cat. This time anyway," I said, feeling lucky.

Cat owners with cats like Rickenbacker suggest I place the cat in a room with the door shut before I exit with the dog and then let the cat out of the room after I return from a walk or backyard play. This is a great strategy when the cat is visible and you can catch it. Easier said than done, right? Rickenbacker knew he would have two opportunities to try escaping the home every time I exited with Smooch.

Rickenbacker enjoys jumping up on the top of the couch when I am watching sports games on television. Some cats begin purring loudly before they are touched by a person, and Rickenbacker is one of those purrers. "Felines, start your purring engines!" they say at the Feline Indianapolis 500 cat motor speedway. Jumping up on top of the sofa a couple feet from me, Rickenbacker starts up his purr engine revving it immediately in high purr RPMs (revolutions per minute). Rickenbacker saunters along the top of the sofa and proceeds to walk onto my shoulders before he jumps onto my lap and sits up against my chest as I scratch him for minutes at a time. He enjoying the warmth and cuddling of human contact with the benefits of my hard nails. I enjoy his thick hair and purring body resting against me. Rickenbacker stays in this position for a while unless I let out a yell like a sports fan!

I find it is easier to see cats' movements when I am inside a home preparing to leave, unless there is furniture near the door with enough room for a cat to crawl under and wait for the door to open. I look under these furnished areas before I open a door and walk backward out of the home, enabling me to see any feline escape artist's attempt for outdoor freedom. Walking backward is enough to stop the most assertive feline escape artists when you block off the door opening with your body. Cat owners often place obstacles under furniture near their home exit doors to deter cats from hiding and then escaping outside when a door opens.

When I enter cat residences, a cat may be waiting near a door under furniture and then, faster than a speeding bullet, try to escape. I open the door only a couple inches, sometimes sticking my clipboard through the door opening, moving it up and down and quickly before entering and then closing the door. The clipboard should be enough to deter even the most brazen feline smoking its rear tire hip muscles preparing for a feline Big Daddy Roth–style escape. Cat owners and pet professionals, start your engines. There are many cat exits to explore and escape artists to out stealth. Watch out for flying cats, clawed and de-clawed!

A TYPICAL PET SITTING SCHEDULE FOR PET OWNERS OVERVIEW

Pet owners should inform the pet professional about their dog and cat routines and needs. The following schedule has been culled from my work with many pet owners during the initial telephone and home visits before beginning a contract.

Many dogs can safely be left in the home for four or five hours between breakfast and lunch or lunch and dinner. Some days I am away from the home I am pet sitting in for only a couple hours. Pet professionals have normal working and personal lives to be attended to outside their job location between the end of breakfast and the beginning of the midday walk, and between the end of the midday walk and dinnertime. The following is a schedule for pet sitting one or more dogs and one or more cats.

6 a.m.–8 a.m.: Pet sitter wakes up. Dogs fed breakfast. Cats fed breakfast. Dogs walked in yard or in neighborhood. If dogs don't poop, dogs may need to be walked a second time or let out into

the yard a second time. All water changed for cats and dogs. Litter scooped.

8 a.m.–12 p.m. (or 1 p.m. depending on bathroom needs of dogs): Pet sitter may be out of the home walking other pet owners' dogs, visiting cats, or doing personal errands. Or the sitter may be in the home doing activities that are enjoyable and restful.

12 p.m.–1 p.m.: Midday walk for dogs in neighborhood or exercised in fenced yard. Water refilled if necessary. Treats for dogs and cats or as directed by pet owner. Puppy may be fed a midday meal.

1 p.m.–5 or 5:30 p.m.: Pet sitter away from pet sitting home or at pet sitting home relaxing and doing things to care for him- or herself and the animals. This could include time outside with dogs in fenced yards. Sunbathing or playing in the snow or rain is enjoyable for some dogs. Sunbathing is something many dogs like and is generally safe as long as they have access to shade and water under their own power without being restricted by a leash too short to reach the shade or being loose in a fenced area without shade in the enclosure. Grooming those cats amenable to grooming and using cat toys is great fun and stimulating for the cats.

Dinnertime 5 p.m.– 5:30 p.m.: Dinner put out for dogs and cats. Dogs walked after dinner or let into fenced yard. If dogs don't poop during dinnertime walk, the pet sitter will remember this and try again with a bedtime walk or yard outing. Water refilled.

9 p.m. or bedtime (Owners can inform pet sitter when dogs are walked at night or let out into yard before bedtime.): While attending to the needs of cats and dogs during pet sitting, it is important to have some direct undistracted time with the family pets daily. This assures the pet sitter that he or she is fulfilling all of the responsibilities required as well as freeing him or her for self-care.

The following are important focused activities a pet sitter could be asked to do for the four-legged family members whose own family is traveling: scratching and petting, combing and brushing, talking to the pet, quiet time, enthusiastic playtime with most dogs, cat toy use, dog toy use, and prescribed treats from the homeowner. (Don't bring outside pet treats into other people's homes. Pets' digestive systems are used to what they normally receive. Also, some animals have gastrointestinal tract sensitivities or allergies to certain treats known [or un-known] by pet owners and their veterinarian.)

Pet sitters who have children, who are not allowed by the pet com-pany they work for to be brought into the pet owner's home, can sched-ule three to five hours of time with their child or children between breakfast and lunch and lunch and dinner. Four to five hours of bond-ing is a fairly good way to balance the needs of parenting and the pet-sitting contract.

DISPENSING MEDICATION IN THE PET FAMILIES' HOMES

Extreme care and focus are necessary when dispensing medications for cats and dogs. Pet professionals must be sure they understand the in-structions for this crucial pet-sitting task. Pet owners need to be sure to leave detailed instructions and review the medical protocols when they initially meeting the pet professional.

I worked in adult group homes for years dispensing medication for developmentally delayed adults. We had to pass tests in order to be able to learn to properly dispense medication. The key factors in dispensing medication for animals in pet owners' homes are similar to those used for people. The pet professional dispensing the medication to a family pet must give:

- *The correct medication*
- *The correct dosage* (medication amount)
- *The correct time and frequency* (once daily or two times daily, a.m or p.m., or once every other day for one week, etc.)
- *The correct animal* (if more than one animal lives in the home)
- *The correct place* (ears, throat for swallowing, nape of neck for diabetic injection, ground up into food, etc.)

Certain pet families own two to four cats or two or three dogs. Two dogs of the same color and the same breed, like two black Labrador retrievers or two Golden retrievers, often live in the same home. Some homes may have two short-haired black cats with the same eye color. Cats and dogs may need ear-applied medication, either rubbed into the inside of the ear or sprayed or poured deeper into the ear. Other medications are applied topically to rashes on elbows or other skin areas. Some oral medications need to be either crushed if they are pills or poured if they are in liquid form. Pills and liquids may be mixed into wet food or given in whole form manually in a pill pocket. Diabetic shots need to be given where the pet owner has clearly indicated and how their animal is most amenable to shots, including gently rubbing the area after the shot is dispensed.

Be vigilant about preventing medication from polluting the food of other animals in a home. Cross-contamination needs to be avoided when giving medications. You do not want a spoon with one pet's medication on it being dipped into a can of another pet's cat or dog food. I always use a fresh spoon after mixing liquid medication into food for one pet. Medication spoons should be rinsed, loaded into a dishwasher, or hand washed. While this might sound like common sense, owners and pet care professionals need to guard against letting their stressors get the best of them, making them rush too quickly in their work. Being overly tired can also cause medication dispensing mistakes.

MEDICATING CATS IN THE PET FAMILY HOME

Pet owners can rest assured that competent pet professionals will medicate their pets properly. Cats on medications may behave very differently with a pet visitor or sitter than they do with their owners. Let's imagine a cat receiving two medications daily, once in the morning around breakfast time and a second time around dinner. If this cat stops appearing in the morning and at dinnertime to receive the medication, a cat pet visitor usually has only thirty minutes to find and administer the medications. A pet sitter sleeping in a pet family's home has more time to find a sleeping or hiding cat. This problem can be solved if certain rooms or floors are shut off for cat access during the pet owner's traveling schedule.

The pet professional takes steps to prevent animals other than the medicated cat from eating the medication that has been mixed into the cat food when other animals live in the house. Certain moody cats are not approachable by the pet care professional. Ask the cat owner what his or her medication strategy is.

During a thirty-minute cat visit where other dogs or cats live, I immediately place the cat in a room by itself, with all its necessities—water, dry food, wet food, a litter pan, and windows—to make sure I know whether the cat eats its medications during the thirty-minute visit. I open the door before leaving the home so the cat can circulate and I can see if the food with the medication has been eaten. Exceptions to isolating the cat include cats amenable to oral medications given through a liquid dropper or eating pills from my hand. Cats may eat medication easily by approaching me or letting me approach them. I give them a pill wrapped in a pill pocket or in some nice, wet, fishy food on a plate, and the mission is completed with a happy sandpaper tongue lick and twitching whiskers.

CATS NEED SCRATCHING

The single cat living alone in the home doesn't have another cat to socialize with when its owners travel. The single cat need physical affection from the pet visitor if it is amenable to a stranger's affections. It concerns me that some pet professionals who visit a single cat spend little or no time scratching a cat. It is below standard work for a cat visitor to enter a home, feed the cat, change the litter, and leave. Single cats need the visitor to sit down near them and be touched, scratched, held if possible, and treated more like their owners would treat them. Pet owners will inform pet professionals about a cat's favorite toys and how best to use them for the cat's benefit. Many cats benefit from a combined playtime of aggressively pursuing a toy and wrestling and biting it followed by relaxed scratching and purring.

I suggest cat owners not hire people whose visits are only ten to fifteen minutes. The cat cannot receive the socializing it needs during a short visit. The cat visitor may need fifteen minutes just to scoop litter, change water, portion out kibble or meat, take in mail and dry cleaning, and locate the cats that don't come out when the visitor arrives. Fifteen-minute visits are too short when the owner is out of town more than twenty-four hours. Twenty-five to thirty minutes is a better time frame for cat visits unless the owner wants a fifty- to sixty-minute visit one time a day or every other day.

I spend twenty-five minutes minimum, even when the cat is very shy or has other cats living with it to provide affection and a social life. I sit in the room where a shy cat may be hiding, providing the cat with some human contact, even if it is in an open closet. I take cat toys and try to engage the cat. Long feathers, often a great cat toy, are invaluable for stimulating shy cats hiding in a closet! Earlier I mentioned reading cookbook recipes to cats, just to allow them to hear a calm and kind human voice.

Scratching a cat is something I may do before I do the chores and again after I finish the chores. I like the repetition of scratching to create more bonding for the cat when their pet family is away. Cat owners know the difference because a well-scratched cat is a happier cat when their owner gets back from traveling. Cat owners who hire an independent or nonindependent cat visitor can ask him or her to write down what the protocol would be at their residence. The cat owner can add to the cat protocol list, including some sustained scratching of the cat. Discuss this with the cat visitor and let him or her know that is something that is expected. I visit families that have more than one cat and I pet or scratch all of them—if they are amenable to being scratched.

Pet owners should always remember one thing: the pet professional works for you. If you ask him or her to do something reasonable, a professional should do it. If you ask a professional to do something unreasonable or impractical, he or she should respectfully let you know that it cannot be done. Pet professionals follow specific customer service guidelines from the pet company they work for regarding pet care or their own experience as independent professionals.

TAKING A PET TO THE VET

Pet owners who hire an independent pet professional must be reachable by phone for emergencies. If pet owners are unreachable due to travel and cell phone restrictions, pet owners must work out an emergency response plan with the pet professional in advance so that all parties know the step-by-step emergency protocol.

A responsible pet company or independent pet professional will ask the pet owner to supply, in writing, information about whom to contact in case an emergency arises with the pets. This written information is left at the pet owner's home in an envelope marked "Medical Emergency Protocol." The information should include the business name, address, and phone numbers of the pet owner's veterinarian, and a credit card photocopy and expiration date. The owners should write down the amount of money they are willing to spend on their pets in an emergency that requires a visit to the vet. Pet owners who won't leave a copy of their credit card must put in writing that they have an agreement with their veterinarian to treat their animal in a routine or emergency situation. Overnight veterinary emergency hospitals may not be willing to keep a copy of a credit card on file. But the owner can put in writing the specific friends or family members who are willing to be responsible for paying for emergency overnight care. The pet sitter and his or her company are responsible for transporting the pet in emergencies to a veterinary hospital. The independent pet sitter is responsible for emergency hospital transport.

A pet owner may ask a pet care professional to take the pet to the vet for a nonemergency visit. Perhaps the cat or dog has recently had a surgical procedure and needs a follow-up visit, or something of a nonemergency nature came up the day before the pet is scheduled for a dog walk and the pet owner has to be at work that day. I have received a call from an owner the morning I was to begin pet sitting, alerting me that the cat or dog had begun to show symptoms that need a veterinarian's opinion right away, and the pet owner had already communicated with the veterinary office about the pet's symptoms and that I would bring the pet in that day.

The pet owner has the responsibility to provide a clean, working carrying case for the safe transport of all cats and small dogs. The carrying case limits the spread of bodily fluids and substances like vomit, blood, urine, and feces. The carrying case also functions somewhat as a seat belt acts for people in case a car has to stop short or is in an accident. Further, it keeps the transport driver safe from interruptions by a wandering animal that may be exploring the vehicle, eating unhealthy things, or distracting the driver with playful or aggressive behavior.

After hours, the pet owners can expect the pet sitter to be responsible for driving the pet to an after-hours emergency veterinary hospital unless previous arrangements have been made. Responsible pet care professionals always have a map, GPS, or directions to this kind of facility and its phone number to call in transit to the hospital. Emergency visits by a pet professional warrant a call to the animal hospital to share information the staff may need before the animal arrives, especially if it is a life-threatening situation.

The pet care professional is obligated to phone the pet owners immediately if an emergency occurs by calling every phone number the owner has provided and leaving a message on each phone if the owner doesn't answer. Some pet owners don't own cell phones or may not have cell phone service in geographically remote destinations. Pet owners should leave the landline and cell phone number of a friend the pet owner trusts in emergency situations.

The pet owner can expect the pet professional to contact the front desk staff at hotels, motels, and inns about a pet emergency occurring, using the exact phrase "pet emergency." The pet owner needs to be rung in his or her room and informed to call the pet care professional who is transporting the pet to the veterinarian, as well as calling the veterinarian's office.

The pet owners may not be in their rooms during the daytime hours when the front desk at their vacation facility rings them on their room phone. The pet owners may be off the property without cell phone transmission, having left for a boat, local air or train trip, walk, or hike. In these cases, I would ask for a manager to oversee a note being left on the pet owners' door as well as a message on their room phone, asking them to call the front desk, the pet care professional, and the veterinarian about a pet emergency. The pet owner can expect more than one message in an animal emergency as a backup. Emergencies can also occur with a home, for example, a leaking roof.

Emergencies rarely occur during pet sitting or pet visits, but when something unfortunate occurs, these protocols are important for everyone's safety, health, and peace of mind, and so the sitter can maintain professional standards.

VET EMERGENCY OR NONEMERGENCY?

Pet sitters and visitors must know the difference between a medical emergency and a medical problem that is not an emergency. In many situations, only a veterinarian can distinguish between an emergency and a nonemergency that still needs some medical assessment and follow up. If I have any concerns about an animal's health, I immediately call the owner of the pet company I work for, even if it is after hours. I also have the phone numbers of each pet's veterinarian on the key tag where the dog's house key is attached. With my independent clients, I call the owner directly to ask how he or she wants me to proceed. If I can't reach the pet owner, I immediately call the animal's veterinarian. After hours, I call veterinary hospitals that assess and treat animals after hours and overnight. I have the local phone number of nighttime veterinary hospitals for emergencies.

One Monday morning, I arrived to care for a ten-week-old puppy for the third week in a row. As I entered the door, I saw the puppy had gone to the bathroom on the floor and left a substantial amount of blood in her poop. This puppy had previous problems with intestinal bleeding. I called my boss immediately on her cell phone number, then cleaned up the mess and gave the puppy a short walk outside. My boss called the pet owner who left work and would be arriving home in less than thirty minutes. The pet owner made an appointment with the veterinarian that morning soon after the time she would arrive home. The ultrasound showed a problem that called for surgery and was fixable, barring any complications. The surgery took place and the puppy recovered and went on to grow and thrive normally. I would have taken the puppy to the veterinarian if the owner had been too far away.

The chain of communication that responsible pet owners and pet care professionals follow reflects professional standards initiated by the pet company or the independent pet professional integrated with the pet owner's wishes. It wasn't by accident that I saw the health problem the puppy was continuing to exhibit and followed a quick protocol of direct communication to the necessary people. The chain of communication is a chain of accountability, and my boss, the pet owner, and I all fulfilled our roles because we had the proper infrastructure in place. Teamwork is great, isn't it? Teamwork builds pride, competence, safety, customer service, and customer loyalty.

Veterinary hospitals schedule daytime hours. Many family pets have nonemergency symptoms and emergency conditions that can be served during regular daytime hours. Certain veterinary hospitals schedule overnight hours. Medical conditions that are not life-threatening and can be treated during regular veterinary hours include mild sneezing, runny eyes, coughing, raw skin, itching and scratching, short-term vomiting without a fever, and loose stools for less than three days in healthy animals with no preexisting condition. I recommend pet owners to ask their veterinarians before traveling if their animal could be seen after hours during an emergency at the vet's office.

5

PET OWNER'S COMMUNICATING WITH PET PROFESSIONALS

Minor conflicts can arise between pet family owners and the pet professionals they interview and hire. Misunderstandings can arise simply because of the laws of probability in human relationships. The more often a pet owner hires a pet professional for their pets, the more success and minor conflicts they will have. Pet owners and pet professionals must remember there is no perfection in life, only perfect imperfection. Adversity is good and necessary if we respond appropriately and with mutual respect and effective strategies. We are all lifelong learners. Pet owners are lifelong learners about their pets and have the best day-to-day view of their lovely cats and dogs in their life stages. Pet professionals have the most accurate understanding of how a particular cat or dog might respond to them in the context for which the pet professional is hired.

INITIAL MEETINGS AND SIGNED AGREEMENTS

Good communication is the key to minimize conflict and empower the pet owner and pet professional. Pet owners may feel comfortable with an unknown pet professional before agreeing to hire them. But they can find some reassurance through positive references or referrals from their friends, colleagues, or veterinarian.

In my independent business, I set up an initial meeting with the pet owner to see if we are comfortable with one another and how well their pets interact with me. When working for the pet company I meet the pet family after the owner of the pet care company has met them. The pet owners invite me to their home at an agreed time where I meet the pets, talk to and play with them, and mingle in the backyard with the dog or give the dog a short walk. I engage with cats, closely following the guidelines the cat owners have informed me work for them, allowing the cat owners to even prompt me by guiding me. The meeting lasts about twenty-five minutes, and I leave a questionnaire with independent clients if they haven't received one in the mail.

Pet owners should receive a written and signed agreement for all pet services: sitting, dog walking, cat visits, bird visits, doggy daycare, and dog playgroups. This agreement contains many questions, and it clarifies up-front protocols for the companion animal's health and safety, the security of the home, the financial terms, and the needs of the pet owners and pet professional.

Most conflicts that arise between the pet owner and pet professional are minor. Even major conflicts can often be ironed out with kind, respectful words and conversation that restates feelings, wishes, and expectations. Pet owners stating their concerns about their pet's care is a very important part of their role, and the pet professional can address specifically each point of the owners' concern. Sometimes an owner may become disappointed with some aspect of the pet service being offered. The professional may have a different opinion than the pet owner or may never have thought of an owner's suggestion or concern until the subject came up.

Pet owners are placing themselves, their property, and their animals in a vulnerable situation with pet professionals. Pet owners are counting on the professional to do the right thing or the expected thing all the time in meeting an animal's needs. Pet owners, like everyone else, have their life struggles, extreme stresses, and changing situations regarding family health, finances, vacations, births, deaths, employment, separation, divorce, and so on. Positive statements and strategizing are important when conflicts arise. Statements like the following go a long way toward conflict resolution:

Pet Owner: We are worried about Georgie and her needs. Please don't forget to use her raincoat, even if it is not raining but the sky is gray. She was too wet after her walk.

Bob: I think you know exactly what Georgie needs. I'm sorry I missed that detail. I'm glad she has such a good home. I'll write down your suggestion here on my pad. Thank you for your input.

Pet Owner: We feel like DeGaulle needs a short bonding with you before transitioning to your playgroup car. Could you just sit for a short moment and give him a treat?

Bob: You're right. I'm glad you brought this up. What are his favorite treats?

Pet Owner: I found some white road salt stains on the wooden floor. I was really shocked. They come up easily enough, but I thought you folks were going to always try and clean your boots off before you enter our home?

Bob: I understand you don't want snow and road salt on your carpets and wooden floors. What are your suggestions? What would you like me to do?

Pet Owner: Maybe you could take off your boots at the front door?

Bob: Are there other options that won't diminish the time you want me to spend walking Arno? The front door is near the crate. If there were some old towels spread out from the front door to the crate I would walk only on the towels.

Owner: That's a possibility. We sure have enough old towels around to use some for the hound.

Bob: That's great. I'll be sure to use the towels on the floor when I arrive here for dog walks.

Pet Owner: We are really frustrated about the wrong leash coming home with Napoleon from playgroup. This is the second time. When can we expect the correct one back?

Transporter: Napoleon's leash is one of four red leashes at dog play-group. We have telephone calls in to two other families to see if the leash can be returned in two days, on Wednesday when Napoleon is back in playgroup.

Pet Owner: It's an expensive leash and we hate losing track of it. We probably should have his name written on the leash. We'll get that done.

Transporter: It looks like an expensive leash. Thank you for your patience. We get frustrated too when we put the wrong leash on a dog because there is no name on the leash.

Notice the pet owners express themselves openly and the pet profes-sional acknowledges the pet owners' wishes and frustrations empathi-cally, taking responsibility for his or her own mistakes while also sharing some of the same important goals for what the pet owners wish. No one is made to feel bad or intentionally careless or uncaring. Both pet owner and the pet professional are seen to be on the same page with a com-mon strategy: for example, write the dog's name on the leash and return the correct leash to the customer.

Figure 5.1 presents the independent pet care contract form I use with pet family owners. It can be used as a guide to the types of issues to be covered when contracting with a pet professional.

Figure 5.1. Sample Pet Care Contract and Client Questionnaire

Pet Care Services
Today's date: / /

Dates of animal service:
Start: month_____ date_____ year___time_____
End: month_____ date_____ year___ time_____
Day and approximate time owners leave for trip:

_____

Day and approximate time owners return home:

_____

Pet sitting to be done in your home? yes____no___

Dog walks? yes___no___
Dog walks (weekends only) yes___no___
Dog walks (Monday–Friday only) yes__no__
Cat visits? yes___ no_____
Dog behavior playgroup? yes___ no_____
Doggy daycare? yes___ no_____

Pet owner trip transportation mode: train__ car__ plane ___boat__
(Inform me about delays in planes, trains, and other travel. If you need
pet care extended beyond our agreement, I'll try to provide extra walks,
meals, visits, and overnights if my schedule allows.)

Pet owners' names. Include all household members:
Owners' address:

_____

_____

_____

Contact information:
Cell phones _____
Residence land line _____
Travel contact information:

_____

_____

Veterinarian name, address, phones:

_____

_____

_____

DOGS
Name(s), breed, age, sex, neutered date/spayed date:

_____

_____

_____

_____

_____

Feeding, Exercise, Medications, Sleep
Dry food? yes___no___
How much? Frequency? Brand?

_____

_____

_____

Wet food? Yes___no___
How much? Frequency? Brand?

_____

_____

_____

Where does your dog usually sleep at night when you are home?

_____

_____

_____

Where do you want your dog to sleep when I pet sit?

_____

_____

_____

Current or recent medications?

_____

_____

Is your dog(s) a breed needing 1–2 miles of exercise daily? yes__ no___
Is there a harness to walk your dog with or a collar? Where is the harness or collar located?

_____

_____

Does your dog's collar include a name, phone number, and updated license tags?

_____

What is your dog's walking/exercise/feeding routine every day?

_____

_____

_____

Describe your dog's personality, favorite things, and least favorite things.

_____

_____

_____

_____

_____

_____

Does your dog(s) enjoy car rides? yes___no___
Beaches? yes___no__
Swimming? yes___no___
Grooming? yes__no__

Is your yard completely fenced in? yes__ no__
Are the dog's shots updated and current? yes___no__
When being walked on a leash, how does your dog react to children, adults, and other dogs?
Has your dog ever been attacked by dogs or cats ?
Does your dog have any history of onleash or offleash aggression toward other dogs, adults, or children? yes__no__. If yes, explain:

_____

_____

_____

Is your dog(s) gated at home when you leave, between breakfast and lunch or lunch and dinner? yes__no__
If so, in which room(s)?

_____

Is your dog(s) crated when no one is home? yes____no____
If so, which room is the crate in?

_____

Do your dogs' crates usually have water or food in them? yes___no___

CATS
Name(s), breed, age, sex, neutered date/spayed date:

_____

_____

_____

Feeding, Exercise, Medications, Sleep

Dry food? yes___no___
How much? Frequency? Brand?

_____

_____

_____

Wet food? yes___no___
How much? Frequency? Brand?

_____

_____

_____

Describe your cat's personality, likes, and dislikes.

_____

_____

_____

Are cats indoor___or outdoor?___
Is there a cat door?

yes___no___

When visiting cats while you're away, I may ask you to shut off the basement and parts of the second and third floors of your home for cat safety. Is this acceptable to you?

yes___no___

For safety reasons, I'd prefer that outdoor cats be kept inside during your trip. Is this acceptable to you?

yes___no___ maybe___

Hiding places cat(s) frequents:

_____

_____

_____

Does your cat enjoy grooming?

yes___no___

Is your cat up to date with all shots?

yes___no___

BIRDS

Name(s), breed, age:

_____

_____

_____

Care Instructions

Sprayed with water 1x daily?

yes____no____

Birdseed shells blown off seeds daily?

yes____no____

Dried bird seed replaced daily?

yes____no____

Digestive aid placed in small quantity on floor of cage?

yes____no____

If yes, how often?_____

Cover on birdcage(s) overnight during house sitting?

yes____no____

Enjoys shoulder/arm perch?

yes____no____

Other bird care instructions:

_____

_____

_____

_____

RODENTS

Rodent(s) name(s), breed, age, instructions

_____

_____

_____

_____

_____

_____

SPECIAL NEEDS PETS

I have experience caring for animals with blindness, stroke, diabetes, advanced hip weakness, and rescue history, as well as puppies and those in the last stage of life.

Does your dog or cat have a rescue history? yes___no___

Does your pet have disabilities or special needs? Describe.

_____

_____

_____

Is your dog a puppy? yes___no___

If so, is it house trained? yes___no___usually_____

Has your puppy or dog received ongoing training in the last 12 months? yes___no___

Training improvements:

_____

If your pet has been behaving abnormally before your trip, let me know whether or not they have been evaluated by your veterinarian.

Has your pet any recent bathroom accidents? yes_____no_____

Explain:_____

EMERGENCY CARE INSTRUCTIONS

Please 1) leave in your home an envelope labeled "emergency care," containing a photocopy of both sides of your credit card, with a dollar amount limit allotted for emergency medical care for each pet or 2) set up an agreement directly with your veterinarian about paying for emergency services.

HOME INFORMATION

Landlord

_____phone_____

Plumber_____

phone_____

Electri-

cian_____phone_____

___

Heating/gas   company_____

phone_____

Trash/recycling day _____

Friends and neighbors (names, addresses, and phone numbers) who could help in emergency:

_____

_____

_____

_____

_____

_____

Circuit breaker location:

_____

Sump pump?
yes____no____
If yes, where does water exit home?
Front of home____side of home____rear____
Ice melt/sand location(s):

_____

Laundry facilities on second floor?
yes____no____
If yes, consider turning off water to washing machine before you travel.

Number of cars left in driveway:
0____1____2____3____
Number of boats in driveway:
0__1__2__3__4__
Any cars expected to be towed, serviced, or used by relatives/friends not living in your home during pet sitting?
yes____no____
For safety reasons, friends and family members should not visit your home when I am pet-sitting without prior agreement between you and me.

You are responsible for removing snow from the driveway and walkways so I can safely enter and exit your home during pet sitting. Is there a snow removal plan in place?
yes____no____

Do you have a garage I can use? yes____no____

Garage door opening: electric____manual___
Will you leave me an automatic garage door opener? yes___no___

Plant and garden care needed:
1st floor__2nd floor___3rd floor__basement____outside___
    Plant and garden care instructions

_____

Mail delivered__ mail held__ newspapers delivered__ newspapers
held___

Will there be any visitors to the house or property during your trip? Any
packages or dry cleaning expected? Gardeners, housekeepers, oil delivery, etc.? Describe. Include names and days when possible.

_____
_____
_____

When I leave your home, I prefer to leave a radio playing classical
music 99.5 FM, or a television playing Animal Planet, for pet stimulation until I return. Is there a radio available on the first floor?
yes_____no_____

MY COMMITMENT

- Dogs receive a minimum of 4 walks or yard times daily (breakfast,
  midday, dinnertime, bedtime).
- If you have a fenced yard, I will exercise your dog daily in the
  yard.
- I will scoop cat litter 1x daily.
- I will groom and scratch cats if they enjoy it.
- Your pets will receive fresh water, fresh food, conversation, and
  kindness every day. They will feel loved and cared for.
- Be sure to leave balls, toys, and grooming tools for play/exercise/
  bonding.

MY SELF CARE

What room will I be sleeping in?

_____

_____

How many thermostats are there? Where are they?

_____

_____

_____

I like to cook on the stove. This replicates some of what your pets are used to with you, their family. Please leave part of a shelf in the refrigerator free for my food.
Please leave ample paper towels and antiseptic counter/floor cleaner.
Dishwasher instructions:

_____

_____

_____

Simple directions for television use:

_____

_____

_____

What TV channels do you receive? Animal Planet___Red Sox___ Celtics___ Patriots___Bruins

SECURITY AND SAFETY
Number of yard gates? 0_____1____2_____3____
Please secure yard gates before your trip.

Are there any aggressive dogs that roam loose in your neighborhood?
yes_____no_____
Hawks frequent some neighborhoods, endangering toy or miniature dogs in fenced yards. Does this apply to your dogs? yes___no___

Are there any doors or windows on the first floor that don't lock correctly? yes___no___
Do the house keys work both front door and rear door entrances?
yes___no____

For my safety and the pet's, I prefer key access to both front and rear doors, and a key to each door if locks differ. I will label the house keys with only the first name of your dog/cat.

Are pets gated with pressure gates? yes ___no____
With hardware-attached gates? yes__no___
Please note that pressure gates are unsafe at stair tops for cats, dogs, and children.

It is normal for you to call me when traveling to see how your pet is. I may also call you if I have some questions or just to reassure you every-thing is going well. Is this okay? yes___ no___
Is there an alarm I must disarm or arm? yes___no____
Please leave the alarm directions and password on a separate sheet of paper for me when I begin.
Alarm company name and phone number:

_____

_____

Does the alarm company need my name, password, and phone num-ber? yes___no___

PET SITTING FEES/CAT VISIT FEES/DOG WALK FEES
Per day:
one (1) dog _____
two (2) dogs _____
three (3) dogs _____
one (1) cat _____
two (2) cats _____
three (3) cats _____
Note: When I pet sit for a dog or dogs, there is no extra charge for one cat.
A non-refundable deposit of _____percent payment is due when we sign this agreement. This secures your reservation for my services.

I/we, the below signed pet owner/pet family, agree to indemnify and hold harmless Pet Care Services from all claims, demands, liabilities, suits, actions, damages, (whether immediate, consequential, or other-wise), costs and expenses (including but not limited to attorney's fees) with respect to injury, harm, loss, or damage to residence, and family pets on or off our property. We promise not to sue Mr. Berkelhammer for any reason.

Pet owner signature/date

_____

Pet owner signature/date

_____

Pet Services/date

_____

LOGS AND NOTES FOR PET FAMILY OWNERS

Separation anxiety is felt by the pet owners and pets themselves. Pet logs documenting the animal's daily behaviors, health, happiness, medication, and so forth are a professional standard for pet professionals when addressing separation anxiety. Pet owners should feel comfortable and confident in asking for one from a pet care professional, even if one is not offered.

Pet owners enjoy reading logs of their cats' or dogs' activities when they return from travel. I enjoy log keeping in the pet owners' home. Log keeping helps me integrate and understand the needs of a particular pet family as I learn by doing, especially serving first-time pet owners and their pets. The information contained in the logs helps pet owners feel better about themselves, their animals, and the pet professional.

Pet family owners who read a log see substantive positive events that nurtured their pets while they were traveling. The log allays concerns, guilt, and uneasy feelings, including any separation anxiety, they experienced while traveling. Communication logs show customers that the pet professional diligently accomplished responsibilities while nurturing the pets and following the owners' directives. The log creates a basis for dialogue and improved customer service and is useful for future pet sitting contracts with a pet owner.

Pet owners generally express strong appreciation for the logs and enjoy reading them. Children in particularly enjoy reading about what their pets were up to while the family was traveling. A log can help create a happy new customer who seeks the pet services again and who refers other people to the pet professional. Logs educate pet owners about small business customer service standards and protocols for pet sitting and invite members of pet families to communicate with one another and the pet professional. I include below some sample logs from some of my pet sitting experiences. The word "conversation" in the following logs means I talked to the animals I visited.

SAMPLE LOGS

Log for Two Days of Cat Visits

11/1 Sunday: Litter, mail, dry cleaning, water, dry food, wet food, newspaper.
  A.M.
  Stew and Vegas together under bedspread. Vegas came out for treats. Scratched Vegas, Stew shy under bed. Conversation with cats. All food from 10/31 eaten. House warm and cozy at 65 degrees.
  11/2/07 Monday: Vegas out for scratching and some purring during scratch time. Conversation with both cats. Litter, mail, water, dry food, newspaper. Intense cat play with balls and feather. Increased heating system two degrees to 64 degrees, kind of cold at 62 degrees as you told me it might be. Small pile of vomit with no cat hair or any inanimate objects visible today.
  Hope your trip went well! Please leave a phone message informing me you have returned home.
  Thank you! Bob

Log for Pet Sitting Dog with Intestinal Sickness

1/23/08 12–1 p.m.: Arrived for pet sitting. Dylan left diarrhea on kitchen floor. Dark brown soupy mess with pieces of something in it. (Barbecued chips? Dylan's owner told me that morning Dylan had eaten a delicatessen sandwich off the counter with bag of barbecue chips.) Dylan not wagging tail as usual, though spirits pick up when I pet and talk to him. (There had been one previous case of loose bowels this morning according to owner.) Owner put down two pee pads and Dylan left mess on one pad and the rest on floor. I called my boss, who suggested a diet for three meals of cooked chicken and rice, one cup each meal. The meals would be one for tonight, and two tomorrow. I cleaned up floor using disposable gloves I store in my car. Pet owner had plenty of paper towels, liquid cleaner, and garbage bags under kitchen sink. I walked Dylan outside. If Dylan continues soiling problems the day after tomorrow, I'll take him to veterinarian for checkup and possible medication. Called Dylan's owner to inform them of situation and our approach to try and remedy the situation. Dylan's owner appreciated being informed and felt this would resolve itself over time with the nutritional measures planned.

1/23/08 4–5 p.m.: Fed Dylan chicken and rice for dinner. Walked Dylan in backyard. Left for three hours.

1/23/08 8 p.m.: Second incidence of diarrhea since I started pet sitting and third time today. Cleaned it up, walked Dylan in backyard, and called to tell owner about Dylan and starting him on rice and chicken diet precooked from my bosses freezer. (Dylan's owner apologetic and appreciative of strategies to support Dylan.)

1/23/08 9:30 p.m.: Walked Dylan in backyard. Dylan in bed at 10 p.m.

1/24/08 4 a.m.: Checked on Dylan before my early morning writing. More loose stools on floor in master bedroom area. Walked him in backyard. Cleaned up mess. Water bowl filled in master bedroom area. Hydration very important. Spirits seem quite good.

1/24/08 8 a.m.: Chicken and rice for breakfast. Walked Dylan around neighborhood and he received plenty of exercise this morning.

1/24/08 1 p.m.: No stomach problems between breakfast and midday walk at 1 p.m.

1/24/08 5 p.m.: No stomach problems between 1 p.m. and dinnertime. Plain rice and chicken dinner without kibble.

1/25/08 8 a.m.: Good news! No loose stools overnight and poops this morning in yard firm and well formed. I'll gradually mix in kibble with chicken and rice over the next couple of days. With no more loose stools evident for over 24 hours, I won't have to bring Dylan to the veterinarian.

1/25/08 5 p.m.: I cooked up some organic steel-cut oats for myself for breakfast and fed Dylan some of the oats gently warmed up with some chicken. Dylan showed great enthusiasm eating the oats and chicken and stood over the bowl afterward licking his lips.

Telephone Updates from the Pet Family Owners

Pet owners and pet professionals work together to achieve great customer service. Pet owners enjoy updating me about their pets' health after I complete my pet sitting or pet visits. Once they do, it feels like the owner trusts me and my good work has come full circle via the pet owner's conscientiousness. Below is an example of communication with a pet owner, the pet sitter, the veterinarian's office, and the owner of the pet care company I work for, with all cooperating to solve the medical problem of a pet I was sitting for.

Mrs. Taggart left a message on my cell phone the morning I started at the Taggarts' home, where I would be sitting for their cat, Rickenbacker and their dog Smooch.

"Bob, this is Mrs. Taggart. My husband and I saw some blood in Rickenbacker's litter box this morning. He was squatting outside the litter box, sometimes without success. I hate to inconvenience you because you are just starting pet sitting for us this morning, but I've made a 12:30 appointment for him at Dr. Rockwell's. I hope you can fit this into your schedule today. Please call me when you receive this message and after Rickenbacker's examination. Please leave a message if we don't answer."

I have my cell phone on all the time during pet sitting except during sleep. I immediately left a message for my boss, informing her of Rickenbacker's medical issues communicated to me. My schedule was filled around the 12:30 p.m. time, but I was able to reschedule the appointment on the same day. I returned the following message to the owners after letting them know I would bring their cat to Dr. Rockwell that day.

"Hello, Mrs. Taggart. The veterinarian didn't find infection in Rickenbacker's urinary tract, which was not surprising to Dr. Rockwell because Rickenbacker is three, younger than the age cat urinary infections occur. The doctor placed him on antibiotics. The ultrasound found evidence of gravel like matter that needs to dissolve. The veterinarian hopes to accomplish this with medicated food instead of surgery, which I brought from your veterinarian to your home in the form of both dry and wet canned food.

"I'll feed him the medicated food until you return from vacation. Your veterinary visit with him is in three weeks. I'll watch him closely every day. As you told me, and both the doctor and I concurred, Rickenbacker has a lot of energy and his general mood is good. If there is a marked decrease in his activity and spirits, it could mean a blockage is developing in his urinary tract, which is a very critical medical situation, needing immediate veterinary intervention. Could you please call me back confirming you received this message? It's 5 p.m. Thursday. If you wish to call your veterinarian, the office the number is 999-999-9999. Thanks." The Taggarts confirmed later that day they had received my message.

Three weeks later I received an additional phone call.

"Hello Bob, this is Wendy Taggart. How are you?"

"Hello Mrs. Taggart. I'm fine. How is Rickenbacker?" I asked.

"I wanted to update you. We took him back to the doctor's office for his three-week checkup. The new ultrasound shows very little left of that gravel like matter in his bladder. He's almost completely well, and I wanted to thank you for taking him to the vet the day you started pet sitting for us. You saved his life!"

"That's very kind of you. I don't think I saved his life, but I appreciate the comment. I am just glad you and your husband saw some blood in his urine the morning you left for your trip, called the veterinarian, and set up a veterinary appointment."

"Thank you Bob, and we'll be in touch."

"Thank you Mrs. Taggart."

E-mail can also be used for long-distance communication between veterinary offices and traveling pet owners. Pet owners appreciate this level of good communication with independent and company-based pet professionals.

NOTES BETWEEN PET OWNERS AND PET VISITORS OR PET SITTERS

Notes are another way a pet owner communicates with pet professionals. Notes can be left at the end of each visit or shared via e-mail or even text message, depending on what the pet owner would like. Feel free to state your preferences, and indicate how often you'd want updates of this kind.

1/23/09 Is your puppy [Bingo] having fewer accidents in the home? Bob

1/25/09 Hi Bob! Bingo is starting to ring the bells on the back door when she needs to do her business. Thanks for staying in touch. (Bingo's owner.)

4/12/2010 Simon is coughing during our walks. He irritates his trachea by pulling. A Sensible Harness or Easy Walk Harness eliminates this because the leash attaches to the chest area. You and your kids will also have more control of Simon using a harness, when you wish to slow him down or take a turn in direction, or when he lunges at a dog to play. Bob

4/19/2010 Thanks Bob for your 4/12 note. As you saw today, we started Simon with a harness last week and there is no more trachea coughing! Simon's Mom and Dad.

6/30/10 Willow is not eating the pill in the pill pocket or when I wrap it in food with or without a pill pocket. He eats the cheese or tuna fish around the pill pocket but avoids the rest. Do you have any other suggestions? I can grind it up and mix it into food, unless you have found that doesn't work. Bob

6/30/10 Okay Bob, why don't you grind it up and we'll see if Willow eats the pill? Thank you! Willow's Mom

2/12/11 Rocket fit in quickly to dog behavior modification playgroup today as he did on his first day yesterday. Rocket seemed like he knew more of what to expect and jumped into action quickly after an initial looking around. Rocket played ball, wrestled with other dogs, and smelled his new friends. The familiarity factor is growing for him. Rocket is responding well to staffers and we really like him. Rocket's confidence is growing and should continue over the coming months. Bob

5/22/11 Rocket started his third playgroup month today, running confidently next to larger dogs—a Rhodesian ridgeback and a Newfoundland. Rocket even faced them with playful growling. Rocket chased balls with larger dogs and is more confident than ever in his expanding play style. Bob

5/23/11 Bob, thanks for Rocket's playgroup update. He is more relaxed at home and easier to be with. He isn't a terror anymore in the neighborhood. Rocket rarely barks loudly or pulls on his leash around other dogs.

8/30/2011 Puffin and Glory behaved very well during the pet sitting over the past three days. They are peeing and pooping regularly, drinking plenty of water, eating food, and enjoying being scratched and talked to. They really like the peacock feathers to paw at and chew. You're right, the red mouse is their favorite toy! Alfalfa ran around in circles in the back yard with his favorite tennis ball. He was in happy spirits, enjoyed the grooming, ate, drank, and did his bathroom trips daily. Dry cleaning is hanging on the laundry room door per your request and I signed for the two packages you said would arrive. Please call me when you arrive home to let me know Alfalfa is under your care. Thank you, Bob P.S. I noticed some very small ants around your kitchen drain in the left side sink.

5/29/2010 Today Barbs built on her confidence over the four months in playgroup and ran up and down the play yard for the first time. She was very excited with her joyful running as staffers were also. Barbs' play style is changing! Water checked and treat. Bob

DOGS LIVING IN TWO PET OWNER HOMES DURING SEPARATION AND DIVORCE

There is good news for pet owners and their children going through separation and divorce. Certain dogs can successfully live in two pet family homes after spouses separate or divorce. This success is a wonderful thing for the pet owners and the children. I don't believe adult cats would be successful moving between two homes. However, a kitten being exposed to moving back and forth between two homes might be able to adjust, but I have no proof of this.

The best way for a dog to have the greatest potential for normalcy in two homes with children is when the co-parents of the children establish a baseline of functional co-parenting over a period of time in each home. Certain former spouses will be unsuccessful at this because of unresolved hot-button issues. Over time, healing can occur if people choose to heal and the spouses may be able to function at a level that would support the family dog living in two homes. Feelings and desires for sharing the family dog in two homes are not rational bases for a dog living in two homes. Feelings and desires can be motivators, but functional parenting means developing skills on a consistent basis that can support a dog's welfare. Feelings alone cannot take care of a dog.

My didactic studies in marriage and family therapy introduced me to the use of duplication in the lives of families. Duplication and harmony support the pet family dog receiving what it needs in each family home. It's difficult to say how much time this may take because of many variables. It is best for the family pet to begin going back and forth when the former spouses are able to provide for the dog's needs consistently. Initially, spouses need time to adjust and endure a new and extremely difficult situation. This includes overseeing the children's elevated levels of upset over the loss of their old lives and the practical issues of having to adjust to new schedules and geographic change.

The family dog can become an elixir for the children during the heartbreak and chaos of divorce, by traveling with them between the two homes and maintaining the fabric of stability and identity that a pet family brings. Children in separation and divorce need their companion animals around them, preferably every day. Dogs are adaptable and need relatively little, but dogs need daily consistent routines in their pet family homes, including food, water, shelter, human love, bonding with family members, limits, security, exercise, and contact with other dogs. When these basic needs are met in a new two-home context, a dog can successfully live in two homes. Separated and divorced spouses who place the needs of their children above their own unhappiness are more likely to create a better life in two homes for their children and family dog.

The following items of duplication should be available for the dog in both pet family homes: pet bed, toys, dog food, feeding and drinking bowls, treats, leash, and harness. There should also be provisions for schedules for playgroup transport and dog walker if applicable; veterinary bills and clinical findings; calendars for routine checkups, heart worm protocols and scheduled follow-up veterinary visits; first-aid kits, thunder medication (if the pet fears thunder) or any other medications, and poison control phone numbers. Newspapers are also important if the dog is used to retrieving them!

Parents in two homes make sure their child has a comfortable, pleasing bedroom that is decorated with things the child feels an affinity for, such as posters, artwork, and bedding. By the same token, a dog certainly feels at home with a doggy bed or a similar sleeping arrangement in each home, which may be in a human's bed, on a sofa, or on the carpet or rug next to a bed. If the dog is most comfortable in a doggy bed, then the second pet family home should also provide a doggy bed if resources allow.

Children are acutely aware of things in their environment. Children often keep similar toys and books in a two-home situation as a way to ease the adjustment. Duplication of important possessions increases bonding, healing, and stability. A dog will also benefit from duplicate toys in each home. Both homes need to have the same regular food and treats that have worked for the animals in the past, all appealing to the animal and free of allergens. If the food and treats are different from home to home, it is more difficult to deduce which food may be causing allergies or other symptoms. Both a harness and a leash are necessary in each home for a dog. Harnesses, as I've said, are a safer way to walk the dog for both the adults and children, and decrease throat trachea irritation when dogs pull on the leash.

Both pet family owners should have all the paperwork related to their pet's medical care, even if it is agreed upon between the two homes that one pet owner is paying all or a majority of the veterinary bills. Veterinary bills and clinical findings should be duplicated by the veterinarian at the request of the parents and sent either via e-mail when possible or through the mail to the two residences. Duplication of bills and medical finding reports allows children who are old enough to learn about those aspects of pet owner care and responsibilities. The yearly license for a dog needs to be bought and placed with secure hardware on the collar.

Co-parenting Conflicts in Two Home Pets

The children of divorce in the two homes are better off if the pets' parents never share conflicts about the pets (or anything, for that matter) in front of the children or the pets. By conflict I mean strong disagreement with a high degree of emotion, tension, inappropriate language, anger, or fear. However, if the co-parents have matured to a consistent baseline level of civility in their conflicts with each other, they can have a polite disagreement in front of the children who are old enough to understand their parents are actually resolving something in a respectful manner. Dogs and cats can also become upset around uncivil fighting. Cats and dogs don't like screaming or rage, which can elevate their anxiety and fear. Divorced pet parents who sanely resolve conflicts set a good example for the children of divorce to learn how to resolve conflict. Separated and divorced pet owners can develop the discipline to avoid airing strong conflicts over a cell phone speaker, a computer, e-mail, or at transitional times like drop off and pick up of children and pets between the residences.

Pet parents prone to chronic conflicts with each other after separation and divorce may consider talking with a trained clergy member, attending religious services, or seeking the services of a licensed marital and family therapist. These resources may create more peacefulness, which is something of great value for the children and the pets. Pet owners who see problem behavior in their pets after divorce may seek out an animal behavior professional for consultation.

Veterinary bills and money responsibilities in general can be a negative stressor for co-pet parents. Veterinary bills can be difficult during underemployment, job loss, sickness, or when large veterinary bills come in after pets have undergone testing or surgery. A recession can severely strain resources available for pet care.

Professional Dog Walkers for Dogs Living in Two Homes

Divorced pet owners can hire a pet professional to walk and help transport their dog. I've had the privilege of walking a gorgeous dog for a family who lives in two homes in the same town. I often walk Mexi at his dad's home a number of consecutive days and then drive Mexi over to his mom's home. This dog walking protocol helps the family in maintaining the daily needs of their family dog and the children living in two homes. The following is an example of a schedule for walking Mexi while living in two homes.

Monday: Mexi at Parent A home. Walk and leave at Parent A home.
Tuesday: Mexi at Parent B home. Walk and drive to Parent A home.
Wednesday: Mexi at Parent A home. Walk and return to Parent B home.
Friday: Mexi at Parent A home. Walk and return to Parent B home.

Dogs living in two homes could also apply to the grandparents of children whose parents own a dog. Grandchildren visit grandparents overnight, and the dog walker may be contracted to walk the dog at the pet owner's home and then transport the dog to the grandparents' home. This is a wonderful three-generational pet family model enjoyed by the family and the dog.

Co-pet parents in two homes with a baseline of good communication and parenting skills make it possible for a family dog to move safely between homes. The children and parents are the big winners and the dog is very happy too! The family dog's companionship warms everyone's heart, including the canine's heart!

PET SITTING OR PET VISITOR WRITTEN COMMUNICATION BETWEEN TWO PET COMPANIES WORKING THE SAME HOME

Pet owners often hire two separate pet companies or independent professionals to care for the animals in a home during the same time period with different responsibilities. The pet owner may hire a pet care company for the dogs enjoying a thirty-minute walk sometime between 11:00 a.m. and 2:00 p.m. The pet owner may hire a second independent professional for pet sitting overnight and be responsible after 5:00 p.m. and for a breakfast meal and walk. Pet owners require professionals from different companies to communicate between themselves for the overall safety and security of the pets and the home. The pet owners can also make it clear that both pet professionals need to read each other's notes and leave all the notes for the pet owner to read when he or she arrives home from traveling. The pet owner is paying professionals to do the job right, and that includes communication between the pet professionals and the company they work for, whether the professional works for someone else or is independent. Notes written by pet professionals for the pet owners should be left in a safe place that wind, fans, water, or animals don't have access to. Notes are best stapled or paper clipped together.

Strangely, pet professionals don't always follow through with these protocols. Here's one example. During my 11:00 a.m. walk of Mookie, the ambassador dog, a neighbor approached me and said, "Part of the backyard fence between my property and the dog owners' property has fallen down. Do you know when the owners are coming home?"

"I'm not in communication with the owners," I said. "They are traveling and someone else is staying there overnight with the dog. I'll let the home guest know and ask him to contact the owners immediately about the fence," I said. "Thank you for bringing it to my attention."

I wrote a note for the pet sitter, asking him to notify the pet owners about the fence and to confirm via my cell phone that he had passed the message along. The pet sitter never contacted me, but when the owners returned, they told me the pet sitter had called them. I told them that I would appreciate their instructing the other pet professional to communicate with me when I request it. When a fence breaks between two properties, the security and safety of both the dog and the neighbor's property is at risk. Pet professionals can be liable when situations are amiss.

CASE VIGNETTE: SALENE AND PAPARAZZI

Two lovely heart-warming Yorkies I care for live in a very large treed area. Salene is a teacup Yorkie, and Paparazzi is a regular Yorkie. Their pet owners have instructed me about their daily exercise routine, including letting them out into the fenced front yard or rear yard. Salene and Paparazzi cannot be left alone outside because a family of hawks lives nearby. A hawk can easily lift a small dog off the ground and carry the beloved and terrified pet away. Their owners asked me to be vigilant when I am outside with Salene and Paparazzi. I am prepared to act in a split second if a bird of prey ever swoops into the yard and attempts to cause every dog owner's worst nightmare. I set up a chair in all seasons and sit outside as these two gracious Yorkies sniff the grass, look around curiously, and rest, and I've mentally rehearsed using the chair to fend off an attacking hawk.

Salene and Paparazzi have filled me with fond memories. Salene can fit in the crook of my arm. She is anxious toward me for the first two to six hours that I pet sit and will not leave her yellow and blue madras plaid doggy bed to sit near me until usually the evening of the first day. Salene's owners have written a four-step routine that encourages her to sit on my lap and lick my face the first night and Paparazzi to snuggle next to my leg. Having them lick almond butter off my fingers is the first step when I enter the home. Then Paparazzi and Salene walk around the neighborhood on leash for pooping and overall stimulation. I talk in a low enthusiastic voice to draw both dogs to me after the first few hours pass. I also sit with the dogs in the evenings on the screened porch off the living room, listening to a water pump make a pleasing sound in a backyard pond where an occasional heron lands.

Most pet owners communicate well, either orally or in writing, and I make sure to read and review the information about their pets every time I visit their homes so I can integrate updates and changes since my last visit. I don't rely solely on my memory and experience, because it's human to forget things. Pet owners who prepare notes on a printed computer document or typewritten letter make it easier for pet professionals to follow their requests.

Pet owner updates might include new pets in the home, medications added or dropped, instructions on gating a dog in a room when I am out of the house, new dry food or wet food or a change in serving size, and new plants that need watering.

At one juncture, I visited Salene and Paparazzi for dog walks without pet sitting them. The visits were for thirty minutes three days in a row, with a second visit on the first and third days. Salene seemed quite uncomfortable around me and was unwilling to leave her bed to sit with me. I decided to temporarily move her bed out of the room, and I returned to sitting on the sofa. She decided to come sit on the top of the sofa, near my head, where I couldn't see her. I spoke with her gently and petted her as she sat behind me. I placed her on my lap after a few minutes, because I realized she was shaking. The shaking subsided and she relaxed in my hands, leaning against my belly. After ten minutes of this bonding, I felt very close and quiet with her. She turned around and looked at me and began to crawl up my chest to lick my face. Mission completed!

Moving Salene's bed had accelerated the process of her bonding with me. It seemed potentially risky in some ways, but I followed my instincts. I thought that if she got closer to me, she would remember how to relax and feel safe with me as she had in the past. I thought it was important to speed things up because my visits would be limited to thirty minutes.

Pet owners may communicate very little other than filling out either the detailed forms my company asks them to complete and sign or my own independent client forms. The company I work for places a business pad in each home so that owners can comment.

I also ask questions of the pet owner at times, but a small percentage of owners rarely respond to questions a pet visitor has about their dog or cat. Occasionally I notice that a dog needs to have its nails cut or a cat has a cough, and my notes to the pet owner about this may go unanswered. As frustrating as this can be for the conscientious pet care professional, we can't change other people and can only try to inform and educate. The pet professional can learn to value everyone's communication style, even though the desired response from the pet owner may not be forthcoming.

REPORTING POSSIBLE NEGLECT OR ABUSE OF PETS

A pet owner or pet professional may suspect that neglect or abuse is occurring in their neighborhood. Sometimes this information is just neighborhood gossip, springing from malice rather than concern for animal welfare. The pet owner or professional can look for signs that indicate real trouble and that call for intervention from family neighbors, an animal control officer, or the police.

Visual cues aren't always available because the animals are kept indoors or behind opaque fencing. But if the animals are kept outside, a concerned person should check for these signs:

- Open sores that are pink or red and seem not to have been medically diagnosed or treated
- Open wounds and cuts that are not stitched up or bandaged

- Prominent bony ribs (a possible sign of lack of food or an undiagnosed nutrition or digestive problem)
- Visible fleas or ticks on the animal's hair and body
- High concentrations of flies, feces, and urine smells and stains outside
- Dogs chained outside for long periods of time (and possibly dehydrated and overexposed to heat and humidity)
- Metal or wire collars that cut into dog's flesh
- Chronic limping or coughing
- Presence of hazards such as broken glass, nails tacks, and open containers of dangerous fluids

Concerned adults have three choices: ignore the situation, talk to the pet owner, or contact an animal control officer through the local police station.

A pet owner or pet professional might decide to approach the owner. Asking questions in a kind manner about an animal's welfare is better than blaming or being hostile. Remember that individuals, couples, families, and businesses can go through a major crisis in which animals may suffer. Destabilizing life changes in a pet owner's life may include economic recessions, physical illness, mental illness, substance abuse, fighting among the pets, divorce, underemployment, unemployment, and natural disasters. The pet owners may be trying and failing to reorganize themselves in such a way that their animals' needs are taken care of.

A pet owner may be unwilling to divulge anything, spurning help or communication. It may be best to call the animal control officer at this point. Let the police or the animal control officer know you are a pet owner or pet professional living or working in the area and you have a concern that you can't fully validate. Police and animal control officers are respectful toward sincere people who step forward with concerns. Police know concerns are not always fact based. Once summoned, the animal control officer follows protocols that allow him or her to gauge whether the animals are suffering or in trouble, accidentally or intentionally, and whether medical intervention or rehousing is necessary based on care standards.

The animal control officers will visit the residence and ask to see the animals because they have the legal right to assess situations. The pet owner may feel offended or betrayed by the anonymous whistle blower if no problems are found. Their privacy has also been compromised.

If the pet owner is not home to answer the door, an official document is left giving the owner a deadline for contacting the officer. The pet owner who responds within that allotted time may learn that their home needs to be revisited, and the assessment continues. If the deadline passes, the officer may have the right to enter the property without the owner's permission.

The animal control officer may find a level of neglect or abuse that warrants removing the animals from the owner immediately. Pets are transported in a special animal transport and taken to a veterinarian or a shelter for medical assessment. The pets whose lives can be saved receive treatment to see how much they can recover their health. Others are medically judged to be beyond saving and are put down.

THE UPSIDE OF BARKING

A dog's repeating bark is annoying to many people. But have you ever thought about what that bark means? Gordon Newell researched and wrote about maritime history, and a lecture he gave contextualized dogs' barking in maritime history.

Heavy fogs along the California coast would eliminate the visibility necessary for ship captains during the day and night. Radar and other technology had yet to be invented in the 1700s and 1800s. Captains navigating in fog had trouble locating islands and shallow ocean waters in high and low tides. Boats were ship wrecked in fog after hitting rock formations in the water, crews imperiled, and cargo lost.

Newell said that sea captains became familiar with the sounds of different pet owners' barking dogs on land, and where those dogs lived on the California coastal towns, villages, including farms. Sea captains learned through repetition on their voyages that a certain bark corresponded with a location. In dense fog, the captains would recognize the barking dogs and know where they were in relation to the coast line and the dangerous ocean reefs they needed to avoid. Dogs indeed were ship captains' best friend in fog!

6

TRANSITIONS IN THE LIFE OF A PET

Pet families experience many of the same lifestage transitions as humans. They go through conception, gestation in the womb, and birth; some period of time nursing from the mother, socialization with littermates, moving from exclusively liquid food to solid food; adoption; maturing physically and socially, aging, and passing on.

Certain pets are involved in lifestage transitions that demand higher levels of love and professionalism in their daily support and interventions from pet owners, pet sitters, and pet visitors. A pet in its last stage of life may need to be diapered or carried outside for fresh air and bathroom needs. The story of Layla later in this chapter delves into this type of lifestage transition.

CASE VIGNETTE: NELLIE: A NEW PUPPY

Pet care for puppies is exciting and hard work. Nellie, my focus here, was introduced in chapter 2 in the discussion on behavior modification playgroups.

Nellie was an eight-week-old Golden retriever when she was adopted. I began caring for her within a week of her adoption. Nellie's mom worked outside the home twenty-five hours a week. Nellie's mom had owned another Golden retriever who had passed away in old age, so she was an experienced Golden retriever owner with clear ideas on how she wanted to proceed with Nellie. Pet professionals can learn from pet owners who've owned the same breed previously. I've worked with pet owners who have owned bulldogs, Golden retrievers, Scotties, German shepherds, Coonhounds, Pointers, Corgies, Persian cats, Siamese cats, and Maine Coon cats for much of their adult lives and sometimes childhoods.

When initiating association with a pet care company, the owner or independent professional schedules an initial visit with the pet owner and puppy. The discussion includes how the puppy care is proceeding, strategies, note taking, and what options to pursue. The independent pet professional will give the pet owner some forms to fill out. (See chapter 5 for sample forms.) The pet company owner will provide the information shared in this meeting with all of the pet company employees who will be involved with the puppy care and, possibly at a later time, dog playgroup transport, pet sitting, dog walks, or cat care, as the owner's needs continue to evolve. Many puppy owners will already have family dynamics of competing needs with children and the spouse in the home. Puppy family owners can relax more with competent pet care professionals helping out.

During my initial visit with Nellie and her mom, we discussed house training, food, water, treats, medications, designated yard areas for pee and poop, playing, exercise, neighborhood concerns, and walk routines. Neighborhood concerns can include loose dogs off leash with aggression problems.

Puppy care requires setting up a daily schedule based on the pet owner's needs. Puppy parents may be outside the home during puppy care; however, a spouse may be home, telecommuting, or parenting. A sample schedule for puppy care is provided below. In this example, three different staffers took part, on the basis of their availability and the discretion of the company's owner-director.

Monday–Thursday
10:00 a.m–10:30 a.m. 1:00 p.m.–1:30 p.m. 4:00–4:30 p.m.

Each thirty-minute visit involved one or two walks in the backyard and teaching the puppy to pee or poop in a specific area of the yard. Fresh water, a meal, and playtime were offered. Puppies are usually crated when the pet professional arrives and are recrated when leaving.

"What words are used for her bathroom business?" I asked Nellie's owner. We decided I would use the phrase "Get busy," followed with

"Good get busy" after Nellie went to the bathroom. I would give Nellie treats only after she went to the bathroom outside. Nellie became excited when I said "Good get busy, good get busy," and gave her a treat for a job well done. She would wag her tail and jump up on me, eat her treat, and then jump up on me again. I would often pick her up and give her a hug. As Nellie aged, I encouraged her to stay seated without jumping on me by placing my open hand extended toward her, signaling her to stay. "Good stay, Nellie." I would also turn my back to her if she refused my command. Dogs become unhappy when people turn their back to them, feeling separated from the warm playful communication they prefer.

I left notes for Nellie's owner after my four to eight hours, reflecting an authentic positive regard for their pet family and the company I represented. Knowledge and respect help the puppy development progress as smoothly as possible, strengthening the owner–pet professional relationship.

I kept a bathroom log one day of Nellie's progress for Nellie's owner.

Nellie August 27: 8 a.m.–4 p.m.
Pees outside:

- 8:15 a.m.
- 9:15 a.m.
- 10:30 a.m.
- 11:45 a.m.

Pees inside home on pee/poop mats:

- 11:32 a.m.

Poops outside:

- 10:35 a.m.

Nellie was a magnet for the children's and adults' attention during our walks around Marblehead. I repeated the socialization process day after day that summer because Nellie was thrilled with the attention of being petted and hugged by children. I held Nellie on a tight leash to teach her not to jump on people and to limit her puppy biting.

RESPONDING TO NELLIE'S PUPPY BITING

Redirective discipline is part of owning a puppy. A puppy's biting of people or property other than toys is not acceptable. Responses to biting include "Ouchie, no biting," giving the puppy a spray of water, turning your back, or quickly blowing air into the puppy's nose after gently touching the snout. Puppies learn best through repetition. Age-appropriate children can be taught these measures by their parents.

Nellie often looked for a favorite couple to greet her on our walks. Nellie would lead me to their driveway, pulling me ten to fifteen feet up the driveway whether or not they appeared. The husband often appeared first, and Nellie would wag her tail and hips and greet him enthusiastically. "I'll get my wife," the neighbor often said. His wife would then appear and Nellie would bond with her. Puppies are a wonderful member of neighborhoods. I occasionally knock on the door of an elderly neighbor for a five-minute visit while performing puppy care. "You made my day" is a response I often receive during these visits.

Puppies are life educators, helping children realize things about their own developmental stages. Puppies are small, as are children, after birth. Children are thrilled by puppies' miniature size. Everything physical is tiny on puppies: heads, feet, legs, paws, and tails. Puppies are huggable the way children are huggable. They also grow quickly, the way children grow quickly. Every four to seven days, puppies are noticeably bigger. It's not unusual to hear someone say "I haven't seen your puppy in a week. Look at how he's grown" or "Is that the same puppy? Look at how long her legs are!"

Puppies, like children, are much larger in their internal qualities than their external features. Both puppies and children have a curiosity that overflows their cereal and water bowls and makes a lot of noise through barking or yelling. Kids and puppies cover a lot of real estate with their scampering and running. Puppies pedal with four paws, while children pedal scooters and bicycles. Owning a puppy and raising dogs are part of the American dream.

Pet owners and pet professionals set limits on puppies and people around them regarding treats. Puppies need to eat their regular food until they are full grown to maximize their nutrition input, without diminished appetite from eating treats. Puppies may be confused by receiving treats from a stranger for something other than toilet training. Some treats from well-meaning neighbors may have allergens in them.

Nellie had major surgery before she was ten weeks old to correct a genetic problem. After her surgery, the veterinarian told Nellie's owner and me to reduce her exercise by discontinuing walking Nellie around the neighborhood for at least two weeks to expedite the internal healing of her intestines and soft tissue areas and to keep her staples in place at the site of her surgical incision. In the early stages after surgery, I checked Nellie's staples along her long incision site daily to make sure they were still in place. The staples would eventually start loosening and eject themselves from her incision as the tissues healed more fully. Neighborhood children were fascinated by Nellie's large abdominal incision.

I spent three weeks at Nellie's home during her owner's working hours, sitting quietly with her as she ate, slept with her head on my shoe, and took sunbaths in the backyard while rolling on her back in thick grass and clover.

Nellie grew quickly, and one day I noticed her harness was too snug along her back and ribs after I put it on her. The device was becoming harder to snap shut. I loosened the harness and off we went! Harnesses that are not properly loosened as a dog grows impede the normal movement of a dog's shoulders and the expansion of the ribs when inhaling, causing them to walk with less coordination and sometimes tripping and falling, especially when descending stairs.

Nellie was six months of age, and her owner was waiting for her to finish some worming protocols before entering her in dog behavior modification playgroup. Nellie's need for social interaction was obvious: she relished her dog neighbors Telly, Felix, and Cinnamon, as well as their owners. Nellie began to roll over on command, give paw, climb onto a big flat rock on a hill, and sit for treats. A typical very intelligent dog in a Golden retriever's body!

A NEW PUPPY: CONSISTENT STRATEGIES FOR HOUSE TRAINING

Some puppy owners may already be in the process of house training. Other puppy owners may be overwhelmed or unclear about how to guide a puppy in house training or how to work with a pet professional team or individual to train the puppy. Professional experience begets confidence and helps to create clearly stated strategies for the puppy family.

Puppy owners and pet care professionals reward the pets' going to the bathroom outside the home with praise and a treat. Pee and poop mats in the home can be a practical tool toward house training and sanitary floors. However, certain dogs may be confused by pee and poop mats, slowing down a dog's house training. If a puppy begins to rip up and possibly eat pieces of the pee and poop mats, it may be best to discontinue using them for a while. The pet owner and pet professional would place mats in a previously agreed-upon place where the puppy can see them and is encouraged to use them. The pet owner and pet professionals must be on the same page and be consistent with bringing these soiled mats outside on the property. This simple, powerful strategy allows the puppy to see where they are supposed to relieve themselves—outside. Because of young children's needs or overwhelming scheduling factors, pet owners may be inconsistent, and this can influence the puppy to be inconsistent. Pet companies with great customer service make themselves as aware as possible when a pet family is inconsistent in house-training protocols.

The pet owner and puppy caregiver can try a second strategy by forming a small but visible pile of the puppy's feces in an agreed-upon place in the yard, intentionally walking the puppy and showing it the pile.

Puppy Care Yard Safety: Pruned Healthy Trees

Pet owners generally wait for their puppies to receive shots from their veterinarian before exposing them to other dogs. Therefore, the pet owner and pet professional should walk in the pet owner's yard until the puppy is ready and old enough to walk around the neighborhood. Accordingly, trees on the property can be a safety hazard, with limbs falling if not pruned and inspected by tree professionals. Tree limbs weigh a lot, and their mass and velocity as they fall to the ground can seriously injure or kill a puppy and a pet walker. The independent pet professional or the owner of a pet company should review the trees in the yard with the owners before puppy care begins. Arborists recommend home owners have trees on their property inspected once a year. I have personally had two close calls with falling tree limbs.

Adoption

Recently adopted pets entering the pet family home is another lifestage transition for the pet family. Pet professionals usually recommend that the adoptive parents of new animals postpone any unnecessary travel soon after the adoption. The newly adopted animal is in the early stages of putting down new roots, and building routines takes time and requires repetition. Pet owners may have scheduled business or vacation trips before they adopted a cat or dog, only to realize later the new pet can't go on vacation or a business trip.

How does the pet professional support the routines and needs of adopted dogs or cats when pet owners travel? Pet professionals are not the pet's parents. They must strive to create a bond of trust and security.

CASE VIGNETTE: CUMIN GETS ADOPTED

Experts on trauma believe that traumatized people live their trauma, not their lives. I am inspired by the partial healing of trauma in rescue dogs and cats, influenced by adoption, behavior modification play groups, and doggy daycare.

Cumin is a dog I met formally soon after her family adopted her from a local no-kill shelter. Coincidentally, I had seen Cumin myself before her adoption, when I visited the same shelter with my youngest children. I remembered Cumin's hollow, unhappy eyes looking emotionless and withdrawn, and her lying down toward the back of the cage, isolated and forlorn. She didn't come to the front of the cage when my children and I offered her a finger to sniff or lick. I felt depressed in her presence and wished to give her some affection, which she rejected. Cumin was a picture of true misery and unhappiness, a dog begging for love but without any perceptible hope. Cumin's pained eyes showed very low expectations for her future. I remember stepping back from the cage and visiting other dogs and cats at the shelter before returning to the front of her cage. Again I felt her internal energy waves of misery project outwardly from her forlorn gaze. Little did I know I would be walking her, pet sitting her, and eventually driving her to a dog behavior modification playgroup as she gradually became trusting and happy, because a fantastic adoptive family would love her, and the company I work for would aid the family! God works in mysterious ways!

Cumin's success with a stable, loving adoptive family is the type of feel-good success story shelters, pet owners, veterinarians, pet care professionals, and all others involved in animal rescue like to tell. I appreciate the vast network of people in the animal rescue process that come to the aid of dogs, cats, horses, rabbits, and others. Cumin's story occurs over and over again in America because so many private Americans invest time and emotional and financial resources to rescuing animals with the adoption process.

Cumin may be part Rhodesian ridgeback and part Viszla, with the requisite brownish-orange, short-haired fur of those breeds. When I met Cumin to begin walking her two times a week, she appeared extremely anxious and fearful of me, a stranger. Cumin didn't wag her tail, and I found it difficult putting her leash on because of her anxiety. I sensed how fearful she was as my hands moved closer to her with the leash. Was Cumin afraid of my hands hitting her? I sensed my own fear as I felt the energy in her body as extreme unease. I was concerned about being bitten as her head regressed further back like a snake's and a look of fear, dread, and confusion filled her lovely brown liquid eyes. They still begged for hope, showing some sweetness in her spirit waiting to express itself. I was freezing up myself in response to my fear.

Beyond Cumin's visible fear, dread, and confusion was something else I hadn't been able to notice in the animal shelter as clearly. Cumin's eyes had the blank, frozen look that develops over time from the chronic emotional pain of a loveless life, in which material and social needs were not met consistently, a blank look of expecting the worst to happen to her again as it had previously, over and over. Does trauma unhealed in a dog reflect in its posture, affect, and behavior? Yes. Did trauma influence Cumin's excessive flight and fight responses? Yes. Cumin's adoptive family was going to make a gigantic difference.

When visiting her, I tried different strategies on certain days. I would open her crate door, move my body away from the entrance door so as not to intimidate her further, and encourage her to leave it. Cumin would quickly exit the crate and run around the one-floor house looking for her family. Cumin searched quickly in the living room, the family room, the office, the kitchen, and the master bedroom, before finally settling in a lower bunk bed. The bunk bed was used by the family's eight-year-old child. Cumin moved me emotionally as I watched her try to re-create the growing bonding that was occurring with her loving adopted family. Hopelessness was being replaced with the adoptive strategy of family bonding through love and caring. I saw how Cumin turned her back to me as she snuggled in the bunk bed before and after our walks.

Cumin was bonding very strongly with her new family. Through these important relational objects, she recognized the familiarity of her own smell, her family members' body smells, and of course the familiar shapes, colors, and locations of the family home furnishings. The bunk bed below the family's one child was a magnet for Cumin. Cumin's excitement and relief was reflected in her eyes as she settled into a place of nurturing security. How comforting for Cumin to have routines every day of sleeping near a young boy who helped care for her in a dry, warm, comfortable, safe home, where fresh food, clean water, and daily human affection among all occurred. Dogs and cats relish and need sleeping areas that provide safety, comfort, and warmth.

Cumin had lived as an abandoned dog in Puerto Rico. She became pregnant and had a litter of puppies in an abandoned building. Cumin would come and go from the building, gathering food for her puppies. Two of Cumin's puppies were killed by dogs. A good samaritan rescued Cumin and the remaining puppies.

Before adoption, rescue dogs like Cumin and her puppies are prone to neglect of their basic needs: human warmth, affection, food, water, safe shelter, a healthy social life with other dogs. Abandoned dogs and cats can be hit by cars or have near accidents with cars and buses. They may drink water out of rain puddles and gutters polluted by toxic chemicals from sewage, lawn fertilizers, engine oil, and gasoline. Abandoned dogs like Cumin have sometimes been kicked and beaten or had objects thrown at them by cruel adults or children. Attacks by other loose dogs can also occur.

Cumin was learning how to soothe herself as comforts in her home became a daily norm instead of the exception. Self-soothing for a rescue animal is a mode of self-care that continues to condition the nervous system to feel better through integration of nurturing habits in the rescue home. Self-soothing is how animals learn to respond more normally in life.

Cumin appeared very uncomfortable when I would enter her home. She appeared anxious when she failed to find her family. In those early days of visiting her, I found Cumin had a soft place in her taste buds and stomach for cheese before and after her walks. The cheese helped her relax.

Cumin's Challenges in Being a Relaxed Dog

The first couple months walking Cumin, she would literally jump off the ground a couple of inches when a sanitation truck drove by or a loud noise occurred. Even a muted car horn would stir her into acting startled. Cumin would also bark fearfully and sometimes aggressively at adults. Trauma had overstimulated her nervous system, as her fight and flight responses showed. Cumin was unable to maintain a visual focus for more than a few seconds during our early walks. Her eyes and head moved quickly back and forth as if she was back on the streets of her former life, avoiding cars, trucks, and buses, looking for food in back alleys, and going without human affection. This excessive eye and head movement was an adaptive behavior she used as an abandoned dog, learning to survive a life in which her basic needs were not met.

Cumin was unable to walk on one side of me, unlike most grown dogs. Most dogs are easily corrected if the walker prefers them to be on the left or right side of the pathway. Cumin would move back and forth in front of me quickly, full of anxiety, imitating a windshield wiper's sweeping range of movement. I used the Easy Walk harness, which decreased being pulled forward and allowed me to temporarily correct the multidirectional walking, if only for a few seconds.

Cumin's adoptive family communicated well with me, keeping me in the loop about her progress and their areas of concern. Cumin's adoptive family told me Cumin was generally comfortable with children and that they would walk her to their son's school in the morning. The family left informed notes for me, and we intermittently spoke on the phone the first couple months of my contracted dog visits. This communication helped to keep everyone on the same track. Every couple weeks of dog walks, I saw improvement in Cumin's ability to calm down and receive nurturing from me and also returning some companion-ship. Cumin grew more relaxed and began to sit next to me on a stone wall when we stopped for a breather, instead of sitting three to five feet away from me as she had previously!

In a seated position, Cumin had the opportunity to look at her neigh-borhood and become familiar with roads, homes, trees and shrubbery, people, and smells. Cumin began enjoying when I scratched her jowls and rubbed her back, without cowering in fear as my arm and hand approached her body. Cumin also started to let me know some of her preferences by insisting on transitioning away from some activities to new activities.

For example, Cumin enjoyed jumping on top of a retaining wall and taking sunbaths. The sunbaths looked very soothing for Cumin. I could see her eyes and body relax more in the heat of the sun, and Cumin would refuse at times to move on in our walk until she had experienced enough sunshine. I was proud of her ability to soothe and nurture herself and to set limits with me about what she needed for self-nurtur-ing. Cumin's loving adoptive family was helping her trust her growing capacity to self-sooth. Cumin began jumping up on me to lick my face and wag her tail during our walks.

Cumin began to slow her head movements and spend time smelling and looking at her surroundings without my prompting her by pausing. She decreased her barking at adults pushing baby carriages, noisy trucks driving down the street, and cars driving by. Cumin began to look curiously at neighbors without physically freezing up in tension or barking. Cumin even allowed her neighbor across the street, a World War II veteran with a calm, syrupy voice, to pet and scratch her.

Cumin absorbed her neighborhood in a positive way her first three months in her new home. The adoptive family's routine helped Cumin learn to begin trusting again, and they offered her care of her basic needs, relaxation, and pleasure. My walks and bonding with Cumin were a small but significant part of her higher quality of life.

I walked Cumin for a couple of months, satisfying an initial goal agreed upon by Cumin's parents and my company's director. Cumin's bonding with her family, neighborhood, and me meant she was ready for the dog behavior modification playgroup! I was scheduled to drive Cumin to playgroup, providing her continuity through familiarity.

I remember Cumin's first day in my car for playgroup. "Do you know where we're going Cumin? You are going to meet lots of buddies and friends to play with," I said. I guided her into the front seat of my car, where she rode with me until she was ready to be with other medium-sized and large dogs in the backseat months later.

The playgroup director requested I arrive after the other transport vehicles, so all the other dogs had already moved through the transition pen into the main fenced area. I left Cumin in my vehicle to walk my other dogs into the playgroup yard, and then brought Cumin in last to the transition pen where my boss sat in a chair. My boss talked with Cumin, petting her, scratching her, saying sweet words, and hugging her. A few minutes elapsed and the director asked me to let in a small dog, which immediately approached Cumin's face. Cumin backed off and the dog went to smell Cumin's rear area. Cumin quickly moved away from the dog again. Cumin would make it clear over and over to many dogs for years that she didn't want dogs smelling her rear. A second dog and a third dog were allowed into the transition pen. Cumin was excited and interested but also ill at ease.

After about twenty minutes, the director leashed Cumin, walking her into the main fenced area with the rest of the dogs. Cumin's leash was removed, and dogs came up to her, sniffing her and licking her. Her shyness was palpable and visual as she quickly moved away. Cumin would communicate this discomfort to many dogs through her first couple years at dog playgroup, although she eventually became amenable to close eye-to-eye contact and brief nose-to-nose proximity.

Cumin's anxiety decreased over time and she became excited about entering the main fenced area with her dog friends, spending more time with other dogs in closer proximity to them. Cumin looked excitedly forward and to the side toward other dogs more frequently, inside the fenced areas and also as I walked her to and from my car. Cumin's frequency of initiating contact with dogs increased and she separated herself less from other dogs.

Cumin became less introverted in transport with other dogs. She would look up from her front seat location and meet the gaze of dogs in the rear seat, especially Sporter, a wonderfully social and playful Labrador who placed his paws upon the dividing fence between the front and rear seats. Sporter would look down at Cumin with eyes of curious honey sweetness, and Cumin would return the gaze sweetly.

A Technique to Accelerate Cumin's Healing and Social Skill Development

I began knocking on the front passenger window as I brought another playgroup dog to the car for transport. This technique helped Cumin, who sat up front with me, transition from generally lying down in her chosen self-soothing posture to looking out the window. I did this to include Cumin in the visual and geographic social system of transport.

"Look, Cumin, here's Sporter! Here's Mookie! This is Surething's house." Cumin would look puzzled at times, but I believe it was helpful for her and the other dogs. Some dogs may remember where certain dogs live, deepening their social bonding in transport to playgroup.

Cumin began showing an increased interest on her initiation for backseat dogs. Cumin started to make eye contact with other dogs without my tapping on the window as I walked them to my car. Occasionally Cumin would sit up and look into the rear seat to make eye contact, and she would return eye contact more vividly when a dog in the rear seat looked over into the front seating area. Dogs were modeling relaxed behavior for Cumin!

High-anxiety dogs like Cumin are challenged by transitions. Cumin would act like a torpedo, exiting and entering transport vehicles quickly, showing panic on her face. Occasionally I would bring the other dogs to the rear seating area first, before Cumin, for safety reasons. Dogs jump into the rear seat one at a time, and Cumin sometimes jumped in unsafely when another dog was also jumping, risking injury.

After six months of dog playgroup, I saw Cumin experience more relaxation, leaving my vehicle with two or three other dogs on leash and entering my car with less rushed anxiety. Dogs eventually learn to walk socially in a small pack to and from the playgroup area at drop off and pick up. Cumin was developing a tendency to stay close to the other leashed dogs with little pulling forward or to the side. After keeping Cumin separate from other dogs in transport for months, I began placing a small relaxed dog on the floor in front of the seat Cumin sat on. Cumin was fairly comfortable with this except when the dog tried to share the seat with her. She became more relaxed with sharing the seat, and eventually I introduced two small dogs to the floor of the car, Shana and Fredrick. These lovely dachshunds were highly socialized and licked Cumin on the face and helped her become more open to normal dog relations.

Many times Cumin fell asleep in the front seat, resting her head on the arm rest between the two front seats. I have never seen Cumin so relaxed with me as when riding in my car after playgroup except when sunbathing on walks. I began placing Cumin in the rear seat with other medium-sized to large socialized dogs, and she adjusted well to this new arrangement. The dogs were all very kind and gentle to her, nuzzling and occasionally licking her face.

One of Cumin's favorite things to do at dog playgroup was to catch bugs with her mouth. This looks absolutely hilarious, and her technique is really fun to watch. Standing still or sitting quietly, she uses little body movement, waiting for a bug to be close to her mouth and then we hear her jaws make their sound. When Cumin gets the bug on the first bite, she remains still. If not, she turns her head if necessary and pursues the bug. Cumin has a neat look of determination on her face when bug eating.

Obviously I have great respect for Cumin's adoptive family. Cumin's story shows the wonderful synergy of Cumin's pet family, who do most of the caring for her, combined with the dog walks and dog playgroup. What a success! And success is what a pet professional's commitment to customer service is about.

The following is part of a note I left her family after a walk one day.

Dear Family,
I am so impressed seeing Cumin becoming happier and more re-laxed. Cumin enjoys being walked, smelling and seeing her new neighborhood. She is lucky to have you as her family! Cumin is feeling loved and safe with you. What a wonderful home you have provided for her. Thank you so much!
Bob

AGING AND DYING

Case Vignette: Lightning's Navigational Adaption to Blindness

Rosie greets me at the front door like a bowl of very happy gelatin doing the twist, wagging her whole white pug body in opposite directions, waiting to be picked up to lick my face and hands. Rosie loves to sit on laps like a cat and go to sleep snoring away through her septum. Lightning, a senior bulldog-pug mix, is like a vacuum cleaner, sucking up treats off the floor after being rewarded for her bathroom trip to the side yard. Lightning enjoys sunbathing and being in the shade during summer sun. Jean Claude, a black Persian cat with lime green eyes, is the Archie Bunker possessing the living room chair. I have pet sat for these three many times and find them inspiring and fun.

Lightning's Special Needs Support During Pet Sitting

Lightning has been sightless most of her life, and her hearing is diminishing. She has adapted to blindness by using her own navigational system, slowly moving about the house and outside in the fenced yard. Lightning uses her nose, snout, and jowls, touching and rubbing against wall baseboards and doorways, to walk carefully from the kitchen, to the living room, and down the hallway to the master bedroom, exiting with Rosie to the backyard. Sometimes Lightning makes a mistake and walks directly into a chair leg or doorway, hitting her thick, hard, brownish-black skull. Lightning's head and jowls sound like fine sandpaper rubbing along the wallpapered halls. I also tap my foot on the floor as I walk ahead of Lightning to use sound and vibrations to guide her in reaching a destination and finding floor treats.

Occasionally I use a leash in the home, when Lightning navigates from the sofa to the kitchen and down the long hallway to the backyard. I use the leash intermittently indoors to keep her from walking straight into a wall or piece of furniture and to turn her in the correct direction if necessary. Otherwise I keep the leash very loose, respecting Lightning's independence as she navigates herself. She knows what she is doing with her blindness and navigational abilities, and I never want to hinder or disrespect her abilities. I would rather she use it and not lose it. Before I leave their home after breakfast and lunch, I lead Lightning to her water bowl to hydrate herself if she needs to. After Lightning is finished drinking, I lead her to the sofa, where she jumps up and lies down. Lightning loves to relax and sleep on the thick, soft, black sofa. Sometimes when I return hours later, she will be in the same place I left her. I scratch Lightning's muzzle and jowls, which delights her, and she holds her head up off the couch as I scratch her, with a look of pleasure on her face. Lightning looks so relaxed on the soft sofa I think about how astronauts must feel in zero-gravity chambers training for space travel.

Over thirteen years old, Jean Claude is a very cool cat, acting like he purchased the easy chair in the living room, paid for it with his own money, loaded it into a cat mobile to drive it home, and carried it into the living room. Rosie, Lightning, and I never sit in that chair because it is clearly Jean Claude's domain. Jean Claude has that look of authority in his eyes.

I wake up at night sometimes and walk through the living room. Certain nights all three animals are awake, holding court. Jean Claude sits in his golden yellow chair facing Lightning and Rosie, who are stretched out on couches with their heads up. I sense they have their animal conversations and communication going on. I sense a tangible excitement among them, a closeness of animal family, and a social energy. I actually feel like I don't belong, so I don't intrude by staying there.

Would they be communicating about me? If I were in their furs and a pet sitter replaced my real owners for a few days, I'd be talking with my fellow fur family members about that. Here is an imaginary conversation among Rosie, Lightning, and Jean Claude.

"This pet sitter snores louder than our two owners and there is only one of him," Rosie said.

"I wish he would put a cork in it, but this is a dry house. I can't stand his singing either. He's no Lassie or Rin Tin Tin, I'll tell you that," Jean Claude said.

"Yeah, smells like garlic and beans too," Lightning said. "He doesn't give us as many treats as our owners. How do we get rid of him?" Jean Claude asked.

"Actually he gives Rosie and me plenty of treats when we come in from outside after our bathroom trip," Lightning informed him.

"Yeah I know. I hear you two dogs bark for your kibble after the sliding door closes off the family room in the backyard. I don't get anything from this dude except my daily boring dry kibble. How about a fresh mackerel, or at least a smelt?" Jean Claude said.

"Jean Claude, you know our owners switched you to kibble to help your digestion, and it's better for you. You have fewer tummy aches, don't you?" Rosy asked.

"Less cat gas too, right, Jean Claude?" Lightning asked.

"Yeah, yeah, that's easy for you kibble hounds to say!" Jean Claude said.

"Doesn't he know it's okay to spoil us a little, like our owners do? Don't these pet sitters go to school and get educated about us critters?" Jean Claude asked.

Lightning loves the outdoors in the backyard and takes sunbaths of three to seven minutes on hot summer days. She regulates the amount of time she can tolerate the sun on a hot July day the same way a child or an adult does by moving out of the sun into the shade when she has had enough direct heat. I've seen Lightning roll on to her back and wriggle on the grass before completing a sunbath, the way she did as a puppy many years ago. Lightning stands up after the wriggling and lopes over to a shaded area for a shade bath. Her tongue hangs out of her mouth as she sits there breathing and smelling.

Lightning appears to be thoroughly enjoying herself, not letting her blindness get in the way of relishing a dog's life. I recently scratched Lightning's jowls outside for the first time after she moved from the sunbath to her shade bath. I swear she put a big smile on her face the way she does on the living room couch.

The devoted owners of Lightning and Rosie reward them with a treat after their backyard bathroom stops. The dogs begin barking immediately for their treats before I can reach into the treat bin. I place Lightning's kibble treat on the floor in front of her and tap the floor loudly so she can find her treats through smell and through hearing and feeling the sound vibrations of my tapping foot. I also keep the treat opportunist Rosie away from Lightning's treats.

When I first met the pet owners during my initial consult, they told me the only source of conflict in the home was Rosie and Lightning fighting over the same toy. "Please don't play with both dogs at the same time with toys. If the dogs feel they are in competition with each other for a toy, they fight," the owners informed me. "What we do is place one dog alone in a room for a few minutes, close the door, and play with the other dog using a toy."

Wow, that was so true! Soon after the pet sitting began, I was going about my business washing dishes in the kitchen, when an intense amount of loud barking and growling erupted between Rosie and Lightning in the living room. Feeling fearful, I trotted into the living room. A toy was on the floor between them and they were lunging and nipping at each other aggressively. I was afraid to get near the dogs with my legs or hands, so after they didn't respond to my asking them to stop, I decided to take a chair and place it between them. They both continued growling, lunging, and fighting.

I started to move the chair back and forth, and this forced them to stop lunging at each other. I kicked the toy away, picked it up, and placed it out of sight while the growling and fighting continued. The dogs were still fighting, so I moved the chair legs between them again, and this pushed their bodies farther apart. I saw no bloodshed. Lightning and Rosie separated and there was peace once again in the home. I hadn't been using this toy during pet sitting—it had been left on the floor. Over many days of pet sitting throughout the years, I never saw them fight again.

CASE VIGNETTE: LAYLA'S LAST FEW MONTHS

Pet professionals help pet families function better through major life transitions. Life transitions include kittens, puppies, adult pet adoption, dogs recovering from surgery, aging dogs, separation, divorce, pet human family illness, substance abuse, and under- or unemployment, among others. Pet owners appreciate pet care professionals visiting their homes, especially during difficult times. Customer gratitude escalates exponentially when a beloved family pet is in its last months—like Layla, whom I took care of in the last stages of her seventeen-year life. I visited Layla on average four times weekly.

"We couldn't have gone to work every day without your help. We knew Layla was in safe hands," her parents told me after Layla passed away. "We couldn't have extended her life without the pet care company. We couldn't have done it ourselves."

These are very moving and poignant statements from experienced and loving pet family owners. Can you imagine having to put down a beloved family pet prematurely because of your work schedule, an illness in the family, or a move from one home to another? Pet owners wish for their pets a full life, with the least possible loss in quality of life as their pets age and approach and enter their last stage.

Layla was a gray miniature poodle who loved the harbor's salt water alongside a seafood restaurant in Marblehead, Massachusetts. "Look, Mom, the dog's swimming. That man has a leash on her," a child said sitting above the swimming area on a restaurant's outside deck.

"Is that your dog? She's cute," a child said.

"No, I'm a pet care person taking her for walks," I said.

"Can we feed her a French fry?"

"Layla doesn't eat French Fries," I said.

"Tommy, come sit down and eat," a woman urged the inquisitive boy.

Layla was in her last year of life when I took her swimming on warm walk days. She paused at the water line where dry beach transitioned to wet tide waters, lifted her snout, and took a few breaths. Then she walked straight into the water up to her hips, turned around, and headed back to shore. Layla had coal black eyes and deep gray-black hair. The water dripped off her like silver mercury, turning her hair to glistening gray in the midday sun. As droplets dripped through her curling poodle coat, she looked like she was having a bad hair day. Layla would be dry within twenty minutes, except for her "undercarriage," which I would towel-dry back at home, where the air conditioner was on for her midsummer comfort.

Layla was an unenthusiastic walker some days, displaying a stubbornness I grew fond of and expected. Her stubbornness affording us time to pause intermittently, and then off Layla went churning her legs with senior dog power. I'm sure all the exercise her owners and the pet care company guided her in contributed to her longevity of seventeen years of life. Like people, dogs enjoy their routines. Senior dogs can be adverse to new adventures. They pick and choose what they want to engage in. Layla would often lead me on her routine left and right turns up and down streets bordering Marblehead harbor. Layla enjoyed smelling ivy, flowering plants, and shrubbery in the spring and summer.

The snow-white Bichons down the street would begin their watch-dog barking during my daily walks with Layla. We would move to the side of the road when the vehicles of carpenters, electricians, plumbers, masons, landscapers, the postal workers, delivery drivers, oil deliveries, and others slowly navigated Marblehead's narrow streets, which were formerly horse paths. Old colonial towns really keep dog walkers, pedestrians, and vehicle drivers on their toes, sharing narrow commercial and residential roadways with dogs on leashes and watching for car and truck doors opening. One beautiful old colonial is built so close to the old horse path road that occasionally large trucks brush the top of the roof when driving by.

The last three months of Layla's life, she lost strength and coordination, before gaining some back and then becoming weaker again for the last time. Layla always enjoyed her food and water, especially in those last months. In the last stage, I would occasionally need to lift her up and hold her in front of her water and food bowls. Layla and her parents made me feel honored that I was entrusted to help her perform functions she had mastered in her seventeen years.

Layla would rifle her snout, jaws opened aggressively, into the fresh smelling home-cooked red meat and food paste prepared by her owners. Layla would initially reject the kibble on her plate and finish the home-cooked meat first, honoring her parents' home cooking.

My heart was always touched by Layla's gentleness during eating. She had difficulty keeping too many pieces of meat in her mouth, and a piece would sometimes fall out. I would pick the fallen meat piece up off the plate and feed it to her by hand. Layla would carefully open her mouth and deftly take the small pieces from my fingers without ever accidentally biting me. Then she would return to her chewing. What a dear. How humanizing for me as a pet caretaker for an aging dog. Layla's poise deepened my adoration for her and my respect for her parents.

Pet professionals caring for a senior dog have to be alert to changes, such as a lack of water intake or a fever or shaking in the body, and report these behaviors and symptoms to the pet owner. Layla's owners asked me to call them at work and leave a message each day. I really liked making the calls because excellent pet care and customer service are my goals as a pet care professional. I also left notes after each visit regarding water Layla drank, the food she ate, her bathroom behavior, and so on. These notes were essential communication to inform Layla's owners about her daily condition and quality of life.

Layla needed a diaper for a short period of time. Her parents had talked with me about this. I assured them it was simply another reasonable challenge to respond to professionally.

In a previous career in the holistic health field, I had worked with a wide range of people, including patients living with cancer. I used my hands and yoga science stretching techniques to help them develop better posture and deeper breathing, to walk greater distances, and to feel less pain. Until I started working with people living with cancer, I had not seriously considered certain aspects of my own needs that cannot be taken care of when caring for other people. Layla's lifestages brought back some important reflections and made me examine a number of existential questions. What is my purpose in life? Am I fulfilling my responsibilities to my kids and myself? What needs to continue and what needs to change?

As dogs age and become in need of diapers, a feeling of the inevitability of aging becomes palpable between pet owners, their children, and pet professionals. This heightened sense of Layla being in her last stage of life was occurring. I felt a deeper sense of empathy and love for Layla when I saw her in a diaper. It also made me think about my own mortality. "Wow, Layla, this is your last stage of life. I don't want you to die. Someday I am going to die. I hope that isn't for a long time. I want to see my children's children and my great-grandchildren. And be a successful writer, too. I still have so many things I want to do with my life," I said one day, talking out loud to her like I often do with animals.

Pet care professionals ask for the tools they need from pet owners for pets' particular needs. I asked Layla's parents to buy me some sanitary wipes, and I bought myself some disposable gloves that fit me properly. Disposable gloves come in at least three sizes—small, medium, and large.

At walk time, I removed Layla's usually clean diaper, helped her stand up on her soft blankets, and readied her for a special harness purchased during her last three months of life. The harness slid under her belly area and latched shut on her back. There were straps I could hold above Layla's back supporting her in a standing and walking position. As I lifted the straps, the harness would support her trunk, hips, and shoulders, offering her protection from falling if she lost her balance. This ingenious harness also protected some old leg joint injuries she had had surgery for in the past.

Independence is important in an animal's life as it ages. The harness allowed Layla to have more independence and to stand outside in the fresh air and sunshine. Layla was able to continue activities she had done all her life, and the harness allowed me to exercise Layla on short walks.

At one point I realized Layla might pass away soon. The last couple days I cared for Layla, I made sure she stood in the afternoon sunshine and smelled some ivy leaves. Layla still looked beautiful in the sun, the light making her hair glow like gray embers. I'll always remember Layla smelling those ivy leaves in her yard, as the sunshine illuminated her coat. I remember saying to her, "Thank you Layla for teaching me so much about living and aging. You and your parents are wonderful."

I received a tearful phone call a few days later from Layla's father. "We had to put our little girl down this weekend. Too many things were going wrong for her at once and she couldn't handle it. It was time," he said.

"Thanks for being such loving pet owners," I said.

Layla had a great love for her owners. I recalled a visit to Layla's house one day to walk her when her owners came home unexpectedly. I saw and felt the deep bond Layla had for them as she looked at them and turned her body to face them, and the kindness and sweet words they returned to her as she wagged her tail. Sometime after Layla passed away, her owners invited me over to thank me. They told me how they met, which had involved Layla. Layla's owners lived in two separate urban apartments in the same building. Layla went out of the open door of the apartment one day and went into a different apartment door. Layla brought the tenants together in her own unique, charismatic style. Layla the Matchmaker!

I received a phone call from her owners about six months after Layla passed away. "Is it okay if we use you as a reference for an adoption agency we are trying to adopt a brother and sister poodle from?" Layla's dad asked.

"That is really exciting. I really appreciate being asked for a reference," I said. I had written references for people in the past, and a telephone interview reference was welcome.

Interspecies Mourning

Bereavement and healing from loss are very personal things. As I reflected on Layla's death and completed this chapter, I remembered that I had not been geographically close to my father or to two of my grandparents in their last stage of life, and how I regretted this after they passed on. Surprisingly, playing a small but important role in Layla's last lifestage has given me some peacefulness about missing out on my relatives' final stages. Professional pet care brings with it unexpected companionship and gifts. Layla and her parents gave me these unintentionally and I am grateful for them.

Goodbye, Layla. Hello, Dad. Hello, Grandma and Grandpa. May your souls rest in peace.

MOURNING TRANSITIONS AND STRATEGIES FOR PET FAMILY CHILDREN, ADULTS, AND SURVIVING PETS

The passing of a family pet triggers a mourning process for the pet family's adults, children, and surviving pets. Surviving pets suffer their own loss of contact with the deceased pet and changes in the socialization with the entire pet family. Surviving pets feel some of the suffering their human family is feeling, in addition to their own loss. Pet professionals also mourn the passing of a family pet they have been caring for.

During their pet's last stage of life, pet owners sometimes begin an anticipatory mourning period, preparing for the inevitable. In this last stage, pet owners suffer because the pet is suffering, experiencing declining health and chronic or acute diseases before it passes away. Pets may exhibit limping, slower movements, swollen body areas, serious digestive problems, excessive weight loss or weight gain, or other symptoms. Pet families are saddened to see pets lose some of their vitality, take medications for failing health, experience surgery when that can be tolerated, or be denied surgery because of a weakened ability to tolerate it or recover safely. Pet families know when the end is approaching for their beloved pet.

Pets' passing helps their owner fathers and mothers teach the children about mortality, a huge gift for pet families. During this transitional stage, parents can talk with their children about grandparents the grandchildren know who are aging and the changes in their own lifestyles. This sharing of interspecies facts of life makes things more understandable for children.

The loss of a pet includes the swift and sudden ending of daily routines. The rituals of caring for a pet, firmly integrated into the pet family from sun up to bedtime, seem to cruelly vanish.

Adult pet owners have muscle memories of their pets, like reaching for a leash hanging on the wall, only to remember their beloved pet has passed. Dog owners may feel conflicted about what to do with a leash, either deciding to leave it on a hook or placing it out of sight in a drawer or closet. Both decisions involve pain and suffering.

Cat owners no longer have their cats rubbing against their legs or sleeping in the hollow of their lower back on the bedspread at night. Pet owners find it painful to see water bowls or litter boxes standing unused, but may not be ready to store them. Pet owners ache in their beings seeing the empty floor spaces where their pets' supplies functioned so well for many years, nurturing their beloved companions. Litter boxes in attics or basements may stay in their same place for months after the pet passes. Family life is lonelier without our pets and isn't as rich.

Pet families have the private freedom to mourn in their own styles, traversing through memories, feelings, conversation, and rituals. Younger children usually have less experience with a family pet member dying, contrary to older children and their parents. The child–pet bond deepens as the pet's health declines and passes. The significance of an entire life, from birth to dying, becomes magnified by the loss of a beloved pet. Gratefulness and respect for the pet's place in the family's lives take on a newer reflective and emotional significance after a pet dies. Sadness reflects the *pain* of what has been lost, but gratitude reflects *appreciation* of what was lost. Gratefulness is a core religious value, and sensitive reminiscing is a strategy parents can use to help their children mourn. Pet family memories can last forever.

Children whose pet family has lost a pet may need encouragement to use multiple resources inside themselves and in their family to help in the mourning process. Talking or spending quiet time with parents, grandparents, uncles, aunts, cousins, siblings, and peers is helpful for children mourning a pet. The family knowledge base really is a great resource for kids in the pet mourning process. Engaging in artwork is helpful. Family photo albums that include photographs of the deceased pet, when the child is ready to look at these, can be a useful tool. These photo books can remind the family of good memories from marriages, vacations, and other events.

Praying at home or attending religious services helps all family members unburden some of the upset and connects people to a source of God's support and a congregation's support that can feel encouraging and healing. The Jewish people have a prayer called the Mourner's Kaddish that has parts for both the mourners and the congregation to read aloud, allowing the community to support those who are mourning the death of a person.

Sports and physical activity are always an excellent outlet for children during mourning. Soccer, baseball, basketball, football, skating, skiing, and other sports help children literally move forward in life, learning how to embrace challenge and feel joy.

Children can also be encouraged to share their emotions, write in a journal, or visit other families with pets. During seasons where animals are giving birth and visitors are allowed to see newborns, farms can buoy the spirit a great deal. Being around young lambs, rabbits, chickens, pigs, foals, calves, and other farm animals can be inspiring for children and adults.

Parents need to be sure children are eating well and meeting their sleep needs. Parents and grandparents know that more sleep can be very medicinal during a time of mourning, partly because feeling loss takes quite a bit of energy physically and psychologically. Kids should not be made to feel bad if they don't want to talk about or express feelings about the deceased pet. It can be helpful for parents to inform a younger child's teacher when a family pet has passed. The empathy and understanding a child experiences from the adults who know and care about her or him is a balm in this mourning process.

Additionally, this is a good time to continue to eat properly. Eating fewer spicy foods and ice-cold foods during a mourning process is easier on the stomach and nervous system. Hot or warm soup is always a relaxing way for the bereaved to start a meal. Having the whole family sit and enjoy soup as a first course is a good ritual during mourning.

Parents may see levels of difficulty in a grieving child that alarm them and should seek professional help if needed. Children may be experiencing multiple adversities in their lives in addition to a family pet passing. These other stressors could include puberty, a parent's separation or divorce, the illness of another family member, or school academic or social problems.

Death is an ingrained part of life, and the difficulty pet family children and adults have fully mourning loss in their lives can create hindrances throughout the lifestages if the grief is internalized when it needs to be expressed outwardly. The passing of a beloved family pet is a silver-lining opportunity for all family members to gain greater insight, understanding, and wisdom about how individuals, couples, and families react to and understand life and death.

CASE VIGNETTE: CHANTEL: A CHARISMATIC DOG-WALKING COMPANION ON A HORRIFIC DAY

The companionship of pets often provides humans with more than we offer the pets. Chantel is a Havanese of Mediterranean and perhaps Cuban heritage. She is a small dog with layers upon layers of beautiful, thick, white hair with black and silver colors mixed in. Chantel exudes a sweetness from her dark eyes and face when greeting people. Chantel has a loving nature with her family and an intelligence I find moving. I have seen how excited Chantel becomes with her pet family's children as they ask her to do a trick like "High Five" or "Sit." Chantel has great eye contact when performing tricks and exchanging affection with the children, her parents, and the grandparents.

There is a spiritual connection for me between Chantel and my late father. My father was a veterinarian for over fifty years, educated at the University of Pennsylvania and Rutgers University. One of Dad's favorite dogs was named Pumpkin. Pumpkin was a Pekingese, with a golden orange-brown coat and brown and black highlights in her face. Like

Chantel, Pumpkin's disposition was sweet as buckwheat honey. My father always told us when he had seen Pumpkin. "Pumpkin was in today at the hospital, kids. She is so sweet, such a sweet doggy." Forty-five years later, Chantel may be to me in some ways what Pumpkin was to my late father.

Chantel loves to run and jump on a leash with me during my walking visits with her. Down the street from her home is a metal utility box about knee high. I began to approach the box one day from about twenty feet away and ask Chantel, "Jump up? Chantel jump up?" I directed her to the box, but she didn't want to jump up. I tried it again and she refused.

"That's okay, Chantel," I said. Next I lifted her on top of the utility box to let her become accustomed to it. She seemed both curious and anxious, looking around the top of the utility box and down at the ground. She wasn't relaxed being at what I thought was a short distance from the ground. To Chantel, being fourteen inches off the ground may seem a lot higher than for a grown man like me. I gave her a treat then lifted her off. On the way back from her walk, about twenty minutes later, I approached the utility box again. "Chantel jump? Jump?" I ran toward the box and Chantel jumped up on top, wagging her tail and looking nervous as she surveyed the top area and her surroundings. "Good Chantel, good Chantel," I said giving her a treat and petting her.

I sat down next to her while she ate her treat and thanked her for her new brave adventure. Chantel was still looking around and toward the ground, now perhaps with more curiosity than anxiety. "Jump, Chantel, jump?" I said standing up and Chantel jumped off the utility box. She wagged her tail as I petted her. Chantel repeats this ritual with me on most of our walks. I enjoy this as much as Chantel does.

Chantel and I have other rituals that we follow on her walks. Two dogs around the corner are usually inside their homes behind large bay windows. I thought bay windows were for sunlight and plants and for homeowners to gaze out of. Now I know bay windows are for barking dogs to jump into so they can say hello to canine and feline friends out for a stroll.

"Chantel, do you want to see your friends?" I ask her as we rounded the curve on the street we needed to cross. Is Chantel wagging her tail because of my enthusiasm, or does she know the word *friends*? A large dog, possibly a Portuguese water dog or Labradoodle, jumps up into the bay windows and starts barking at us, causing the bay window to flex. Its owner has laughed when I put my finger up to my mouth, signaling for the dog to stop barking. I wave a couple times and I say to Chantel, "Want to see your other friend?"

Chantel's tail starts wagging again. We cross the street, and a large mixed breed dog begins barking at Chantel and me from his bay window. Chantel wags her tail barking back.

Short sprints have always been a source of joy and exercise for me with leashed dogs. Much to my surprise and pleasure, I found out that Chantel enjoyed sprinting on leash. One day I said to her, "Run? You want to run?" I began sprinting the length of one front yard, and Chantel came along unenthusiastically. I continued to ask her once or twice a week, "Run? Do you want to run?" Chantel's tail would begin to wag, her tongue would hang out of her mouth with enthusiasm like Michael Jordan attacking a defense, and she would take off with me, running as fast as she could for one property length, her tail wagging quickly afterward. I could see how Chantel passed with flying colors her physical with Dr. Mayer and Dr. Hoyt.

Sometimes horrible things happen to very good people, and animals help humans with their gift of companionship. Chantel provided wonderful companionship for me the morning I learned a friend of mine, along with the baby in her womb, had been murdered. I learned about this only twenty-five minutes before I was scheduled to walk Chantel. I was scanning the town newspaper when I saw a newspaper headline. I read down a few lines, and in the first paragraph was the name and photograph of my friend. I was absolutely shocked and felt woozy and sick. How could this be? When did this happen? Why didn't I know about it? I had been so involved in writing this book that I hadn't been listening to the radio or reading newspapers. Writer's isolation!

I somehow drove over to Chantel's home and unlocked the door. I walked up the stairs and through the kitchen and opened the door of the den overlooking an outdoor pool. I saw Chantel in her play corral. Chantel rolled onto her back and wagged her tail, and I proceeded to scratch her belly before lifting the pen twelve inches and letting her slink out underneath to have her leash fastened to her collar. The walk was a combination of Chantel's usual charm, our normal routine, and me feeling shocked, angry, and upset. "Focus on Chantel, focus on Chantel, Bob," I told myself. "Don't let this wonderful time be taken away by events I have no control over, except insofar as how I react to those events. I can mourn later on."

I watched my own thought process encourage me to focus on Chantel, knowing it was not possible to be totally present with Chantel. I was starting to feel a large reservoir of feelings and thoughts arise in my being after reading about my friend's double murder! I forced myself to watch Chantel in her routine, momentarily keeping my feet under me as my individual world began to spin out of control. I wrote Chantel's parents a note before I left: "Great walk today in the sunshine. P/P [Pee, Poop]. Water refilled, treat given. Thank you, Bob."

That day I had five dogs to walk, and I began the grieving process more fully after I left Chantel's home. I was in shock, angry, and sad. I was so grateful I had wonderful dogs to be with that day to take a small amount of the horror and shock off the day and to help me see the overwhelming beauty in most people, animals, and nature. I remember that was a Friday morning, and by 2:00 p.m. I was done for the day. I dropped my time sheet off at the pet company office and sat outside in my car, unable to drive. Companionship comes in all shapes and sizes and from all sources. Thank goodness for the companionship of those five dogs I walked that day.

PETS MOURNING PETS

Pets are affected by the loss of another family pet in their home. These effects can influence a pet's overall health in both body and mind. Pet owners report behavior changes in their pets after the passing of a dog or cat: "Jory hasn't been the same since Rufus died. He whines more and doesn't wag his tail as much as usual. It's been over six months now." "Charlie seems less active and sad since Dinah died. He mopes around the house and barks more than usual." "Mittens is less active now that Boots is gone. She's putting on weight." "Charlie doesn't like to play outside anymore since Tully passed on." "Mungo is more anxious than ever since Donnie passed. He wants to sleep in our bed and not his crate. He's morose when we leave the house. He is having more intense separation anxiety."

On the spiritual, physical, and psychological levels, the surviving animals need the family to maintain its love and provide basic needs of food, safety, shelter, animal socialization, and exercise, helping the animals adjust to the passing of another pet. The surviving companion animal has lost a whole set of routines it was accustomed to when it lived with its fellow cat, dog, or other family pet.

Interactive social routines and kinetic routines are lost. Animals roughhouse and lick each other, play ball and play with toys together, sleep near each other and sometimes in the same crate or dog bed. Animals eat next to each other, share water bowls, gaze into each other's eyes, greet family members together, bark and meow together, share kitty litter pans, eat food crumbs together underneath dining tables, and take walks together either outside or up and down the stairs within the house.

The four richly interactive roles pets play with each other—leader, bystander, opposer/rebel, and follower—are now lost. Consequently, a remaining pet may seek out or need more interaction with its owners. If your pet is an initiator and leader, it may make this known to you. Other times, with these leader dogs or cats, an uncharacteristic shyness may occur because of the loss. If your pet is more of a follower, its shyness or low-key style of interacting may prevent it from letting you know its increased need for attention after another family pet passes.

The dog or cat left by itself after another family pet passes may experience a vast decrease in kinetic movements. Movement helps a dog's or cat's sense of belonging to where it lives in the home and neighborhood. Two dogs walking on a double leash or next to each other on two leashes have had a daily ritual for years, with the companionship stimulating more exercise and socializing for each other. Indoor cats play with each other and enjoy many activities in the presence of the other, running up and down stairs, wrestling, or chasing a cat toy offered by the owners.

The companion animal's owners should keep their surviving pet's kinetic and social life, in the home and in the neighborhood, active to maintain everyone's health. Placing a surviving dog into a dog behavior modification playgroup or doggy daycare can be very helpful for the dog's healing and overall life.

Here is a conversation with one pet owner.

Pet Owner: "This is our first trip away since Erma's littermate Candle passed on. They were together in our home for seven years. We are concerned about her being alone without us and Candle."

Pet Professional: "I'll keep that in mind when I visit. I'll seek out Erma and be sure to comb her and pet her the way you showed me. Do you have a radio you can leave on?"

Pet Owner: "Yes, we do," Erma's parents said.

Pet Professional: "I'd suggest leaving on classical music for stimulation. I can also alternate classical music with Animal Planet on television if you'd like," I said.

Pet Owner: "That sounds like a good idea. We might want you to visit every day, but visit twice every other day," Erma's parents said.

Pet Professional: "Two visits on alternate days will be helpful for her," I said.

Pet owners should consider consulting a veterinary homeopath for understanding on approaching loss and other physical or behavioral pet concerns.

WHEN PET PROFESSIONALS GRIEVE

Pet professionals are informed by pet owners of recent pet passing in their pet family. Pet professionals may notice pet owners have beautiful photographic portraits of deceased dogs and cats, sometimes with their collar and license hanging from a frame. Grief for a family pet affects pet professionals who have bonded with cats and dogs through their activities. Pet professionals have our own wonderful memories, feelings, and grieving process to go through.

Pet professionals have given and received from the family pets we have cared for. We are their companions for a short time during the week, as they are our companions during pet visits, dog walks, pet-sitting sessions, playgroup transport, and playgroup. I become bonded with the family pets as an adult in their homes during that time. Pet sitting for one day or fourteen days accelerates bonding with these wonderful companion animals. Their personalities and character traits, the roles their breeds have played over the course of human history, their physical beauty, and their individual challenges and sicknesses all command respect and connection in professional pet care. Pets are nourished by our professional activities with them, and they move and inspire us.

Pet professionals talk, cry, and reminisce with pet owners about their loss and our loss. Pet care company owners may make a charitable gift to a local animal shelter or agency in the name of a pet formerly under the care of the business. Pet care professionals often send sympathy cards to the pet family as well. Goodwill is extended consistently by pet professionals to the pet families we serve. Life is precious, love is profound, and customer service is guided, coordinated, and improved by respect for life.

CASE VIGNETTE: MEMORIES OF A GREAT PYRENEES AND THREE DACHSHUNDS

I was blessed to pet sit a Great Pyrenees, Quartz, less than a week before old age won out. I will never forget Quartz, a graceful, sweet, massive dog with thick white beautiful hair lying down in the snow everyday and napping in the sunshine or under the gray winter sky swollen with expectant snow. There are so many things I will never forget about Quartz. She would roll over on her back like she was a giant puppy, not an aging dog. When I would let her out the door, I had to wait for her long body to pass by me before I could close the door. I would look down only to see more of her long back still in the doorway. She would bark at people who walked past the home on the road, sounding like a dog far off in thick fog. She would lay her great length down at night on a reddish oriental rug, framing her head, feet, and tail in its borders. There was the distinctive shuffling sound of her paws moving across the wooden floor, and Quartz's midnight-dark eyes staring at me calmly when I stroked her face and scratched her neck. She would drain the water from her huge bowl in no time flat. The Great Pyrenees was content and happy with her family.

Then there were three dachshunds, Fredrick, Shana, and Hildebrand, that I visited for dog walks and playgroup transport. This dachshund family spent many hours snuggled together in a dog bed about thirty inches in diameter. Most of the day these three slept together, played together, and walked together, except when the two younger ones were transported to dog playgroup. Many times I found the three dachshunds under small blankets they had pulled over their heads to create a homey dog bed nest. Exiting the bed, they looked like they were being hatched out of a dachshund egg.

I remember how the younger dogs, arriving back from playgroup, would enter the dog bed and pull the covers over the older Hildebrand and themselves routinely, just like a window shade being pulled down.

The day before Hildebrand passed away, I knew it may be the last chance I would see her. Hildebrand was twenty years old. She had developed the health symptoms of a very aged dog, and I decided to stay a little longer and spend more time outside with her before I drove Fredrick and Shana to playgroup. I found that her owner had left me a note. "Hildebrand is laboring in her breathing and is weak." I read the note left by the person who had visited early that morning from another pet company and had not taken Hildebrand outside because of her weakness. I carried her outside, feeling her body against me. Hildebrand surprisingly walked spryly about the backyard amid melting snow and stone walls.

I was surprised at her strength. Her breathing became more relaxed and less labored as she scurried about slowly but surely. I watched the footprints she left behind and the way she held her head up in the fresh air and sunshine that blew in off the harbor and toward the west. I looked at Hildebrand's footprints a second time to etch the memory into my mind, recognizing that I might never see her or her footprints again. I wanted those footprints walking across my memory, leaving firm snow tracks in my brain. The prints were clear and well formed in the fresh, shallow snow, leading up to and around a holly bush Hildebrand enjoyed smelling and peeing near. I felt sad yet inspired by her short outing as I carried her upstairs, holding her warm body with my bare hands against my rain jacket. I felt privileged to have known her, her brood of two other dachshunds, and their attentive, loving owner, who relished looking out for her three dogs' best interests.

Before I left, I said aloud a prayer for her and wished the best for her and her family. The next day when I arrived, a very beautiful note was on the counter, along with her photo, which I ignored at first, not wanting to face the inevitable. I looked under the blanket and didn't see Hildebrand. She had gone to Doggy Heaven. It was with sadness I visited the home most weekdays soon after Hildebrand's passing to transport Fredrick and Shana to dog behavior modification playgroup. After Hildebrand died, the two surviving dogs had a whole network of dog friends to enjoy the company of, three to five days a week. They certainly missed dear Hildebrand, but they didn't miss a beat of their already established social life. The playgroup helped them adjust to life as a twosome in their warm fragrant bed with the covers ready to be pulled over them.

REPLACING A BELOVED FAMILY PET

A pet family benefits from sufficient grieving before choosing a new pet. Allowing a grieving process avoids major mistakes. The main questions most people have are: When has enough mourning time passed mentally and physically for a family to choose a new pet? Are we the right pet family for a particular dog, cat, or other animal?

Mourning pet family members become ready at their own pace. Your mental and physical batteries should feel charged up in a strong, steady way. Wanting another companion animal is a sign of adult readiness. Not feeling ready for caring for a new pet is a normal stage to be respected by all adults in the home. Emotion and impulsivity are limited aspects of readiness. Some families have three generations living together under one roof. All adults and children should be heard from before initiating a pet search. If a spouse is not ready, this needs to be respected. Impulsive emotional decisions can result in new pets being rehoused after a failed ownership decision.

What are the needs of a rescue or nonrescue dog, cat, bird, or rodents? Time, money, physical space in the home and outdoors, as well as fencing, walking to respect dog breed exercise levels, feeding, cleaning up, bathroom training, veterinarian visits, grooming needs, animal behaviorists, pet company support, and the list could go on.

Completing the unfinished business of a previous pet is important. Unfinished business includes paying off outstanding veterinary bills, telling relatives or friends about your pet's passing, and cleaning up clutter or messy materials used for your last pet. Cat owners may have basement or attic areas with old litter boxes left uncleaned because of their distress.

Pet owners may be surprised at the process of choosing a new pet after they have mourned a previous pet, because they may have different needs now as an individual, couple, or family with children. Lifestyles will change as individuals become couples and as couples become families. A couple who formerly owned dogs in a home and has since moved to a smaller condo may seek cats instead of dogs, or smaller breeds of dogs.

CASE VIGNETTE: WELCOME HANSEL AND GRETEL AFTER LAYLA

I received a phone reference call from the poodle organization Layla's parents told me about. Here is a portion of that conversation:

"This is Miss Boyer from a poodle rescue and adoption agency. Is this Bob Berkelhammer?"

"Yes it is," I replied.

"We are calling about Mr. and Mrs. Alderson's adopting intent of two poodles through our organization. You are one of the people on their reference list," she explained.

"Yes, the Aldersons told me you'd be calling about their hope to adopt the poodles Hansel and Gretel," I said.

Miss Boyer told me that our conversation would be confidential. Then she asked me about my relationship with the Aldersons.

"I am friends with Mr. and Mrs. Alderson, but my primary role is I took care of Layla as a pet care professional for over a year."

"How was the Alderson's dog taken care in your opinion?" she asked.

"Layla was very well taken care of. For example, they cooked her a lot of homemade food—chicken and meat which she liked a lot," I said.

"Are you aware of any veterinary visits?" she asked.

"Yes. The owners were very proactive in bringing Layla to Dr. Rockwell. They updated me about her visits, which increased in frequency her last year. They asked me to update them daily by phone about Layla by calling them at work. They were excellent communicators. The Aldersons created a comfortable resting and sleeping for Layla," I said.

"Was she clean and groomed?"

"Layla was groomed professionally quite often. She looked quite beautiful."

"Thank you very much," Miss Boyer said.

"What happens now?" I asked.

"We are gathering information and may take steps leading toward adoption," she replied.

A couple of months later, I heard that Layla's owners were granted a one-month trial with Hansel and Gretel, and after that the adoption was finalized.

Layla's owners were sitting in the small backyard of their beautiful home defined by thick slate tiles, varnished wooden benches, large shrubs and trees, and attractive low plantings of wild ginger. I opened the gate, and Hansel and Gretel started barking very loudly. Closing the gate immediately, I sat down on the ground in my yellow rainproof pants to mimic their lower height. Hansel and Gretel ran over, barking, to check me out. Hansel is a phantom poodle with gray hair with some tinges of black. Gretel is very black. Hansel and Gretel had been freshly groomed the day before, and their masculine and feminine characteristics showed strongly with expertly clipped facial hair and body shapes. They began licking my face and sitting on my lap.

"Do you like my poodle cologne? It's by Faberge. I wore it especially for both of you," I said to Hansel and Gretel as their owners laughed. We transitioned over to the benches and Hansel proceeded to sit on my lap most of the time. The couple of times I moved him off my lap, he immediately moved back. "You're in," Hansel's dad said to me. Gretel rested in her mom's arms when she wasn't on dad's lap.

"They are great lap dogs," Mom said. "The main thing is they need to feel like this is their home. When we took them to our relatives, they seemed out of sorts. They looked at us and seemed to say, 'Well, this is nice, but are we going to be left here?'"

"Continuity is the key," Hansel and Gretel's dad said.

I am thrilled to meet a new generation of this family's pets whose previous pet I had taken care of. I appreciate being trusted and I believe my decades in small business and parenting have given me a customer service acumen.

Hansel and Gretel's owners guided me with specific instructions for future visits. "When you visit for walks, I would let them out of their crate and bring them outside into the backyard right away. They may do some of their business right away and then you can put their harnesses on for their walk," Dad said.

"Okay. Do they share a crate or do they have separate crates?" I asked.

"Currently they share a crate. They enjoy sleeping next to each other. It's cute. One moment they can be wrestling and growling with each other, and the next moment they'll be fast asleep next to each other in their crate, or even on top of each other," their dad said.

The first time I arrived to walk Hansel and Gretel, they were crated in the kitchen. Hansel and Gretel barked loudly as I let them out of the crate and walked outside after collecting their harnesses and leashes. Gretel went over to the wooden fence covered with wild ginger plants, and Hansel disappeared under a bench. After relieving themselves, I harnessed them and then followed the route I had walked Layla many times near Marblehead harbor. We passed the Bichon's house who were often in the window barking and tossing themselves at the windows like gigantic windblown snowflakes.

Hansel and Gretel seemed unsure of their surroundings and a bit put off by my unfamiliar presence until the street bisected Front Street. They became compliant, following my lead, and soon were pulling strongly ahead of me while vigorously smelling and looking around. We went up to Fort Sewall with the sun warming the November air. Hansel and Gretel sniffed around a monument overlooking Marblehead harbor, which commemorates the U.S.S. *Constitution*'s historic visit to Marblehead harbor in the 1970s. The dogs chose areas under park benches to poop before returning home.

At this early point in adoption, Hansel and Gretel had a tendency to bark loudly at other dogs on walks, and both would also strain to get closer to a dog being walked across the street. What an antisocial racket! I decided to try to nip it in the bud by calming Hansel before he first saw a dog forty, sixty, or one hundred feet down the road or before he would start reacting nonverbally by stiffening at the scent of the dog. I would see the dog first and begin distracting Hansel by making shushing sounds for five to ten seconds. I wasn't projecting palpable tension that could make the situation worse. This worked much better than my being loud and tense and saying "No" or "No bark." Hansel barked less when I did this, resulting in Gretel barking less too.

I also didn't jerk Hansel's head strongly when he barked. I did pull back gently and kept the leash taut while quietly shushing him, sometimes placing my body in between his eyes and the other dog. I would occasionally also place my open palm in front of his face to distract him momentarily from seeing the other dog. Visual obstruction can't hide odors of an approaching animal, but it can work well. Hansel was learning a quieter response near strange dogs.

Hansel and Gretel became more secure in their home over the next three months and both relaxed greatly around other dogs passing by, rarely barking. The big influence in decreasing the barking and leash aggression was the time, love, security, and limit-setting provided by Hansel and Gretel's adoptive parents.

Hansel and Gretel's mom asked me to help solve a problem early on in the adoptive phase. "When I'm home working, my office is downstairs and the dogs let me know when they need to go out. But my husband works upstairs and sometimes too much time elapses, resulting in toilet accidents." She told me that the dogs needed to go out every two hours.

"How about your husband setting an alarm to go off every two hours? He could use his cell phone or an alarm clock, or perhaps a kitchen timer," I suggested.

"I never thought of that. Those are good ideas. Thank you," she said.

One day I was walking the poodles and Hansel pulled the leash strongly toward the curb. I noticed something thick in Hansel's mouth. (Don't cats and dogs often find a way to pick something up in their mouths?) Did he have a piece of broken siding or a bolt with a long shank in his mouth? Or was it a chicken neck or a turkey neck, since I was walking the poodles less than a week after Thanksgiving? It turned out to be a bone about one and a half inches wide and about three inches long. The bone took up a lot of a miniature poodle's mouth, and Hansel would not let go of it without me prying open his mouth. I did this with much difficulty, and I was afraid of getting bitten.

I thought there must be a safer more effective method for opening an unwilling dog's mouth. I asked my boss for guidelines, and she told me, "Place your hand over the dog's snout and press your fingertips into the jowls, against the dog's upper jaw teeth. Most dogs don't like the feeling of their gums pressing into their teeth. If they don't release the object, keep your hand on their snout and blow into their nose. This should work," she explained. I look forward to trying this method.

Hansel holds on to objects because of his controlling personality. Pet owners can alter this trait by giving the dog some food, taking it away, and then praising the dog when they take it away.

This clearly was a pet family in transition. These pet owners had seventeen years of experience with one dog who was quiet and not rambunctious. Now they were the proud but stressed owners of a fairy-tale duo that packed a lot of energy into their tiny bodies. There were some very difficult days early on. The old adage "Three steps forward, two steps back" is good advice for pet owners to remember in the initial adoption phases.

I have continued to walk Hansel and Gretel four times a week for fourteen months. They are much more comfortable in their skins now than when I first arrived, and they now come to the front of their pen wagging their tails. Hansel and Gretel are excited to go on walks and comforted by returning to their new home, which may feel old to them now.

CASE VIGNETTE: CELEBRATING AND MOURNING MISSY—FROM ONE CAT TO TWO

Missy was a gem of a cat who loved people and grooming. I had the privilege to visit Missy many times while her wonderful owner traveled for work. Missy adored socializing with her owner when he was home from his trips that took him to destinations outside his home state for two, three, and sometimes seven days at a time. Missy bonded with him by crawling all over him, making it harder for him to accomplish work at home. Sound familiar, cat owners?

Missy had a black-and-white coat and had an alert look in her eyes. She enjoyed sleeping on a high shelf in the master bedroom closet, which her owner had cleared and layered with soft bedding for her sleeping comfort. It was adorable seeing Missy sleeping on the closet shelf and lifting her head like a periscope when she woke up. She would utter a forlorn begging meow, hop down from the shelf, and ready herself for wet food and grooming.

Certain cats don't enjoy grooming, but Missy relished it. Her owner provided three brushes in his home. I chose the green-and-white rubber brush because its bristles were soft, yet firm enough to reach into Missy's thickest and deepest hairs. After Missy ate, I would pick up the brush and motion for Missy to jump on the bed for grooming, unless I picked her up and carried her over myself. Her purring would start after a few brush strokes from her head down to her tail area. The grooming often totaled ten minutes of my thirty-minute visits. She would relax and let me groom her, and if she left after a while, I would follow her and start brushing her again. The grooming helped Missy feel much more at peace when her owner was traveling; she felt cared for and less lonely.

On some visits, Missy was sleeping on her closet shelf or deeply engrossed in watching a bird from her windows. After entering the front door, I would hear her meow on the stairway leading to the second floor. "I'll be right there," I often said, opening a can of fresh food to bring upstairs to her wet food bowl in the hallway outside the bedrooms and bathroom.

After Missy died, her owner wondered whether his next cat would be like Missy—social and wanting attention or more reserved and independent? He visited an animal shelter and met two cats that were littermates. One appeared shy, the other more outgoing. Missy's owner chose both, because he cared about shelter animals, owned the resources necessary for two cats, and felt a connection to both when he met them. Lucky for them!

I met Seattle and Dart a few days after the littermates arrived in their new home where Missy had lived. Seattle and Dart were night owls. Their owner told me he had awakened a number of times and heard the cats playing with toys and running around. They also slept late into the morning. Seattle was very tired when I visited, and he stayed in his bed behind the couch. Dart was willing to come toward me, rub against my leg, and lie down on the floor to be scratched and played and then dart (like his name) into another room.

Seattle and Dart continued their night-owl behaviors, as reported by their owner. On my subsequent visits within the first six weeks of their adoption, Seattle was quiet, resting, or sleeping in the top of the cat tree. But Dart approached me as soon as I entered the home, his head up at the front door, making eye contact and looking for playtime. Dart was happily amused by many small cat balls his owner had bought for their adoption. I would kick the balls and Dart would chase them. He is a great runner of stairs, and when I threw the balls down or up the stairs, Dart would move quickly and with precision, his front legs smacking ferociously at the balls like a tiger tearing at meat. I bet Dart liked digging his nails into the thickly carpeted stairs as he tore after the bounding balls.

I enjoyed going back and forth giving attention to both Seattle and Dart when I finished providing fresh water, food, and litter. Seattle, though very shy, let me stroke and comb him a little bit and started purring.

It is always rewarding for me to meet a new pet after the owner has gone through the stages of caring for a pet many years, seen the animal pass away, and, when ready, brought another pet into their home.

7

DOG WALKING AND HANDLING TIPS

HARNESSES: SAFETY AND POWER STEERING

Harnesses are one of the best inventions for the health and safety of a dog, children, and pet owners. Harnesses simplify the pet owner's responsibilities when attached by the leash in front of the dog's chest (not on top of its back). They decrease the owner's feeling of being overwhelmed both physically and psychologically, while lessening worry. Unharnessed dogs pulling hard on a leash create excessive strain on the walkers' arms, wrists, hands, shoulders, and back. Unharnessed dogs can cause the owner to fall on wintry surfaces where there is poor traction. The use of a harness allows better footing on surfaces covered by rain, snow, and ice as well as on uneven topography like gravel, larger stones, rocks, tree roots, and soil.

Walking a dog by a leash attached to just a collar can be harmful to a dog, causing excessive strain and negatively affecting the dog's trachea region, cervical muscles, tendons, and ligaments. Dogs with trachea irritation may begin coughing or hacking from the trachea strain. Additionally, dogs can develop pains in their neck, chest, and shoulders from the effects of leash strain.

Collars can also sometimes slip off of a dog's head. During dog playgroup, unharnessed transport dogs may slip their old collars in their excitement to exit the vehicles. In my transport group, I have two dogs without harnesses who slip their collars once every three or four months.

A person walking a harnessed dog has both power steering and power brakes. A walker has much greater directional control to the left and the right, and the ability to make quicker subtle and sharp turns. The dog walker who is trying to take a left turn down a street while the dog pulls to the right or straight ahead can override the dog's direction.

The harness gives children more safety and control when walking a dog. Elderly people and some disabled folks may also find it easier to walk dogs using a harness because less strength and weight is needed by the walker. In this way, the harness can provide more independence and joy for a wide range of people.

Unfortunately, many harness owners mistakenly attach the leash to hardware on their dogs back, which totally diminishes the walker's control of pace and direction, except with small light dogs. I see this back leash attachment causing a lot of strain for the dog owner. The owner's posture is discombobulated, and the dog is out of control, walking the adult or child instead of the adult or child walking the dog.

The security that a harness provides also provides options for the pet family members. Two people from a pet family can walk arm in arm or hand in hand while walking the pet, which bonds them to each other and to their dog. This is great for those who are unable to walk a dog by themselves or who wish to spend some relaxed time with a loved one at sunset or sunrise. The technology of a good harness certainly supports this bonding, but a leash does not. I have seen many situations in which an unharnessed dog goes out of control, forcing a parent to let go of a child's hand or preventing two adults from walking arm in arm.

Remember to remove the harness after a walk; otherwise, if left on, it's likely to be chewed on. Dogs can also shift the harnesses on their bodies after walks, causing the harness to lodge in their jaws, resulting in serious breathing and jaw injuries, or interfering with their hip and leg movements and resulting in serious and very expensive leg joint injuries.

BUYING AND MAINTAINING EQUIPMENT

There are many types of brand-name harnesses for dogs. My favorite brands are SENSE-ible and SENSE-ation, made by Softouch Concepts, and Easy Walk. The SENSE-ible harness is the easiest to fit to your dog, yet it has all the strength and security necessary. Consider buying collars with steel hardware, which cannot be damaged when dogs play bite. Buy collars of thick, wide, hard cloth or very sturdy material, appropriate for the size of your dog.

Some "designer" leashes and harnesses, which come in exotic materials and colors, may be manufactured with weaker materials and are structurally inferior. Fancy designs are not a substitute for the safety and structural integrity of leashes and harnesses. To be an informed consumer, compare the thickness and hardware of designer products with that of nondesigner products.

Maintaining your harnesses, leashes, and collars is essential so that they don't break while you're out walking or jogging with your dog. Hang leashes and harnesses out of a dog's jumping reach and the reach of young children tall enough to stand. Pet owners don't want their kids wrapping leashes around their own necks or limbs, a sibling's neck or limbs, or using them to tie up cats or dogs. A dog's chewing on leashes and harnesses can cause rips or breaks in the fabric and plastic hardware.

GETTING OUT THE DOOR

Leaving the house with your dog can be a tricky proposition. You have to hold the dog safely so it won't run away while you are busy closing doors, sometimes both a main door and storm door, locking the door with a key, and so forth. In high winds, storm doors may blow open or closed.

Some dogs will pull strongly when you leave a residence with them. They are very excited to go outside to relieve themselves and to get exercise in their neighborhood, or they know they are going to dog playgroup and can't wait to see their friends in the transport vehicle. The dog may be so excited that it can barely stand or sit still long enough for its harness and leash to be placed on and secured. Once leashed and harnessed, the dog runs to the door and starts to pull very strongly as the door opens. In this situation, a medium or large dog presents safety concerns for the person and the dog. Even small dogs can present hazards to owners who have some weakness in their limbs or back. A dog that pulls too much can become tangled on the storm door or pull the leash right off your hand.

I've found a way to slow the dog to a halt for ten to twenty seconds while I attend to the front door key, lock, and storm door. I take the leash loop opening and place it around the inside handle of the storm door, keeping my hand on the leash below the opening so it can't come off the door handle. The storm door, not my hand and arm, is resisting the pulling dog. This routine can help a dog become more compliant when leaving the house. Another strategy is to place the leash loop over the handle and wrap the leash around the inside storm door handle a couple of turns. This way, the leash is secure enough that I can take both hands off the leash for a few seconds.

This strategy helps tremendously when you encounter door locks that need oil, making them difficult to turn, or doors that have swelled from weather changes and must be pulled sharply shut while you turn the key.

EXTENSION LEASHES: FOR DOG OWNERS WITH DISABILITIES

One March day I drove down a main road that separates Swampscott from Marblehead bordered by a golf course. Suddenly, a dog appeared from the sidewalk alongside the golf course. The dog crossed off the sidewalk, scampered over the grassy area between the sidewalk and the curb, crossed the curb, and ran into the street in front of me. I slammed on my brakes, and my grocery bags spilled over onto the floor. The adult walking the dog took her cell phone away from their ear and pulled the dog's extension leash back toward her with her free hand. Finally, she put the cell phone in her pocket. She fumbled with the extension apparatus and shortened the leash, pulling the dog toward the shoulder of the road and the curb, and locked it.

This is an example of the improper use of extension leashes by a dog walker totally disassociated from the dog's and automobile safety needs. I walk dogs on sidewalks with the extension leash locked to prohibit the dog from wandering or running into unsafe areas of a street or parking lot. I am also ready in an instant to push the mechanism that locks or unlocks the leash. On a walk, shorten the extension leash and lock the mechanism when:

- A pedestrian or cyclist is approaching on a path or road shoulder.
- Children approach your dog. That way, you have time to see if they approach wisely: hands out, palm up below the dog's head height, allowing the dog to smell their hands.
- You walk a dog through a parking lot or crossing a street.
- You are approaching a train or subway tracks.
- You walk in busy commercial areas, so your leash and dog are next to you and not impeding other pedestrians or the exits of stores.

Extension leashes are not for distracted adults, nor are they for children who don't practice proper safety in areas where cars must be avoided. When using your cell phone, lock the leash.

I often see teenagers, younger children, and adults walking dogs on extended leashes while texting. Parents should consider not allowing their children to use extension leashes when walking a dog. Younger children are better off using extension leashes in yards, in parks away from people, in cleared forest areas, and in areas devoid of cars than on a sidewalk. Teach age-appropriate children how to use the mechanisms on the extension leash that lock and unlock the leash. Ask your children to demonstrate walking the family dog with a cell phone in their pocket, and locking the mechanism on the leash when answering the phone.

Extension leashes are a great invention for people with certain physical limitations due to age or weakness. Walking your dog with an extension leash allows you and your dog more exercise while respecting human limitations. The extension leash allows your dog more distance off the sidewalk or path to explore lawns, wooded areas, hilly terrain, or steep areas that you may not be able to walk on.

Snow- and ice-covered areas on either side of a walkable path are another place for a dog to roam while their owner stands or walks on the path. Extension leashes allow a dog to run in a circle, semicircle, or other kinetic pattern while the owner simply holds the leash apparatus, rotating his or her body as needed.

An adult in a motorized scooter can use an extension leash when parked to let the dog explore. Extension leashes allow for the whole world of aromas to be explored with greater access than a short leash. I have also seen seniors with extension leashes letting their dogs swim in the water.

HOW TO HOLD A LEASH WHEN WALKING

A leash is a loop leading down to hardware that connects to a harness or a collar. A leash is also a social and technological tool for safety, discipline, exercise, and affection for the dogs you walk. Leashes can make the difference between life and death of a dog, preventing car crashes and avoiding runaway and lost pets. Leashes show that pet owners respect other dogs, people, and private and public property. When you add the positive reinforcement of words and treats, leashes help your dog learn what is safe and expected in the yard and around your neighborhood. What an amazing, simple invention, with such far-reaching family, social, and health effects!

The dog walker needs security and control to avoid rare circumstances when the walker falls and the leash comes off his or her hand or when an off-leash dog or leashed dog that is not controlled lunges toward you and your dog. Using more of the leash other than the loop will empower your fingers and hand. Try these steps:

1. Place your hand in the loop.
2. Where the loop ends and leash line begins, bend your second and third fingers completely, with the leash line between the fingers.
3. Form a relaxed fist, with the four fingers flexed and your thumb either closed over the others or out to the side.

This grip gives the dog walker an almost vise-like grip that gets tighter the more a dog pulls. The grip has helped me in many situations, when a dog has lunged toward a squirrel, a car, or another dog, or I have started to lose my balance on ice or snow. My hand didn't come off the leash, even if I did fall.

If the leash loop is too large or if you want even more control over the leash, wrap the leash around your hand once or twice and then make a relaxed fist with the second and third fingers.

Leash chafing and leash burns can occur when you are walking dogs in cold weather, particularly large, stronger dogs and puppies who are not yet leash obedient. I have had to apply Calendula lotion for as many as four days after receiving cold-weather leash burns. Warm, thin gloves made of fleece or a similar material are useful for protecting your hands in these conditions. Older folks or people with pain and weakness in the fingers, hands, arms, or shoulders can gain some support from wearing thin gloves year round. Gloves can reduce some pressure from the leash on sensitive swollen skin and muscle-skeletal areas, and owners can continue bonding with their dogs and receiving their own cardiovascular exercise benefits.

POSTURE FOR WALKING OR CARRYING PETS

I am currently developing an educational video called *Healthy Posture for Blue Collar Workers, Parenting, and Most Occupations*. I have borrowed from this future videotape for this chapter.

My dog playgroup colleagues are often surprised that I can safely walk four big dogs from my parked car to the playgroup area and vice versa. I do this by integrating a yoga science posture that protects my muscles, tendons, ligaments, vertebral discs, and bones from injury when dogs pull with great force. Posture health is available for all people through beginning yoga science classes for children, adults, and seniors.

Sporter, a Labrador retriever, lunging after Monarch butterflies, exerts force through the leash into the dog walker's body. Good body posture helps the dog walker to walk and guide the animal safely as he or she reacts to the animal's movement changes. Safer positioning of the feet, knees, hips, back, shoulders, chest, and head protects these body parts from sprains, strains, disc problems, and falls. Better posture decreases the negative force on certain anatomical areas when other underused muscles and joints assume more of their rightful share of movement stresses. Flexibility in the musculoskeletal body can act as a shock absorber, protecting people from fractures and bone breakage after fall. Cat owners can also benefit from posture improvements when scooping litter, picking up their cats, carrying them on their shoulder or in front of their upper body, and placing them down on the floor or furniture.

Many pet owners and pet professionals would benefit from decreasing the wear and tear on their skeletal and soft tissue areas. Musculoskeletal problems can build up over time, leading to tendonitis, bursitis, hip replacements, knee replacements, and a general weaknesses and loss of vitality that make caring for animals very difficult. Your companion animals need you to be healthy, so they can receive love from you as long as possible, and vice versa.

You can protect yourself from some pain, weakness, and injuries by learning the postural cues below. Go slowly. Choose one of these to improve on for four to eight weeks before moving on to the others. If you work on more than one of these before you are ready, you may be discouraged and quit the process. Cues 1, 2, and 3 are within the scope of this book, but cues 4 through 8 are not, and they are not explained fully here.

1. *Make feet parallel.* Having your legs and feet properly aligned while walking is analogous to having properly aligned car tires. Better alignment reduces wear and tear on the tendons that insert into bones, the ligaments that connect bone to bone, and the muscles that cross skeletal areas.
2. *Lift the sternum.* Lifting the sternum, or breastbone, in your chest helps you breathe more deeply, rotate your shoulders back, and lengthen your back muscles.
3. *Rotate shoulders back.* Doing this, especially on the leash side arm, significantly decreases negative forces on fingers, palms, hands, forearms, upper arms, shoulders, neck, and back areas when a dog pulls or lunges.
4. *Extend and lengthen back muscles.*
5. *Do a slight pelvic tuck by tensing your buttock muscles.*
6. *Bend your knees.* Keep knees normal, walking in a relaxed way, if the dog isn't pulling; slightly bent or very bent if the dog is pulling slightly to excessively. Bending the knees protects your balance.
7. *Lift head up like a marionette puppet attached to a string.*
8. *Take occasional deep breaths.*

Practice 1: Make Feet Parallel

While walking your dog, look down at your normal foot position. Your feet may habitually rotate inward or out to the side. Start guiding your feet to be more parallel. Try making your feet more parallel for a while, and then forget about it. Later on in the walk, check your alignment again. Notice where your feet are, and don't get upset if they are out to the side. Awareness is the way to gradually improve this over time; having truly parallel feet may take two to four months to learn. A goal of perfectly parallel feet is not practical for people with some histories of hip, leg, and foot injuries. More parallel will be good enough—we are not after perfection! Women need to wear flat shoes, not high heels, to learn this.

Practice 2: Sternum Chest Lift with Deeper Breathing

Lift your chest from your breast bone and take a deep breath while walking the dog. You can assist yourself by placing your free hand on your heart and lifting your sternum area against your hand. Notice your chest breath moving your hand as you take two or three breaths.

During the walk, continue to take some deep breaths and place your hand on your chest for two breaths. Return your focus to your dog, occasionally practicing breathing. This biomechanical posture is also used to calm down anxiety, anger, and sadness.

Practice 3: Shoulder Rotation

Our shoulders tend to move forward when we use our arms, including when picking up a cat. Try rotating your shoulders back for the time it takes to walk up a flight of stairs, then relax and let your shoulders do what they want. As you're carrying your cat or small dog from one destination in your home to another, repeat the shoulder rotations. You should continue to do this in other situations, such as sitting at a personal computer, lifting a child, carrying a child on your chest and shoulder, eating a meal, or using a hammer. Muscles running from the shoulder blade to the shoulder move the shoulders back, not the bones themselves.

CHILDREN WALKING DOGS—*NOT* DOGS WALKING CHILDREN

Children can learn to walk the family dog properly without the dog walking the child. Dogs walking children causes unsafe situations for the child and the puppy or dog. Children are pulled along faster than their normal pace of walking, leading them off sidewalks into grassy medians or the road and causing them to trip and fall. Runaway dogs and walker injuries can occur. Poor walking manners learned by the dog are common. Proper walking posture strengthens a child's body. I have overheard children giving feedback to their parents and the dog when the dog is controlling the walking: "I can't keep up! Stop it, Clancy!" "Stop pulling Spot!"

Usually, the child's upper body is excessively forward (hyperflexion), and the child's back is bent, with the leash arm rotated excessively forward (medial rotation) in front of the child. The child's lower body weight and strength are uncoordinated and being overcontrolled by the dog.

In most cases, unless the pet is truly too large and strong for the child, pet owners can teach their children to retain their intrinsic normal erect back and strong leg control while walking a pet. Most children have wonderful posture. Their legs and hips are underneath their upper body, their torso lifted, shoulders slightly back, and their head in line with their shoulders.

Puppies are very small and light. To teach children how to walk a puppy, parents should use these statements:

- "You are in charge of your body."
- "Walk slowly. Let the puppy follow your pace."
- "The right pace is your slow speed in walking, not your dog's pulling speed."
- "Yes, the dog wants to pull on the leash and go faster. But you are the boss. You are in charge."
- "Please don't yank hard on the leash. Let's be safe with the puppy's throat and neck. Walking at your pace is how you control the puppy."

Then model these postures for your child, walking the dog back and forth while your child watches you:

- Freeze your walking and stop.
- Space your feet apart a comfortable width with one foot in the rear, one foot forward. Bend the front knee forward. Bending the front knee has a braking effect and will stop most pulling dogs.
- Bend your leash arm at the elbow and tuck the arm into your body when the dog pulls hard.

After you have modeled these positions, watch your child demonstrate them.

OFF-LEASH DOGS?

A small percentage of dog owners follow an antisocial creed. "I am entitled to be undisciplined and not discipline my dog because I am a dog owner." Wrong. This chapter includes three examples of the worst dog owner behavior I have seen in public places. All these situations stemmed from a dog being off leash. Surprisingly, no one was seriously injured by the unleashed dog in each scenario.

Off-leash Scenario I

A mother and two daughters were playing catch in a park on a sunny day. The soccer field was not being used, and most people had left for dinner. The mom and the two daughters each had a baseball glove and were throwing a tennis ball to one another. The kids were about thirteen and nine years of age.

A dog owner appeared in the park with a Golden retriever, which began running back and forth at great speed, having what looked to be great fun crisscrossing the empty soccer field. Very quickly, the dog changed direction and ran toward the family playing ball in the last moments of daylight. Was the dog going to try and play ball?

Shockingly, the dog ran toward the younger girl at a high rate of speed and crashed into her hind legs. The girl fell quickly to the ground, her legs totally knocked out from under her, as if tackled below the knee by a football player. The force was so great she may have hit her head before landing on her back. The girl began to cry uncontrollably as she was comforted by her mother.

"Mommy, I'm scared," she cried out. "Mommy, my head hurts." The girl's mother held her and her sister looked over at the dog in bewilderment. The child's crying diminished to soft sobs after a few minutes, and her mother began to brush grass and mud off the shoulders of her daughter's jacket and to pick dirt and grass out of the girl's hair.

Two women, one being the dog's owner, came over to the family after a while. The owner said she was sorry and, strangely, asked the dog to apologize too. The dog was still off leash.

"Why isn't that dog on leash in a public park?" the bystander asked.

The dog owner leashed up the dog, then said something so shocking that the mother and bystander became infuriated. "This is a rescue dog, and he's ninety percent blind."

"The dog is ninety percent blind? What is a ninety percent blind dog doing off leash in a public park running loose?" the mother exclaimed.

The bystander said, "You are uncivilized. This is a public park, not a dog park! Don't you care about other people? Also, your dog could run into a fence or that swing set over there and seriously injure itself! What were you thinking?"

The dog owner had made a senseless decision to allow a near-blind dog run free in a park where people play. The dog was clearly a danger not only to others but also to itself. If the dog had hit the side of a knee instead of the back, the child could have been seriously injured and required reconstructive surgery. The dog could have run into a toddler or an elderly person, causing a concussion or worse, or into the street, getting hit by a car and causing an accident.

Off-leash Scenario 2

Since 1948, Marblehead has been the home of Shubies, a local beloved American family business that offers wonderful home-baked breads, freshly roasted fish, meats, vegetables, whole grains, wines, artistically designed plates, cast-iron pans, and other food and kitchen products. One afternoon I had just bought grilled organic chicken breasts, sautéed asparagus, and my kids' favorite bread, a sourdough loaf called whole wheat boule.

This restaurant furnishes a stone bench in front of their establishment. As I sat munching away, I saw a series of events unfold, highlighting the need for undisciplined dog owners to leash and control their dogs. A pedestrian was minding his own business walking down the sidewalk with his music-listening device in his ear, a newspaper tucked under his arm, and a beverage cup in one hand, which he drank from intermittently. Suddenly an off-leash dog appeared, quickly running down the sidewalk about 150 feet from the pedestrian, decreasing the distance between itself and the pedestrian quickly.

I heard some people yelling for the dog from hundreds of feet behind it, as it continued to run, now about thirty feet behind the man. The dog noticed the pedestrian and increased its speed. The dog ran up to the pedestrian and jumped high enough in the air to almost touch the man's ear. I saw the dog's rear feet well off the ground. The gentleman became startled and jerked his head and upper body away violently. His newspaper dropped to the ground, along with his drink. I was quite startled myself, sitting about a hundred feet from this. "Get down!" he yelled to the leaping dog, which probably thought this was a game to be played. This could have been terrifying for the man, and could have given him a whiplash-type injury, all because of an undisciplined dog owner who let a dog off leash in a commercial district.

Off-leash Scenario 3

A dog walker was walking two small dogs on leash in an urban neighborhood. A pet owner opened a front door of an apartment building and made his way to an automobile with the family dog off leash. The dog sprinted away from its owner toward the leashed dogs and dog walker. The charging dog agitated the leashed dogs and the dog walker's leg buckled after being tangled up and pulled by a leash. The dog walker fell to the ground and needed surgery to reattach leg tendons. He missed two months of work during his painful recovery.

I dislike seeing these thoughtless dog owner events. If you see this occur, be sure to remind the dog owners that they have a public responsibility to keeping the dogs on leash.

Pet owners with outside dogs must leash them or fence them on their property to avoid safety problems for passing cars, dog walkers, bicycle riders, baby carriage traffic, pedestrians, mail carriers, package delivery people, and others.

Certain dog owners welcome strange dogs to jump all over them and lick their faces in public. Certain dog owners think it is cute when off-leash dogs race toward the street or across the street toward dogs on leash. Certain pet owners have no boundaries in this sense and expect everyone else to be like them, even children. This may be how they allow themselves and their dogs to behave at home on private property, but other factors are in play when they are in public, called public etiquette, courtesy, public safety, and laws.

It is important for dog owners to practice boundaries in public. There is nothing cute or respectful about off-leash dogs jumping on adults and children who are seated or walking by, scaring or disturbing them, but some dog owners get perverse joy out of this. Perhaps they have some type of entitlement psychology or attitude that causes them to disrespect other people's privacy and boundaries, sometimes even their own boundaries and those of their spouses or children in the home. Conversely, the more a dog owner develops boundaries in the home, the more respectful their dogs will be outside on leash.

Occasionally in a park a dog owner will politely ask people if they can let their dog off leash. This really irks me, as if this person thinks no one else will enter the park while he or she is there. Soon other dogs or people appear in the park who have not been asked by the dog owner about unleashing his or her dog, and the dog off leash runs over to the new park entrants, acting poorly toward a dog on a leash, the children, or the adults. I have seen children become terrified, reduced to scream-ing and tears by loose dogs in parks jumping on them. I have also seen mindful dog owners immediately leash up their off-leash dog as new people enter a park.

DOG BITES FROM UNCONTROLLED DOGS

Dog bites trigger a whole bureaucratic network of people to address the situation, both rationally and sometimes irrationally. First, puncture wounds to an animal need veterinary care, including sutures if neces-sary. Antibiotics and pain medication are sometimes prescribed by the veterinarian. Sutures and rabies shots are often needed when an adult or child is bitten.

Then animal control officers visit the homes of those dogs and people involved. Animal control officers have the authority to enter private property to investigate situations, whether blood has been drawn or not. A dog may be placed under quarantine for a period of time, meaning that it cannot be walked off the owner's property until written permission is granted by the animal control officer. Quarantine time periods can be as long as a week or two weeks, depending on different factors.

When a dog bites a person or another dog, negative neighborhood tensions increase. Upset neighbors react, including neighbors who own dogs as well as those who don't. Lawyers may enter the fray, bringing civility or inciting incivility into a given situation. Lawsuits can be filed, in some cases reasonably motivated and based on relevant facts, but sometimes filed on a baseless motivation. The very reason people choose to live in neighborhoods—safety and peace of mind—is altered for a period of time by dogs not being properly disciplined or cared for.

WALKING ON NARROW AND POORLY LIT ROADS

I almost suffered a horrible accident with a customer's dog one day. I was walking the dog in daylight when a car sped by about three feet from the curbstones, with the driver on a cell phone. I heard the car approaching a couple hundred feet away. Knowing that this road lacked sidewalks, I redirected the dog out of the road onto the grass behind the curbstone separating the grassy area from the very narrow road shoulder. My foot could have reached out and touched the right side of the car as it sped past, with the dog pulling away from me toward the road. I held fast on the leash, using all my body weight.

Rural, suburban, and urban areas all contain roads with narrow or no shoulders, increasing the probability of cars, trucks, and bicyclists traveling closer to the shoulder, sidewalk, or whatever land area is parallel to the road. This endangers the dog-walking citizen in good weather—even more so in inclement weather or darkness. Fortunately, I was familiar with this road, where I had walked this dog often in both day and night.

Situations like this occur less in straight well-lit roadway areas designed with wide car lanes and normal-sized shoulders separated from the roadside by sidewalks. Curved roads add to the likelihood that a car driver will be less aware of a dog and walker until close to them. Curving roads call for more prudent decision making from drivers and dog walkers. Well-lit areas become dangerous when drivers are texting or looking at a cell phone.

Bicyclists, especially those who are training for races, have no choice but to share the road with cars and trucks and the shoulder with pedestrians and dog walkers. Cyclists may be traveling at high rates of speed around curves or hilly straight-aways, partially blinded to dog walkers in the road shoulder ahead. This is a very dangerous situation, and the outcome usually depends on luck and the reflexes of the rider.

Although some dogs, being creatures of habit, insist on walking on one side of the walker, the walker should keep the dog on the shoulder side of the road, rather than on the lane side where bicycles and cars pass by quickly.

Country roads present their own unique problems. Many roads in rural and wilderness areas are narrow and have very little shoulder. Dog walkers may be sharing the roads with farm equipment operators, who usually travel slowly and carefully. However, sports cars, road motorcycles, dirt track motorcycles, regular cars, trucks, and bicycles all share these roads as well. These rural areas may have sparse road lighting, and foggy, snowy, and icy weather conditions multiply the hazards.

On poorly lit country roads, carry a flashlight that is always turned on at dusk and nighttime. Consider strapping the flashlight around your arm, hand, leg, or waist so your hands are free. Some people attach a small flashlight to the leash at night. The flashlight commands visual attention because of the movement of the leash. You can also clip a flashlight to the top of your dog's harness, facing toward either side of your dog or toward its tail. You should not have the flashlight pointed toward your dog's head because the head may block the flow of light. Wearing reflective material is helpful, too, but a flashlight offers motorists and cyclists a visual warning from a greater distance. The combination of reflective material and a flashlight creates a small but very visual light show for approaching vehicle drivers.

In some areas, businesses frequently have commercial vehicles traveling the narrow roads, such as oil trucks, logging trucks, food trucks, laundry trucks, newspaper trucks, and quarry trucks. If you have concerns about dog-walking safety, I encourage you to call the company and talk to the manager or owner about your concerns. Local businesses are usually good citizens and will listen to concerns about walking safely in your area. For example, if you live in an area where there is quarrying or logging, thank the company for all the times the drivers have been careful, but also point out any concerns you have. Always be respectful and try to have a two-way conversation. Many companies care about the region in which they do business. They hire local people and have long historical roots in communities. Many business managers are animal lovers too.

I've found that off-road vehicles, despite negative stereotypes about them, are good at sharing the road. These drivers are often dog owners who slow down near dog walkers. Like you, they appreciate mutual respect.

CASE VIGNETTE: THE ADAPTABLE EBONY: WALKING A DOG WITH SPECIAL NEEDS

Have you ever heard an admiring parent or coach say "She was born to play sports; she is a natural" about an accomplished athlete? Ebony, a black Labrador retriever, was born to play ball. He has the greatest spirit for ball playing that I've ever seen, playing with gusto, despite a limp in his right leg!

Ebony is like a puppy in a ninety-pound grown Labrador body, greeting me at the door with his powerful body full of tail-wagging joy and head bobbing up and down.

"Pick out a ball, Ebony," I'll encourage him before we take a walk. Ebony's mom keeps heaps of dirty green tennis balls in containers inside and outside the home. Ebony's teeth are sunk into the green rubber ball within fifteen seconds, and he rushes toward the door, waiting to be leashed.

The first priority is going to the bathroom. Ebony pulls me like a dog locomotive train because he knows once he goes to the bathroom, we will play fetch. I do not let him play ball until he has relieved himself, both number one and number two.

Ebony suffered a serious accident when he was four years old. He fell down a steep hill and fractured a bone, blocking blood flow to his right hip and causing a permanent limp. Ebony's spirit has not been affected by this physical handicap, but this injury has affected his physical coordination and strength. Ebony's right rear legs and hips collapse to the ground when he takes a turn at a brisker pace than he can handle. He also loses his hip and leg support if he descends stairs too quickly. Yet, like a professional athlete, Ebony recovers his coordination and balance in a flash, lifting his fallen hips and legs from the ground, especially when chasing a ball. Ebony's remarkably quick recovery ability should help him as his age advances.

Ebony's Special Needs Exercise

At the initial meeting with Ebony and his owner, I learned how to support Ebony's exercise and play routine while minimizing any possibility of injury. "Ebony overexerts himself playing ball because of his enjoyment of it," his owner informed me. "Ebony doesn't know when to stop, and then he becomes overly exhausted. I limit his chasing the ball to five to seven minutes."

"Five to seven minutes? Sounds good," I said.

"Also Bob, I'm going to encourage you to roll or throw the ball uphill rather than downhill. Throwing the ball uphill in the front yard strengthens his overall body and is safer than him running downhill after a ball, when his lack of stability could injure him," Ebony's owner explained.

I agreed, seeing how Ebony's mass and velocity could have trouble stopping on the way downhill. I worked and played with Ebony over many dog walks. I saw clearly that his momentum running uphill was much more stable and controlled than running and fetching a ball downhill. The owner's request had been practical and important.

Eventually, Ebony's owner needed to move to another home in the same town. The owner was concerned about how Ebony would adjust to a new home and neighborhood. Thoughtful pet owners have concerns like this; lifestage transitions in pet families are sources of concern.

I walked Ebony many times in his new neighborhood. He was thrilled partly because of the dogs that live in the surrounding homes.

At about sixty feet from one neighboring dog's home, Ebony's nostrils often begin quivering. (If only we could borrow our dogs' and cats' scent abilities for a few minutes, to know what our animals can smell, at what distance, and how strongly!) He started a prancing dance, wagging his hips and head. His front legs lift off the ground in horse-like excitement. Ebony barked, hoping to see his doggy friend barking in return behind the glass storm door. When the front door was shut, Ebony's barking alerted the neighbor of his presence and the joint barking began, which delighted Ebony as we walked past the home.

Ebony was delighted by another dog living diagonally across the street. Ebony stopped at the front gate, looked down the path to the front door, and started barking for his friend. The front door sometimes opened and a Golden retriever appeared behind the green screen door, greeting Ebony with hearty barks.

Ebony and I often entered a boatyard on Marblehead harbor, walking up to a retaining wall overlooking the dock and relaxing while Ebony held a tennis ball. Ebony enjoyed the sea breezes off the harbor, raising his nose slightly and twitching his nostrils. Boaters at nearby dock prepared boats for launching, tipping outboard engines into the water, raising jibs or mainsails as the wind fills the sails like invisible magic, untying ropes, and lifting anchors. There is magic in Marblehead Harbor, where the horizon fills your retinas and salty sweat runs down a cheek.

Ebony was often thirsty after our walks, taking a long, loud drink of water from his ceramic bowl before enjoying the ritual of me throwing a large doggy biscuit into the air, which he caught with the clamping precision of his massive jaws and mouth.

Ebony and his owner have not allowed his physical problem to deny him the tremendous fun of daily exercise during companionship!

CLEANING UP AFTER A DOG

Imagine what it is like to be in a pet family's yard while pet sitting and be packing a snowball for a game of fetch with a dog, only to realize the brown stuff in the snow in your hands is old poop, which is now becoming caked into your gloves.

When I pet sit, I've often been asked to let the dog out into the backyard for both play and bathroom needs. Many yards will be full of old dog poop. By full I mean many piles—not three or four, but fifteen to twenty-five. Why do dog owners allow their yards to get full of poop? Families have competing needs, and the pet owner may be busy or distracted. Or the owner may have an aversion to cleaning up the yard after their dogs use it. Even families with children may have yards full of dog poop. Some homeowners allow poop to pile up for six days and have gardeners clean it up on the seventh day. Wintertime dog waste in many residential yards is often allowed to build up until springtime. At spring cleaning time, the owner or a gardener usually cleans up the poop along with branches and other winter refuse.

Poop is slippery, and people can slip on it and hurt themselves. They may also track it into the owner's home. Loads of poop can really cramp the pet care professional's ability to play fetch or other games.

A dog walker or pet sitter who finds him- or herself in this situation may kindly mention to the pet owner "I slipped on poop and almost hurt myself. Fido just missed rolling in it. Wow, that would have been something! A coat rolled in poop. Fido did step in it, so I cleaned his foot by walking him some more on the grass." These statements show concern about the dog's hygiene, the pet family's hygiene, and your own safety.

A good pet sitter appreciates a clean fenced yard for exercising the dog and early morning or bedtime access. On the first visit with the family, the pet professional might ask, "What have you found is the best way to keep the yard clean?" You might be informed that the owner cleans it up once a week or has a service do it once a week. The owners might confide that they get behind in the poop cleaning, but it does get done eventually. In these cases, the pet care company you work for may offer an initial waste removal for a onetime fee, and if you work independently, you may offer that yourself.

Some pet owners who don't have children leave the yard for dog use only, making a lifestyle decision that works for them. The dogs are trained to simply proceed outside on their own to relieve themselves, and then bark at the door when they are done. Dogs living in this pet owners lifestyle may have the most poop-packed yards, because people don't go outside much and the yard is overlooked if the family is rarely walking in the yard. If pet owners are happy with this lifestyle, they let us know in advance that we can just let the dog out, leave the poop in the grass or snow, and let the dog come in.

An owner might think it odd that a pet care company would ask that the yard be cleaned before we start our service. However, we have our standards of safety and cleanliness, and we ask nicely for what we need. "I don't want to soil your home by tracking poop in, and I want to avoid injuries," I usually say.

A small percentage of dog owners would garner more respect if they stopped driving to beaches, farms, forests, or open fields to let their dogs out to poop, especially on private property.

DOG PARK HIERARCHY PROBLEMS AND SOLUTIONS

Dog parks are an important resource for pet families with dogs. Dog owners are inspired when they see their dogs becoming more animated while socializing with other dogs. Dog parks are a system with great positives and some hierarchy problems. The hierarchy problems arise when dog owners do not oversee their dogs quickly enough because the owner is distracted by socializing with other dog owners or the park may be too large for owners to quickly intervene when their dog needs intervention. Additionally, dogs gather at the gate intensely excited when new dogs enter without an adult acting to disperse the crowd. Dispersing the crowd greeting the new dog makes the transition less anxiety producing for the entering dog.

Dog park owners worry about the behavior of other dogs growling, overly aggressive nipping that is not playful nipping, pushing other dogs too hard or too often, or getting in another dog's face with teeth snapping. Dog park attendees are sometimes knocked over by other dogs running at a high rate of speed. Owner's have informed me of sociable dogs being bullied repeatedly while the owner of the bullying dog stood by talking with another dog owner. Larger dogs may push smaller dogs down to the ground, creating fear and anxiety, the opposite of the goals of a dog park.

Dogs bullying other dogs is unacceptable behavior. Two or three dog owners talking and ignoring their dogs compromises the hierarchy at dog parks. Unsupervised dogs that are behaving poorly, for even a few seconds, without owner intervention to correct them sets a poor example for other dogs and is antisocial. In a professionally run behavior modification playgroup, the experienced staff prevent and correct dogs from acting poorly. In a dog park, the dog owners must take responsibility by disciplining poor behaviors and rewarding good behaviors.

Certain rescue dogs have been traumatized through a difficult past. This dog population may not do well at dog parks off leash or on leash.

One or two dog owners can help new dogs transition more easily into the dog park by standing between the opening gate and a crowd of excited dogs greeting a new dog entering. This will decrease the excessive anxiety a new dog experiences when entering.

Some dog owners may not recognize what poor behavior looks like in their dogs or someone else's dog. A large-sized dog park can make it difficult to differentiate good behaviors and distressed responses.

An owner needs to discipline his or her dog if it uses its head to push other dogs too forcefully. Unintentionally or intentionally bowling over another dog is unacceptable. In both situations, the owner of the bowled-over dog may need to calm the dog that is recovering from the forceful contact. Many dogs develop orthopedic conditions from injury or aging, and these are put at risk with out-of-control play.

Dog owners conversing with one another can force themselves to have less eye contact with the other person and more awareness of their dogs' behavior. They should make a commitment to keep their eyes on their dogs while talking to the other person. If this doesn't come naturally, they should ask the other person to help them practice. Let them know you are training yourself to watch your dog as well as listening to them talk. They should inform the person they are concerned that their dog is doing the right things, enjoying itself, and playing well, and not getting hurt or hurting another dog.

Try using a whistle at the dog park to communicate with your dog. The whistle may distract your dog and others playing with the dog for a moment as you move to leash your dog and separate it from the others, or simply to correct the dog's behavior. A whistle can also alert other dog owners to watch their dogs' behavior. Some dog owners may not like you using a whistle. But be prepared, some owners may feel shocked, embarrassed, or overly apologetic for something their dogs may or may not have done.

CASE VIGNETTE: LACY THE CAIRN TERRIER: SUITING THE WALK TO THE BREED

People commonly ask me, "What is your favorite dog?" or "Do you have a favorite breed?" I don't have a favorite dog or breed, because when you spend a lot of time with different dogs professionally in playgroup, pet sitting, or dog walking contexts, many dogs stand out. Working with animals in the home also defines and brings out a dog's endearing qualities. Still, Lacy the Cairn Terrier stands out as one of my favorites in terms of personality and surprises. She is unforgettable. Cairn Terriers, which originated in Scotland as far back as the early 1800s, are named for the rock piles that occur in the rural areas where these dogs were raised to protect farmers' food and help hunters. These rock piles, or cairns, exist near and around farms, and often house vermin like rats and mice, enemies to the farmers' crops and family. Rats and mice eat farm crops, chew through the strands holding bales of hay together, and have other undesirable behaviors.

The Cairn terriers would sniff out and hunt rabbits, mice, and rats from the rock piles and other structures both above and below ground. A Cairn's physique, with muscled shoulders and powerful hind quarters, is built for chasing and digging into the ground. Cairns have a rough external hair texture that protects them from bad weather as well as the sharp thorns in dense underbrush. Cairns have large teeth, strong nails, and thick padded feet. They weigh between thirteen and seventeen pounds and stand eleven to twelve inches high. Their colors can range between black, gray, reddish, cream, or a combination.

Cairn Terriers have also been used to hunt squirrel as well as rabbit, an important dietary staple at times in European history. The most famous Cairn Terrier, Terry, appeared in the movie *The Wizard of Oz* in 1939 as Dorothy's dog, Toto.

Lacy is charismatic! With her deeply expressive facial features, she could be a character actress with different personalities and behaviors. I experience the unpredictability of this sweet, affectionate, relaxed, and active dog when I enter her home or take her on a walk.

Lacy has a wonderful sunny bedroom to stay in with access to the kitchen. She is usually resting comfortably on her mom's bed, beyond the kitchen safety gate, when I enter the home through the living room. Lacy may roll onto her back to have her belly scratched during our walks in any season or weather. Her sudden rolls in front of strangers have often captivated her audiences and left them giggling and scratching her. Her antics change the moods of people quickly, including strangers in a park.

Lacy's field of vision is a magnet for squirrels and birds. She pulls mightily on leash if a squirrel happens by, and she has very good traction in a sprint, even on wet or snow-covered areas.

Gregory Street in Marblehead is full of bushes where birds often gather, fronted by occasional puddles after rainfall. Lacy often looks inquisitively for a second at a group of birds taking a bath before taking off after them. I hold her back with my arms as the birds scatter quickly like an explosion of chirping feathers.

I have walked many dogs past benches, and they do not jump onto the bench unless I stop and coax them. Only Lacy jumps onto the park bench without my slowing down or coaxing her. She enjoys the benches at Crocker Park overlooking Marblehead Harbor. I no longer encourage dogs to sit on park benches because benches should only be used by people for reasons of personal space and hygiene.

Lacy enjoys climbing up and down the rock formations that pervade Crocker Park and sniffing around the sticker bushes which are laden with roses. Her low shoulder height and small, strong body with its muscular legs help her traverse dirt piles and steep, bare rocks with certainty and ease. Lacy is much quicker and surer of foot than I am on rock structures; she can navigate extreme changes in rock angles, heights, and measurements. (I would almost expect her breed to have goat horns!) I intentionally walk Lacy through the rock structures to replicate some of the terrain challenges Cairn Terriers experienced in their native lands before immigrating to America.

Lacy adores meeting new children and rushes up to them, offering gentle licks and bonding affection. She is very comfortable with the adults who stoop down to engage with her expressive, endearing eyes and licking tongue. Lacy might be an ideal therapy dog for visiting children and adults limited by health or circumstances.

Back at home, Lacy often asks me to bend the rules regarding the living room couch, which is off limits after our walk. The postwalk routine is to remove Lacy's leash, give her a treat, and guide her to the area on the other side of the gate. Lacy opposes this by jumping up on the couch. She gives me a lengthy, forlorn look, as if to say, "Surely you'll let me stay on the couch, my favorite place to be during the day when my mother is home? Surely you won't gate me into the bedroom-kitchen areas, where I spent the entire morning before you arrived for our walk? Look at how sad my eyes are. Please let me stay in the living room on the comfy couch, Bobby!"

What a character! Before I guide her off the couch, she places her head on her paws and looks very sad, knowing I cannot be tricked or manipulated and must follow her mom's house rules—but I might give her an extra treat for her Broadway-caliber canine performance!

8

PET PROFESSIONS AS A CAREER

The growing pet care business includes stores, shows, breeding, pet visits, playgroups, pet sitting, doggy daycare, and many other situations. In the company as well as in the pet family, a strong hierarchy is key. The pet owner is in charge of the pet family hierarchy, and the pet business owner is at the top of the pet company hierarchy. Pet care company owners must maintain high standards for themselves, the staff, and the pet owners they serve.

A happy and safe companion pet family member is at the top of everyone's priority list of importance. High standards minimize the likelihood of animals becoming lost, sick, injured, or killed when in the care of the pet owner or pet professionals and make legal disputes less likely. Having high standards also means that pet professionals and pet owners learn from one another through wisdom and mutual respect, and therefore improve the care of pets.

Human communities have always thrived partly on good honest work with a profit incentive and mutual respect among citizens. High standards in a pet professional company create goodwill in communities.

WHO SHOULD AND SHOULD NOT WORK WITH PETS?

Loving animals and having strong feelings about their well-being is not enough of a standard to qualify someone for pet sitting, dog walking, cat and bird visits, doggy daycare, and dog playgroups. Conversely, the fact that animals respond positively to a person is not enough of a criterion for an adult to be hired as a pet professional.

There are some people who should not work with pets. Pet care companies often run a Criminal Offender Record Information background check on prospective employees to screen out unacceptable candidates. I offer some other parameters as well.

Individuals with too much chronic drama going on in their lives and have difficulty holding a job should not be hired for pet sitting, dog walks, cat visits, or dog playgroup work. Those who need to habitually distract themselves—with overeating, watching television, listening to music, and texting on their cell phones—will not be able to focus on the presence and needs of animals. People with an aversion to animal excrement and picking it up with plastic bags or digging out kitty litter and don't have a deep concern or liking of dogs and cats should not apply.

People who are chronically impatient with people and have trouble with authority will fail to act respectfully toward pet owners, colleagues, and the pet owners' animals. Customer relations is a huge part of excelling at this type of business.

Those who are addicted to drugs or alcohol should bypass working with pets. Those with addictions should not make animals, pet care company owners and colleagues, or pet owners and their homes victims of their poor choices. Pets are dependent on humans. They have daily needs that must be met promptly and completely. Individuals who are impaired by substance abuse can cause innocent pets to suffer needlessly.

Anyone who has difficulty paying attention to details would not be good at multitasking and should find other work.

A person who is incapable of walking dogs due to fear of falling or unhealed physical problems should not be caring for other people's cats and dogs. If a person needs to live on a one-level residence and cannot climb stairs to a second or third floor or traverse basement stairs or cannot easily get down on all fours to look under a bed for a cat or dog, pet visits and pet sitting would not be appropriate jobs.

Parents with young children who would need to have their children with them during professional pet care responsibilities are not suitable for pet sitting. Young children have their own priorities, which must always come before caring for another family's pet. Pet customers' animals should not be placed in a one-down position behind the children's needs when a pet care professional is on the job. These truths may seem harsh, but in the world of pets and proper customer service, pets must come first when one is working a pet care job.

THE RISKS OF LANGUAGE BARRIERS

Although a pet family may be able to work around language barriers when hiring people for other roles around the home, a pet professional needs to be fluent in the language spoken by the pet family owners to guarantee standards of safety and care. Pet sitters and pet visitors should be able to demonstrate speaking, comprehension, writing, and reading ability in the main language used in a pet owner's home. Why is knowing the language so important? Because adults who cannot comprehend a pet owner's conversation, read an owner's notes, or follow exactly the directions on a prescription bottle pose serious health risks for the pets, as well as possible legal risks for themselves and the pet company that employs them. Here are some of the scenarios language barriers have caused:

- Dogs and cats locked out of the house in inclement weather, causing dehydration, distress, and excessive barking.
- Dogs with fear of thunder that have not been properly medicated or have not had their ThunderShirts fitted.
- Cats locked into rooms and closets without access to food, water, and litter trays.
- Medications not properly administered.
- Leash aggression episodes endangering dogs, children, and adults.

Sometimes, pet owners of dogs with leash aggression instruct me to avoid contact with other dogs on walks. On one walk I asked another person walking a dog, "Please stop and let me get to a crosswalk and wait for a Walk signal so I can keep my dogs separate from your dog." The other dog walker spoke only Russian, and my two dogs and her dog ended up about eighteen inches away from possible puncture wounds. The dogs lunged at each other, snarling with bared teeth as both of us strained to keep the dogs apart.

Pet owners, you must take control of these situations before they develop by making sure the people in your home who are not family members understand your wishes for your pets. For example, a family may own two black Labrador retrievers, but one dog needs to take two different medications daily, one in the morning and one in the evening. The pet care professional cannot make mistakes, thus the importance of language literacy.

The pet owner should test a potential pet sitter for comprehension by asking the pet professional to list five or six things you told them about your pet. Many pet professionals bring a pen and paper to take notes when first meeting a pet owner. Even if I have to read something off my notes, it shows the pet owner a level of seriousness and commitment to the details unique to his or her dog, cat, or bird. Make sure that the information the potential pet sitter reports back to you is accurate.

PET SITTER SELF-CARE IN THE PET FAMILY HOME

Pet sitting jobs can be demanding both mentally and physically in the pet owners home. Pet owners expect a professional to be at his or her best with a necessary level of energy and a heartfelt presence for the pets.

A pet sitter may initially find living in the pet owners' home confusing and disruptive. Pet sitting isn't simply a pleasant new adventure to relax into—it is work that requires a great deal of adaptation: strange stairways to be navigated, light switches to be found, noises from animals that are not your pets to be investigated, different kitchen appliances to cook on, and unfamiliar icy patios, stairs, sidewalks, and streets to traverse. Pet owners have rehired me in pet sitting contracts, bringing familiarity, comfort, and increased ease of performance. Familiarity reduces negative stress and makes adaption easier.

Pet owners may begin their travels on a Friday or Saturday. A weekend pet sitting contract means a continuation of a pet professional's workweek, when your body and mind need rest and revitalization. Pet sitting one, two, or three dogs or one dog and a couple of cats is demanding, and a contract may call for three days to as many as fourteen days. In these situations, self-care is very important for the pet sitter in the pet owners' home.

Why is self-care important? Self-care allows the pet sitter access to his or her best judgment and highest level of energy while caring for other people's pets. Things go wrong at times and pets need wise responses from those who are caring for them. Sitters who don't take care of themselves are susceptible to using poor judgment, which makes a situation worse for the pets and the pet owners as well as for yourself and the company you represent.

The pet sitter is invaluable to the pet family and the pet company he or she represents. The pet sitter needs self-care for peak performance, peace of mind, and the safety of all involved.

AVOIDING SLEEP DEPRIVATION IN THE PET OWNERS HOME

Pet sitters working with pet owners' animals need to avoid sleep deprivation, which impairs a person's mind–body relationship and negatively affects decision making, making judgment cloudier and slower. Sleep deprivation impairs coordination of body reflexes and physical balance, making incidents such as traffic accidents and slip and fall accidents more likely to occur. Anger and anxiety problems can be triggered from sleep deprivation.

If a pet sitting job is scheduled to start on a weekend, prepare by resting and sleeping extra before you start the job—either the day before or the morning of. A few cat naps can be helpful. Discipline yourself to go to bed early the first night on the job so you can wake up refreshed. Go to bed early after the pet owners' dog has enjoyed its last walk of the evening.

Working people entering pet professions may have a history of chronic sleep deprivation related to night jobs, young children, or medical problems. These people may consider consulting an experienced holistic health physician with at least ten years of full-time clinical practice using integrated alternative protocols, including metabolic nutrition. A holistic approach is different from taking a sleep medication, whether the medication is a naturally derived substance or a Western medical allopathic drug. Taking a medication without looking at other related lifestyle factors focuses too much on the symptoms. A holistic physician can look at your lifestyle choices and suggest changes regarding sleep, food, metabolic nutrition using supplements, parenting responsibilities, overreliance on caffeine, as well as bolstering those habits that promote good sleep, such as taking walks, practicing yoga, and participating in prayer or meditation.

BEDS AND OTHER AMENITIES IN THE PET OWNER HOME

The pet sitter will be sleeping in a new bed in the pet family home. I have been comfortable in most beds I've slept in, with the exception of a couple of real duds where pillows have been too hard or too soft. Many owners suggest that the pet sitter sleep in the master bed, especially if their dog is used to sleeping in the parents' bedroom. A pet sitter may not want to sleep in the master bedroom. This is personal and doesn't have to be justified or explained to the pet owner. Most owners have a second bedroom. Owners who have children and do not have a guest bedroom often ask the pet sitter to sleep in the master bedroom rather than their child's bed—another personal choice that doesn't have to be explained by the pet owner.

A one-bedroom home may feature a pullout sofa. The quality of the mattress on these is an issue. Many pet owners of these sofas have never slept on them themselves, and some have never had guests sleep on them, so they have no idea of their lack of comfort. Some sleeper sofa mattresses are extremely uncomfortable. They can be too hard, too soft, or they might sag. These mattresses are bad for your body and sleep. Others are excellent. The pet sitter might ask the pet owner: "I'd like to think I would be comfortable on the sleeper sofa. Have you or your guests used it?"

A temporary cot or a permanent cot is generally not acceptable for a pet sitter to sleep on. Cots can be very uncomfortable and unsafe, and they add to poor sleep quality. Most pet owners wouldn't sleep in a cot in their home and wouldn't offer it to a pet sitter.

The room the pet sitter will be sleeping in should be furnished adequately. A basement guest bedroom should be fully finished, not just wooden framed without walls, paint, or furniture. A basement room needs good heat for wintertime and air circulation for spring, summer, and fall. Rooms in pet homes below ground that do not have windows can be dark and claustrophobic and may have high levels of mold and dampness, which environmentally sensitive people feel and notice immediately upon entering the area. If you are negatively affected by mold, dampness, or dust, let the pet owners know and they will have to come up with another room option. The owners may not have similar sensitivities and your asking for an alternative place to sleep in the home will educate them. I once slept in a very nice above-ground basement room with good sunlight and air circulation, with no coldness, dampness, or mold, and I was comfortable. Conveniently, the family dog was trained to exit the home through the basement doors into the backyard.

The pet sitter, not the pet owners, decides whether to allow family pets to sleep in the room with him or her. The pet sitter should not feel obligated by the pet owners' preferences, because sleep quality is important. Most owners say something like, "Our dog doesn't have to sleep in your room unless you want," "There is an open crate in the master bedroom our dog sleeps in. If you wish you can move the crate into your bedroom but you don't have to," or "Our cats can be shut out of your bedroom. If they scratch at the door they'll eventually stop and go elsewhere." An open crate in the pet sitter's bedroom can always be moved out into the master bedroom if it is small enough.

Pet sitters may experience poor sleep if pets are loud at night. Cats may scratch at the bedroom door. Dogs closed out of the pet sitter's bedroom may put their noses near the door bottom and threshold and sniff, making a loud noise if it is a medium to large-sized dog. Pugs and bulldogs have nasally breathing that is noisy in a cute way except when you are trying to sleep. Sleeping in the same room or even the same floor as bulldogs or pugs sounds like an automotive repair shop! The snoring of Juice, my favorite bulldog, on the first floor reverberates loudly into the second-floor bedroom I use when pet sitting.

Dogs' toenails make loud noises when walking on wooden, stone, and vinyl floors at night when they are pacing. Pacers wake up and walk in and out of the room the pet sitter is sleeping in or up and down the halls outside a closed bedroom door. Pacers may create a symphony of sounds at 3:00 a.m., sniffing loudly at the closed door's threshold and scratching their claws on the floor. Occasionally, the house cat and dog will wrestle loudly in the hallway or have a short, loud fight with a bark and a meow full of hisses.

Earplugs are one option. Pet sitters may also consider keeping the dogs overnight in a separate part of the house, such as the first floor if you are sleeping on the second floor. A home with young children may already be furnished with a child-safety gate at the bottom or top of the stairs.

Placing the dog in a closed crate overnight with the pet owners' permission can be a win-win situation for everyone. The crate keeps dogs quiet and secure. Older dogs that have nocturnal bathroom accidents when walking around the house overnight can be crate trained to wait until their morning walk.

A pet professional may enjoy having the animals in bed with them. A content cat curled up next to your body is different from a cat sleeping on your stomach or legs, whose weight may wake you up. Pugilistic cats may enjoy whacking your feet in the middle of the night through the bed covers. I often have dogs sleep on the bedroom floor on their doggy bed. I also opt for dogs sleeping in other rooms when I have been sleep deprived or feel I need a break on the job.

Pet family owners want the pet sitter to use the amenities in their home, including clothes washers and dryers, air conditioners, television, music system, dishwashers, Internet, and thermostat. I inform pet owners who own a second-floor laundry that I shut off the water valve to the washing machine except when I use it. Occasional second-floor laundry plumbing fittings have malfunctioned, causing many tens of thousands of dollars of water damage in the home.

I inform pet owners that I always clean out the dryer lint filter before and after running a load, for fire prevention. I keep toasters and toaster ovens unplugged in the home, especially if I am pet sitting cats. Cats may accidentally turn on a toaster oven during their kitchen counter travels.

Some owners ask me if I would like a guest option readied in their computer so I can use the Internet. This is very thoughtful. Using the home's amenities, within the pet owners' permission, allows the sitter to spend more time happily in the home with the animals. This replicates familiar routines of the pet family, a positive thing for everyone.

CELL PHONE USE

I work better with pet owners' animals when not multitasking unnecessarily. Excessive multitasking distracts me and fragments my connection with a cat, bird, or dog. I feel healthier and caring when I'm less distracted. Pet professionals walk through neighborhoods with diverse architecture, interesting people and animals, and beautiful flowers, trees, and shrubs. Being open to their surroundings helps the pet sitters relax and enjoy the world they live in. I limit my phone use intentionally for the animals' well-being and my own.

COOKING AND EATING

I cook in the pet family home when pet sitting. It is too stressful and counterproductive for me to commute back and forth for meals at my home. I cook breakfast and dinner around the time the cats and dogs eat their meals, very homey, and the animals get to smell fresh-cooked food! I get to relax and eat in the home I am living in for one day to three weeks.

The pets feel that a normal routine is continuing, similar to their usual home life, in which their owners are home cooking and eating and making noise in the kitchen. This replication of normalcy decreases some of the separation anxiety pets have when owners leave town. I believe animals would rather have strangers who are kind to them spending more time in their home during pet sitting than less time.

ENTERTAINMENT IN THE PET OWNERS HOME

Pet owners leave instructions for me on properly using their television. I watch television to relax during pet sitting, joined by the dogs and cats. Pets sleep, nap, sit next to me, or get groomed and receive scratching from me while I watch television.

LEVERAGING YOUR EXPERIENCE TOWARD A COLLEGE DEGREE

Pet care is an excellent foundation for earning a college degree. One of my goals is to encourage vocational school curriculum in their agriculture tracks to integrate this book's content of dog behavior modification playgroups, pet sitting, doggy daycare, dog walking, and cat and bird visits.

Children and young adults can work with animals in many areas where age appropriate. Possibilities include:

- Animal shelters
- Dog training classes
- Caring for cats, in your own or someone else's home
- Dog walking for neighbors
- Veterinary hospital kennel work
- Raising farm animals
- Living on a farm and working or volunteering
- Helping set up country fairs
- Attending dog and cat shows and visiting zoos, and documenting the experience with writing and photography
- Interviewing veterinarians in different settings
- Working for an animal adoption organization
- Creating a portfolio of animal photography

Walter Chandoha is a distinguished animal photographer whose books are a wonderful resource for learning about photographing animals.

When applying to college, students often trivialize what they have done outside of school or in extracurricular activities. Everything of substance counts. Let colleges and universities and other postsecondary school institutions know what your pursuits have been over periods of time.

INDEX

ABOUT THE AUTHOR

Robert M. Berkelhammer, also known as "The Pet Pro" and "The Posture Guy," is the son of a veterinarian and has worked since 2007 assisting in running a dog playgroup, walking dogs, pet sitting dogs and cats, and visiting cats and birds. For two decades, he had an integrated private practice in holistic health, helping patients improve their posture and prevent or ameliorate soft tissue pain and disability symptoms. He studied family systems therapy at the Kantor Family Institute and is a practicing certified Kripalu yoga instructor and muscle therapist. He is also a Massachusetts state–certified guidance counselor for grades kindergarten through twelve. He is currently developing a corrective posture walking class and writing a video series on healthy posture for blue-collar workers, parents, and most occupations. He lives in Marble-head, Massachusetts, and is available for consultation on pet sitting, dog playgroups, cat and bird visits, dog walking, grieving for pets, pet-sitter self-care, and occupational and pet-related posture concerns. You can contact Bob at bobberkelhammer@gmail.com.